JAPAN
YOKOHAMA
KOBE

TIENTSIN

ASIA

CHINA

SHANGHAI

HONG KONG

PACIFIC

INDIA

OCEAN

GULF OF
BENGAL
COLOMBO

BULAN TABACO

PENANG
MALAYA

PHILIPPINES

SINGAPORE

INDIAN OCEAN

OUTWARD BOUND: ———
HOMEWARD BOUND:------

AUSTRALIA

Voyage to the Far East

That the greatest marvels are experienced at home, this we
do not learn until we go abroad.   —Wilhelm Raabe, Old Nests

The shortest road to one's self leads around the world.
     —Count Hermann Keyserling, Travel Diary of a Philosopher

I am beginning to believe that there is a certain view of
the real world which is just as closed to the eyes of many
believers as is the world of faith to those who do not believe.
The Lord preserve my passion for the world and a great
gentleness toward it, and help me to the last to be a whole man.
     —Pierre Teilhard de Chardin, Lettres de voyage 1923-1939

HELMUT THIELICKE

VOYAGE
TO THE
FAR
EAST

Translated by JOHN W. DOBERSTEIN

FORTRESS PRESS   PHILADELPHIA

Translated from *Vom Schiff aus gesehen, Tagebuch
einer Ostasienreise,* by Helmut Thielicke
Verlagshaus Gerd Mohn (1959), Gütersloh, Germany

For My Children
Wolfram
Berthold
Elisabeth
Rainer

Contents

A Bit of Preliminary Understanding With the Reader

Before I begin my story, I must ease my conscience a bit. Those who like to read travel books or even those who read their newspapers carefully will hardly find anything particularly new in this book. This is only the story of a voyage, the people who shared it, what they said, and what they talked about.

Explorers learn and experience much more, and those who have lived in foreign countries for a long time have penetrated incomparably deeper. But the first impression too has its interest, if it is registered with a certain alertness. Sometimes it may even allow one to see things that the experts or even the natives have not noticed because they have come to be too much taken for granted. This applies above all to the "ordinary" people, things, and attitudes we encounter on a journey. If I have succeeded here and there in discerning some things beneath the surface, surely it is only because the commonplace, everyday surface of things became transparent for me. The extraordinary and the so-called things worth seeing which are sought out by the tourist were of very scant interest to me.

Nor did I pursue any particular purpose on this voyage. I did not attend a conference (perhaps the most unusual thing about this journey of an academic man), nor was I bent upon studying strange religions or anything else in particular. I set out simply because the Hamburg-America Line—or more correctly one of its directors, Werner Traber—had the pleasant idea of inviting me to take this journey when I happened to have a free semester coming to me. I had been living an ascetic life for a long time, and after many years of work had just completed the third volume of my *Theological Ethics*. After all these years of lonely confinement to forced labor, I felt that now I might be justified in indulging my hungry eyes with a feast. My one purpose was to keep these eyes as wide open as possible and in the quiet of this sea journey engage in a bit of reflection and find my way back to myself.

Above all, I never had any intention of writing a book about it. The fact that I did so anyway came about in the following manner (which in itself belongs in a small way to the account of the voyage).

Very soon after the trip began I had to write all kinds of notes in my diary to give some order to the often chaotic welter of impressions I was experiencing and allow them to take intellectual shape. The writing of it went on quite apart from any literary designs, like a process of nature going on within me without any intervention of will and purpose. Sometimes, when the ship was rolling and pitching—or when the tropical heat made the paper stick fast to my arm, only to lose its sticky mooring in the next moment and fly away—I actually had no desire to write at all. Whenever that happened I had a feeling of emptiness, as if the voyage were not taking place at all: something like this process of reproduction was needed in order to allow these impressions to reach the conscious mind and become something more than dreamy meanderings.

The very act of writing made this voyage a far more intensive experience, and when I began to note this, gradually the joy of giving it structure came over me. I knew, of course, that it would be presumptuous and dilettantish to attempt to draw great "world historical profiles" or depict "lightning-flashes over Asia" (which was the somewhat melodramatic title a well-meaning editor later gave to my radio broadcasts). After all, considering how meager was the contact that I, a poor tangent on the vast Asiatic circle, had with the East, I should have had to resort to mere parroting of commentators who knew far more than I about those areas.

Instead, I was stimulated to try to capture in words the phenomenon of a sea voyage, with all its peculiar forms of experiencing life. This pleasant form of locomotion gives one a distinctively meditative way of seeing things: after each of his adventures on land, the traveler returns to the homely, familiar comfort of the ship, surrounded again by familiar faces; lying on a deck-chair, he can repeat in reverie the experiences he has had, really go over the same ground again and reflect upon it, and look ahead with pleasurable anticipation of what is still to come.

The ship itself is a microcosm where he can fish for and catch all kinds of interesting things, besides all he catches from the realms of land and water *beyond* the railing. In the quiet tropical nights I carried on many conversations with officers and sailors, for those were times, not to hole up in a cabin, but to sit on deck with others beneath the southern stars. The way other, quite different people exist, the laws of the sea, and the experience of living together for months in confined space— these were of tremendous interest to me, and they opened up quite as many new perspectives as the sight of strange cities, jungles, and exotic faces.

Throughout these months I kept struggling first to under- stand this sharply circumscribed and peculiar world of experi- ence as a whole, and then to visualize it and thus gain from it new riches. My situation is precisely that of many of my readers: I really *know* from books and newspapers more about the countries to which I traveled than I *saw* of them, particu- larly the seething political pot in the Near and Far East, the rattling of the chains of colonialism or the clatter of dragging chains already loosed, the vulnerability of these developing countries to the Soviet message of salvation, and many other things. I could not permit myself to stuff my diaries artificially with all this familiar knowledge, for, after all, my only business was to tell about what I myself had heard and seen. I had to be willing to assume both the burden and the blessing of one- sidedness. Nevertheless, there were many times when the book knowledge I brought with me helped me to notice and under- stand things that I would surely not have noticed or understood without it. On the other hand, I learned how pale and unreal are many things we "know" theoretically, and how colorful, graphic, and aggressive they suddenly become when we meet them in a landscape, in the face of a living person, or in the dim twilight of a temple. I could wish that some reflection of that experience might touch the reader too.

So I shall quite simply tell the reader as well as I can what I saw, and sometimes let him share the thoughts that came to me as I looked and listened.

Antwerp to Aden

July 17, 1958

We have been berthed here in Antwerp for a whole day. It was impossible to load the cargo yesterday because it poured rain all day. It was like a day of the Flood. The people on the dock, the complete silence, which was only emphasized the more by the recurrence of the same noises, the view of streets adjacent to the harbor glistening black in the rain, on which cold-looking automobiles were skidding by—all were very depressing. One could not think of going out. I consoled myself with the thought that at least the general deluge could not flood the cellar, as it surely would have done at our house in Hamburg. At any rate we will always be on top, like Noah's ark.

This somewhat dismal waiting was interrupted by reports of uprisings in Iraq, American intervention with warships and parachute troops, and the threat of counterintervention by Soviet Russia—all very exciting when you are on your way to the Far East and will come near these inflamed areas. Under these conditions, will the Suez Canal even be open to us? I fish these reports out of the air waves with great difficulty, for often I try in vain to make sense out of half-understood Dutch-Flemish announcements on my portable radio. Either complete ignorance or some definite information—even if it were very negative—would be more reassuring than these disconnected and ambiguous scraps of news.

How strange the contrast between these disquieting announcements and the comfortable quiet of Antwerp that surrounds us today as the weather begins to clear. Only the width of the loading ramp separates us from the large plate-glass windows of a dockside cafe in which people are lapping up ices and making short work of tall cream cakes. The couples smile happily at each other, and the middle-aged ladies have the same look of cryptic innuendo in their eyes or the same look

1

of malicious pleasure that they probably show everywhere when, besides the whipped cream, the "human-all-too-human" gets between their teeth. Here too, like the burgher in Goethe's *Faust,* people quaff their glasses "when out in Turkey yonder, far away, the nations clash in arms."

The incongruity between what throngs in upon me from the air waves and the detachment of my neighbors in the cafe from all that makes the mind reel a bit. I suppose people sat quite as peacefully in the cafes "Unter den Linden" on the eve of the great world conflagration in 1914. As for me, I can't get away from it; I am troubled by eschatological moods. It is as if my mind were trying to compensate for my travel fever and anticipation with a few depressing counterweights.

Our ship's neighbor in the harbor looks altogether different: it is a gleaming white passenger ship of Soviet origin, which has brought passengers to the Brussels World's Fair and now serves as their hotel. On the pier are many school classes, local people, and travelers curiously crowding around the ship. The Cyrillic letters and the inscription "Odessa" obviously exercise a stronger fascination than all the other ships or the visitors from the other side of the globe.

Even I catch myself being drawn repeatedly by the attraction of this ship. A fat, somewhat slit-eyed Russian who keeps walking up and down on deck is unanimously declared to be Malenkov by various groups on the shore promenade. In fact, the similarity is really startling.

For the rest, I am struck by the heterogeneity of the people on the Soviet ship. You see a type who might be called the "intellectual man of action," confident and exuding vitality; and next to him another type who—in physiognomy, dress, and behavior—gives the impression of being blatantly proletarian. Racially, too, there are many variations: blond, Western-looking stalwarts mingle with Mongolian and Kirghiz types. All the women are wearing Western clothes. On the street, where I later saw them getting off a bus, they would not be conspicuous because of either their dress or their bearing.

2

I screwed the telescopic lens of my camera to capture a few characteristic portraits, but I was watched very carefully during my attempts, and most of the passengers sought cover or held their hands in front of their faces. Perhaps they think I am a reporter for a picture magazine, or a spy. As ever, old Mother Russia must be on guard!

July 18

In the Channel, just short of Dover. We put out from Antwerp at one o'clock this morning.

Perhaps it was because of the variety in the weather, as well as in the moods I had passed through in these two days—and quite certainly the proximity of the pier cafe, in which I finally got to know every waiter—that I had already come to feel quite at home in friendly Antwerp, and that the harbor still continues to linger in my thoughts.

This is true particularly of my observations during the loading. In the port of Antwerp the operation is still very old-fashioned. The hydraulic cranes are antiquated fixtures which are more an obstruction to the work than a help. The cargo is therefore put down the hatches with the ship's own cranes. Even the little electric trucks that lift and switch tremendous weights with their small forks are not to be found here. The freight is hauled about on sledlike boards pulled by a tractor. The only modern innovation consists in the fact that Diesel motors have taken the place of draft horses. In spite of this, however, the loading proceeds with dispatch. The stevedores in Antwerp have a good reputation.

As you stand at the rail for hours, watching the work of loading, a kind of world-view unfolds before you in which life consists of perpetual loading, unloading, and transporting. Life as transport: this might be a specialization of the theme of man's constant striving and eternal restlessness. Think of all the work that has already been done to get these coils of wire, cases of instruments, bags of artificial fertilizer, and automobiles into the freight cars from which they are now being

3

taken to be restowed in the ship. On how many conveyor belts, hand trucks, tracks, and rails, under ground and above ground, did all these items travel until they were assembled in order to be transported again? Compared with this, the moment of production is actually tiny. Preparation and transport are almost everything; the cooking takes longer than the eating. Life is a long, complicated journey during which everything is unloaded at very few points: that is the philosophy a harbor can evoke.

In any case, it becomes clear to me that a ship does have something metaphysical about it; that is why it has always had the effect of creating symbols.

The microcosm of life on shipboard presents everything in surveyable proportions. Today, for example, I learned a little sociology: rumors run wild on shipboard as well as on land. "We'll probably lie over for two weeks in Colombo: there are always strikes there," says one. "Yes, that's so," says another, "and you'll never get back in time for the new semester." I myself contribute my own two cents' worth: "The Russians have dropped paratroopers in Jordan." (I had misunderstood the report on the Belgian radio; actually it was the British.) "The Suez Canal is supposed to be closed again. We'll have to go around Africa," croaks a sailor with whom I am gassing. Nothing but alarming rumors.

Suddenly it became clear to me how such rumors originate: it is the quiet harbor in pouring rain, the enforced idleness combined with the thwarted urge of the bird of passage to be on its way, that gives rise to these murky thoughts. Boredom proceeds, with the aid of anxieties, to create at least a little emotional excitement.

Still another condition must be fulfilled (and this is precisely what throws light upon a little segment of sociology): only when one is insufficiently informed do these bubbles rise from the murky waters. That was the case in our situation: neither the captain nor the radio operator, the persons who had access to good sources of information, were available to us during these first days. My miserable portable radio was inadequate, and the newspapers were already out of date. We lived in a divided company, those who knew the score and those who merely conjectured, and this was good soil for weird rumors. All these reports were suddenly blown into unreality (one actually has to make an effort even to remember them now), when last evening we sat in the smoking saloon with the captain and the first officer and were furnished with solid information.

July 19

Morning. In the Bay of Biscay. Yesterday was probably the most glorious I have ever experienced on the ocean. The old-timers say that such a quiet, sunny channel passage, when land can be seen on both sides, and France and England salute each other, is very rare. Deep blue sea, light breeze, sparkling light. Everybody was in good humor. Instead of nervous peering into the hazy fog, instead of the gloomy hooting of foghorns answered by many passing ships, only carefree cheerfulness prevailed.

The captain was extremely kind and fatherly and called the passengers up to the bridge to show us the gleaming chalk-cliffs of Dover. The "No Admittance" sign, which hitherto had not failed to have its effect upon our German minds with their authority-complexes, he dismissed as "purely platonic." We received blanket permission to visit the bridge at any time, day or night.

The fabulous feeling this weather creates, of being filled to the brim with vitality, drives away every thought of the somewhat gloomy and disquieting world situation. Suddenly an almost vegetable feeling of carefreeness descends. We go drifting through elements of water, air, and light that seem indestructible. The deep thoughts of the physicists, who remind us that even these primal structures of the world can be toppled by the hand of man, seem at this moment preposterous. The presence of the overwhelming potency of the elements overpowers all reflection.

The passengers have already learned to know one another.

Besides myself there is Mrs. V., with her two daughters, and Mr. N., an official who has been transferred to the German embassy in Tokyo. Mrs. V., who grew up in Japan and speaks Japanese as a second mother tongue, is now on her way with the two young ladies to Hong Kong, where her husband will represent his firm for the next several years. Our first conversations already indicate that Mrs. V. will be a pillar of our small ship's company. She has a highly cultivated knowledge of the countries to which we are traveling. I am glad to be able to sit at the same table with her and the captain, who is also an old Far East hand. To be able to see a country both from the inside and the outside, to be able to measure it by its own standards and at the same time to have at one's command the standards and categories of another culture—this certainly results in the most fruitful perspectives. I could not wish for a better preparation for the Far East.

For reading, I take from my trunk first Thomas Mann's *Joseph and His Brothers.* Here at sea I am hoping that finally I shall again have the long leisure to read some spacious epics, as I once did when I was hospitalized, but the passing ships and the distant coasts are too provocative to the eye to allow me to stay in the deck chair. I walk upstairs and downstairs, from larboard to starboard, in order not to miss anything. In between there is always a bit of talk with the sailors. A good many of them hope to go to a naval school; most of them have clear plans for their lives and, despite their grumbling, betray a certain enthusiasm for their jobs. "Anybody who once gets caught in this mangle never gets out of it," said one.

Evening. Today, after yesterday's sunshine, we went through the west monsoon, which sent white-capped breakers over the deck and made the ship pitch and roll. The ladies withdrew. In this weather I stood enraptured for hours on the bridge, watching the dance of the elements and enjoying the way the ship kept its course, unswerved by the contrary-minded winds. I find it a wonderful thing to be able to withdraw occasionally from the whistling and spouting, the thunderous uproar, and

6

go back to the dining saloon to eat in ordered comfort. For a moment the thought occurred to me that this might be an evidence of the snobbery of civilization, but then I decided to interpret in another way this pleasure we take from experiencing contrasts.

It is precisely these few steps we take out of the wind and weather to a well-set table that permit us to experience culture as a secure and enclosed place. Culture, after all, means that man does not simply accept nature and allow it to push him about involuntarily, but rather keeps his distance from it and asserts his uniqueness over against it. The *Odyssey,* which I imbibe in well-proportioned doses every day, repeatedly communicates this sense of an interior space in which man experiences elevation and superiority over nature. Homer's phrase about the "bellied ships" expresses precisely this feeling of embryonic envelopment that gives the seafarer security in the midst of the elements. The very proximity to the inhuman forces of nature makes us sense with greater intensity this superiority and command that man has over nature. I note how accurately the reading I have been doing in these days reflects this *deinon,* this strange, dreadful power that man has over nature. Gottfried Benn's *Provoziertes Leben* is a struggle with this elemental force (indeed, his entire work is a coming to grips with it), and the same is true of Wilhelm Raabe's *Schüdderump* and most certainly of the *Odyssey.* How fortunate that I have all these books with me and can read them over again!

July 20

A glorious Sunday. Upon awakening we are fanned for the first time by the soft zephyrean breath of the South. The sailors are going about their work in shorts, sans shirts. After the cloudy summer we had in Hamburg, this sunshine is nothing less than a feast. We note at once that everybody is in high spirits, sensing the promise of our distant goals.

Off to port—somewhere off Lisbon—we are accompanied by the chalk-cliffs of Cabo da Roca which we explore with the telescope whenever there is not another ship to be seen on the other side. Since we are only travelers at a distance and are unable to sample the wines of all the countries we pass, I try at least to get a sample of their music with my small radio. From the Spanish coast we get the constant sound of wild dances and the clicking of castanets.

In the evening, our skins burning and glowing from the day's sun, we attended the great welcoming banquet in the dining saloon—caviar on ice, fillet of sole in white wine with mushrooms, Brussels capon garnished with fine vegetables. One would have to be the Thomas Mann of *Buddenbrooks* to have the mind and ability to transpose the experience of this meal into cultivated prose. Passengers in full dress, captain and officers in gleaming white uniforms. A festive evening, after a day that was a festival of light.

Some time in the afternoon, however—this must be added—as we were sailing through the brilliant sunshine, I was suddenly overtaken by the recollection that today was July 20, the same day on which the German resistance movement collapsed with the failure of the attempt upon Hitler's life in 1944, and a day on which many of my friends were swept into the terrors of torture and death. This is the same world in which both of these things are possible: ecstatic happiness in the glistering beauty of the southern sun and the agonies of the torture chambers. There came to my mind the last verse of Psalm 104, that lyric in which earth, clouds, light, and winds become transparencies of the majestic goodness of the Creator. The song concludes—so abruptly that the philologists consider the last verse to be non-genuine—with the staggering words "Let sinners be consumed from the earth, and let the wicked be no more!" Only at this single, solitary place where *man* is mentioned does this somber note appear. It was quite natural that this verse should intrude upon my thoughts just here. Through the midst of the elements, which all unknowingly go on celebrating the praise of the Creator, goes this ship with its cargo of human beings on board, the only ones—and therefore the only lonely

8

ones among all the creatures—who carry their past with them wherever they go, the only ones who live in the present loaded down with the freight of their own freedom, and at the same time the only ones who keep looking to the future with anxiety and hope, because they are burdened with their own knowledge, a minute point of consciousness in the vast, unconscious, creaturely ocean that simply "exists." Every day I remember the brethren who are suffering in Eastern prisons, especially S———. It requires a certain effort at meditation to evoke any real and vital remembrance; the situations are poles apart.

Why is it that this remembering is so much less painful here than it is elsewhere? Is it the euphoria of the moment that almost dissolves the tragedy of life to unreality? Or is it an evidence of that "natural theology" which is so utterly dubious to me in theory but which keeps intruding by brute force in spite of theory—that natural theology which illustrates by experience itself that we are all part and parcel of this cosmos and that the cosmos itself is upheld by the everlasting arms? Perhaps my daily reading of the *Odyssey,* this story of a voyage that tells of the consoling and menacing presence of divine powers, also keeps suggesting to me that we are secure. What would the ocean mean to us if the creative imagination of the poets had not transformed it from a formless elemental flood into a structured image which now gives dimension and order to our own conception of it? Homer took the unruly elements of the world and made them arable. Only then did the flaming skies of daybreak become the signal of "rosy-fingered Dawn," only then did the heave of waves become the rhythm of a controlled event, only then did the horizon become the boundary line of the unsearchable which step by step unmasks its mysteries.

July 21

After an Apollonian night that gave us a sense of calm and amplitude and kept us long on deck, today is somewhat overcast. I feel that this dispensation of alternate cloudiness and brightness is a wise dosage, for another sunny day would make this grandeur almost too overpowering.

At eleven o'clock this morning we passed the Rock of Gibraltar. I was impressed by the ascetic existence of the soldiers, whose habitations were cut right into the rock—into the hard, sterile stone, fruitless and without a touch of green, a symbol of sad necessity and at the same time of petrified mistrust. As if to confirm the thought a searchlight blinked across at us, demanding to know where we came from and where we were going.

The eastern slope of the Rock consisted mostly of a tremendous, smooth concrete wall whose function was to catch rain water. Sea water, too, was stored in order to make human life possible. We passed this menacing mountain of the sea in a light fog beneath a thick bank of clouds, but hardly had we entered the Mediterranean when the sun reappeared.

July 22

Off Tunis at ten o'clock in the morning. Yesterday, from noon on, we sailed through a thick fog that suddenly settled down in a layer about thirty yards deep, pressed down upon the water. Above it was blue sky. The engines ran at half speed, and sometimes we crawled along even more slowly.

Immediately our mood became depressed. The bellowing foghorn that hooted every few minutes, especially, got on our nerves, and actually hurt our ears. At intervals the fog lifted, and suddenly we were pitched into glittering sunshine, but hardly had we gone several miles at full speed when the fog closed in upon us again.

Nevertheless, after supper everything grew light and clear. Instead of the sultry humidity that made the smoky breath of the steam whistle stick to our shirts, an indescribably gentle southern breeze wafted in upon us. To port the gigantic silhouette of the Sierra Nevada still loomed up in the slanting twilight. Dolphins were romping in the water with a contagious *joie de vivre*. The starry heavens rose high above us. Until midnight I stood on the bridge talking with Erwin, the sailor on watch, a little fellow from Traunstein in Upper Bavaria. What a delightful thing it was to hear the Bavarian dialect in the midst of this southern night. He exchanges watch every two hours with Harry, a boy from Cologne, who gives so much of an impression of being a Latin that the girls in Mexico take him for a native—but of course only until he opens his mouth. Nevertheless, he assured me, by that time he has already set their hearts ablaze. The ambrosial night loosens a man's tongue, and we talked about life in general, why we live, and what we can do to cope with life successfully.

I get a real pleasure from the way some of these boys look at life, tackling it consciously and purposefully. By this time they know that I am a minister, and frequently they turn the conversation in this direction. But I do not get the impression that what they say is merely theatrical; on the contrary, I have the feeling they are showing me a side of themselves that they ordinarily carefully conceal, but which is nevertheless their own and therefore genuine. I have given them copies of several of my briefer books, and my guess is that it is not merely courtesy that prompts them to talk about the books at the next opportunity.

Today at breakfast we had a thrilling experience. Peter, the little steward, rushed in and cried, "A Hapag ship is coming!" * With one leap we were all at the window, and sure enough, a short distance away our sister ship the "Leipzig" was passing by. The foghorns struck up a roaring greeting, the flags were dipped, and people on both ships waved for all they were worth. It was an indescribably festive sight to see the "Leipzig" passing by against the background of the mountainous coast of Africa. Suddenly our common homeland became a bond of unity, which, rising above all sentimentalism, was impressed upon us only in these foreign surroundings.

Whenever I turn on the radio, I seem to get nothing but

* That is, another ship of the Hamburg-America Line. (Trans.)

11

the liturgical music of the mosques. Probably it only sounds Moslem to our European ears; it may in fact be popular music.

As we lie in deck chairs at noon, the little tame pigeon that has sought refuge on the ship keeps strutting around us. Everybody loves it, and the passengers and sailors keep running to the kitchen window to fetch food for it. For it too the ship is a place of security. This enclosed, dry place links the small creature with us human beings. We live together as on Noah's ark. But when the pigeon looks out upon the sea, as we humans also do, it does not look upon it from an aesthetic point of view or as an element that imposes tasks and presents a challenge to battle; for the pigeon the sea is the realm of the hostile and the deadly. Perhaps in this respect the pigeon is closer to the men of the Bible than we are, for to them the sea was an element of chaos that swallows up and engulfs men.

After supper I chatted for a while with the little mess boy. I told him about an experience I had had with his counterpart on my trip to America. On the return voyage we were lying in the harbor at Antwerp on May 1, and the poor fellow had such an enormous pile of dishes to wash that he had given up all hope of getting ashore. Out of pity I helped a bit with the drying, particularly since I had learned this quite thoroughly in America. By doing this I won his complete confidence with one stroke, and he asked me somewhat timidly whether I would help him write a letter to his girl friend. Naturally I was glad to do so, and I told him that during my army service I had often helped my comrades write such letters and had even produced some lofty epistles to their mothers-in-law. I made an appointment with him to meet me in my stateroom the next evening and had my typewriter in readiness. When he arrived, his confidence had grown to such an extent that he expressed the wish that I should write not only to this girl friend but also to five others he had in various ports. "You can write one each day, and by that time we'll be in Hamburg." At this point, however, I felt obliged to make a few fatherly, moral demurrals, and said that, considering my calling as a professor

12

of theology, he could not expect me to write to six different "fiancees," and that I was prepared to write at most to *two*. The mess boy to whom I related this today thought this was "nice of me."

July 23

Last night the first really oppressive heat descended upon us and prevented our getting any rest all night. This morning, about six o'clock, we were passing between Tunis and Sicily.

After breakfast the first engineer took us on a tour of the engine room. We had hardly set foot on the top step of the iron staircase when we were assailed by a wave of heat that at first blast could even knock the breath out of an old sauna man. Unless one is a fireman or a cook by vocation, he can hardly touch the iron railing with his bare hands, so hot is it. The farther we descended, however, the "cooler" it became. At the bottom the temperature is only 123 degrees Fahrenheit! The chief said, however, that in the Red Sea the thermometer rises to 185 degrees. In the boiler room it even climbs to 205 degrees. When the young apprentices have to go in to check the instruments, they say, "Now we make our bloody sacrifice for Hapag."

The ship has a steam turbine and therefore develops much higher temperatures than a motor ship. I imagined what it must have been like in the war when a direct hit burst a boiler that develops almost fifty atmospheres of pressure.

Though it was very hot outside, when we finally returned the open air seemed like a gentle breath of heaven.

It is good for us pampered passengers, however, to feel even for a few moments what it means to work down there below, while we stroll about on deck or lounge in the deck chairs. Many of these boys who are making their first voyage find it very hard to stand the heat of the engines. In my conversations with them I can soon tell whether they are unskilled and have only taken on the job as a piece of drudgery to get money quicker than on land, or whether they have a goal and are aiming eventually to reach the position of ship's engineer or something like it. As soon as they have a goal in view, they find their life easier to bear. Then they live for something that cannot be measured merely in terms of money. Still, the idea of sacrifice is not altogether strange to them.

During the night we should pass Malta.

July 24

Yesterday was an enchanting day with a light head wind that took all the heaviness from the heat. In the evening the sailors sat in a large circle on the lower deck, and I could hardly believe my own ears when suddenly, as I was standing at the bow, I heard the spirited singing of some really ancient, old-fashioned soldiers' songs; suddenly hearing these songs about Heide from Brandenburg, Annemarie, and Erika brought to mind my old days in the army. The solution of the mystery was something of a letdown: they had set up a loudspeaker and were only playing records. None of them has an accordion, and, as it turned out when we asked them later, none of them can sing even one song. Even in this bliss of the Mediterranean, beneath a crescent moon that would soften a stone and melt anybody's heart, they did no singing on their own.

What is the reason for this? Perhaps because they have no sense of being a community? (The arrangement of watches on a ship has the effect of keeping the men apart.) Or is it the other way round, they are not a community because they do not sing? Later I met on the quarter-deck three young men from the engine room who are working for wages. We have become good friends ever since I have been treating them to a beer now and then, whenever we chat.

These fellows are almost unimaginably limited in their interests in so far as these go beyond the radius of a crude eroticism and the earning of a few dollars. I am somewhat amused as I look back at myself and think of how people in our position are sometimes shocked at how "dim" the intelligence of some of our students can be. Compared with what I see here, even the most awful cases of this kind now strike me as bright lights.

What I get is an impression of immaturity. And this impression is intensified when these men tell me how they squander their wages blindly and senselessly in port and sometimes even secure advances from the purser for this purpose. They live without care—but certainly not like the lilies of the field and the birds of the air.

All this makes me realize the human dignity inherent in care and concern. Only *man,* as he is distinguished from the animal, can be anxious and concerned, because he is constantly going beyond the present moment, to which the animal is confined; only man knows that he has a future and must die. "That we shall die, we know, 'tis but the time and drawing days out, that men stand upon," says Shakespeare.

To me this absorption in the blind, mad pleasure of the moment seems inhuman, and I become aware of the problem that is inherent in the democratic systems, since democracy depends upon people being mature. Here, if anywhere, it is borne in upon me that these people must be led, must be taken in hand. But where are these thoughts driving me: to a Catholic idea of authority — or even to totalitarian wishes? I note that in this area there is still a great deal of thinking to be done.

Every now and then in my conversations I throw in what might be called rational arguments: do they ever think about the future, do they ever have the desire to go to a merchant marine school, do they ever save some of their wages to make their homes a little more attractive? (I even suggest television, though my attitude toward it is normally very critical, because even this seems to me to be much better for them as well as their families than their asinine bumming around in the St. Pauli dives when they have a few days at home.)

But none of this has any effect whatever upon them. The simple fact is that they are creatures who are motivated more by their impulses and instincts than by their reason. It suddenly is clear to me that with countless people the appeal to

15

reason is an exceedingly impotent undertaking and that, if we are to find a way to these hearts, we shall have to gain entrance at some completely different point. But where is any such exposed flank? Am I perhaps too pharisaical, so that this evening they are not ready to reveal themselves to me? After all, Pharisees, who do not love, cannot understand, and one who does not understand is always confronted with closed doors. It worries me that I might possibly feel superior. But I do not believe that this is so, for I really like these fellows. In their way they are good-hearted boys, and above all very good companions. Their confidence, too, moves me, and I can conceive that if I were in a very desperate situation—in a totalitarian jail or prisoners' camp—I would rather be with them than with many an intellectual sophisticate.

I am moved by a great compassion for these men. (One of them is an eighteen-year-old boy who always beams at me when he comes coal-black out of the engine room, and whose raffish charm is a delight to me.) After all, on what basis should they deal with life? Who has ever given them such a basis of operation? Their parental homes? Or the church (which often does not appear even on the furthest horizon of their life)?

I realize what a liberation the Gospel could be for them, if we only knew how to speak it to them in the right way—simply because the Gospel is not moralism. This experience makes me surer than ever that in this situation moralism cannot accomplish anything whatever. The Law kills. How can one ever combat an urge or a passion by prohibitions, threats, or propaganda? The moral law always operates with frontal attacks, which are much too directly contrived to be able to break through such elementally massed forces. The clamor of the blood and sap of life, the ecstasy of the moment, these can be controlled only by counterweights, that is, by filling the heart with *other* contents which will seize the occupied territory from the hands of these alien invaders. The Gospel does not demand; it fills a person with love and security by giving meaning and purpose to his life.

But I am also thinking of the other riches with which people like ourselves are filled: the fact that we are capable of ordered thinking, of enjoying a poem, a novel, a work of art, the fact that we can dream, and that all of this can constitute a counter-pressure which diminishes the threat of the empty situations when we are vulnerable. What do these poor fellows have in the way of counterweights?

All this was going through my mind in the course of a conversation that was very long drawn out and frequently punctuated by intervals of silence.

Henry, the little eighteen-year-old, brought a guitar with him, but he cannot play it. He also has a fine voice, he says proudly, but unfortunately he does not know any words. It was almost pathetic to see how the lovely night was impelling the men to sing, and yet they were simply incapable of song. From amidships, however, came the sound of "Erika," repeated over and over again, with a few jazz interludes.

I am not at all satisfied with myself this evening. Should I not have said more to the men than I did? Or am I too impatient? Is it possible to speak to them seriously at all, slightly befuddled as they are by alcohol? God alone knows what I have done wrong again and what I have done right, or whether I have done anything right at all. Can persons like ourselves, with our different point of view, with all the inhibitions of the educated, jump over our own shadows and muster up the straightforward immediacy that would be necessary in a situation like this? I went to bed tonight with some oppressive thoughts on my mind. I wanted to make this voyage in order to see something from shipboard. But now I am coming more and more to look *into* the ship and meet the people on it. I am by no means sure that Asia will present me with greater or more moving questions than does this floating microcosm.

July 25

Approaching Port Said, the lights of which, we are told, we shall see tonight.

I was just about to begin writing in my journal and, being called away for a brief time, I inadvertently left the notebook lying in the sun. When I came back it was so hot that I had to let it cool off. Ah, the heat! Since yesterday it has been the center of all conversation and of groaning and moaning, though even they still betray an undertone of pleasure. Up to this time we have always dressed for dinner but last evening we arranged with the captain to make some allowances for the heat. Although air conditioning would make it easy to manage the amenities of custom, we are glad that we do not have that artificial atmosphere on board (though, like most lies, it is very nice). After all, we want to experience the rounding of our planet in the changing degrees of heat too. Since on this freighter we are under no compulsion to dress, we manage well enough. Besides, as one layer of clothing after another is removed, we have the flattering feeling of playing the role of the wise man who accommodates himself to the situation.

Anyhow, the captain and his officers came to lunch today in white trousers and short sleeves for the first time. The wind comes through the front windows into the dining room, two ventilators augment the breeze, and all the apertures in the deck are drawing additional air from above into the room. The old hands are saying that this heat is still quite harmless. The real surprises, they say, will come when we are in the Red Sea. The steward says, as the ladies blush a bit, that the "public" ladies' toilet in the passageway, which is used only by the stewards and guests, since each passenger has his own toilet, is the hottest room on the ship. The seat cover is simply too hot to handle, he says. I chimed in somewhat pedantically, "But after all, you're not supposed to handle it." The embarrassed, amused glances of the ladies intimated very clearly that I seemed to be overlooking the fact that the human skin is indivisible.

Awnings have been put up on the bridge and the radio deck. So we are prepared for anything. I found out yesterday that the iron plates of the ship are already beastly hot, when I took off my sandals for the rather naive purpose of cooling off my feet and blithely proceeded to walk about on deck. In the next few moments I must have looked like a dancing bear being taught by gypsies to dance on hot stove lids. In any case, I tried to secure a bit of compensation by asking the cook, somewhat hypocritically, to show me around the ship's refrigerator room. To be sure, it did turn out to be interesting to see all the delicacies that are stored there. One might have imagined it held the stock of a great packing house, including all the boxes and cartons of a flourishing colonial wholesale firm. But, of course, the main thing for me was its intoxicating coolness. I attempted to make it all the more pleasurable by imagining the heat in the nearby engine room. The tropics and the North Pole—all in one ship. It really is a miniature image of our world.

The cook (who, by the way, is only twenty-two years old and already an admired genius in his trade) may well have wondered about my untiring and persistent interest, for I kept on quizzing him in minute detail concerning the contents of every box and carton, and then went on to philosophize with him on the question whether cooking is an art or a trade. Perhaps with his bright young intelligence he saw through me and was quite aware that I was only trying to prolong these moments in the coolness. With these fellows you can never be quite sure, for these sea-seasoned men have a devilishly clever knowledge of human nature, especially when it comes to diagnosing the "all-too-human."

For a long time now we have seen no ships, no land, and no lights. The endless blue of the Mediterranean surrounds us, smooth as a mirror. I let my eyes rest in this dreamlike vastness that never holds the eye to any fixed point or line. Was it really only the menace of the ocean that caused the ancients to think of the sea as a symbol of chaos? May it not also have been this complete absence of contours, this formlessness, that terrified the Greeks? To the Hellenes, form signified what the Name signified to the Hebrews, namely, the power to cast a spell upon the beholder and take possession of him. They therefore found

19

peace and a sense of security only as they were able either to impose form upon the turbulence of Being or to discover form within it, thus wresting from Being both a sense of their independence of it and knowledge of it.

Complete symmetry, which can be found objectified in the sea, is something that we experience as emptiness, the void. Noonday, of which Nietzsche was so fond, the time when day comes to a stop at its culmination, which on land is ushered in by the irresistible god Pan, bathes everything in a shimmering light that seems no longer to touch any object and that therefore produces no form. It is almost the mystical world of Kant's *Dinge-an-sich* (things-in-themselves), a world of things that have not yet been given form by any process of perception or categorization and seem to remain as they were in the moment before creation. What has no form ceases to be a "something" from which I distinguish and separate myself. At the very moment of blinking, dozing drowsiness this voluptuously glowing formless nothingness draws us into itself. For moments on end we lose the sense of separateness from the cosmos and are mystically absorbed into it. We begin to grasp what the mystics meant by "nihilation," what Schleiermacher expressed in his phrase "the feeling of the universe," and what Goethe's Werther felt as he lay in a flowering meadow and had the sensation in his heart that the tiny insects and blades of grass were a part of himself.

Only at morning and in the evening, when cloud patterns and colors produce forms and structures and when star patterns appear in the firmament, does the world emerge once more from the void like a new creation—sinless, as it were, and in a new primal state, lifted beyond all human history. In the presence of processes like these we may seem to be utterly passive, like an animal playing dead, and yet be full of activity on the inside.

By contrast with this, I have often observed that lavish landscapes, which really have something to offer, simply benumb the imagination and the workings of the mind—especially when we speed through them in an automobile and thus accelerate the rapid change of forms and perspectives. They simply pour out their abundance; we ourselves need do nothing more than remain in a state of pure receptiveness. The rage for traveling exhibited by the general public and by the purchasers of picture postcards is nothing but another instance of the general disease of outer-directedness in our lives, which through television, radio, and managed amusement reduces us to mere bundles of nerves that react only to external stimuli.

All that is changed, however, in this void of shimmering light, which no longer illuminates anything but has simply become an end in itself, or, as Kant would say, light *an sich,* for here begins the world of expressive imagination, the kind of imagination that begins on the inside and moves outward. I can go on end-lessly looking at the two fans circling above me; I can observe how their rhythm synchronizes for a moment, and then how they get out of step and the two mechanisms become polyphonic and begin to dance in syncopated rhythm.

In my reading I have made a curious discovery. At intervals I have been going through a few novels from the ship's library. They are not really bad, and they would certainly give me pleasure if I read them at home during the noon siesta between the busy hours of the day, but here they strike me as insipid and shallow. And whereas at home I often have to brace myself to read the great books—since the beating rhythm of the day's bustle must first be slowed down in order to facilitate a break-through into the "totally other" dimension of stillness—here the great things are near and familiar. I hardly need to make a conscious effort to reach out for them; they are all around me in the stillness. First the Bible, which claims the first hour of the day, and then, separated by a wide margin from all lesser things, the *Odyssey,* the reading of which I have rationed in order to make it last longer. Too bad I have now read through Gottfried Benn's *Provoziertes Leben* and cannot read his letters once more! On the other hand, I have laid aside *Joseph and His Brothers.* I cannot get over the stumbling block that here

21

the author takes these biblical texts with which I am familiar, strips them of their stark, archaic simplicity, reclothes the skeleton with the opulent flesh of imagination and modern psychologizings, and thus turns them into vehicles for his own assertions. With all my admiration for his style, his language, and his mastery of Egyptology, I keep thinking whenever I begin a new chapter: What is he going to do this time; how will he dramatize this or that well-known episode; how will he puff it up to epic proportions? Since I am familiar with Thomas Mann, I know the kind of delicacies that he cannot forgo and that he will allow to melt voluptuously upon his gourmet's tongue. So I cannot muster up the naivete to allow him to tell me the story.

Yesterday at supper we were talking about the Chinese attitude toward death. The captain related what he had seen in a Chinese port, and said that he had heard the same story from others. A coolie, working on the loading of a ship, fell overboard and drowned. Nobody made a move to save him; on the contrary, the others merely uttered catcalls, crying out something like "There he goes." It struck him that they enjoyed the incident as an amusing diversion.

Mrs. V. related some similar experiences, but warned that such incidents should not be too simply interpreted as inhumanity. Out of her knowledge of these things, she explained them in this way. Anybody who saves another person from drowning is meddling with fate and must then assume the responsibility for doing so. If the person who is rescued sustains any injury, the rescuer is responsible for the rest of his life. He has snatched a life from its predestined fate and must pay the costs of his intervention. So everybody is careful not to be caught playing the villainous role of an antagonist of fate.

Regardless of whether these observations and interpretations are true—and whether they are still applicable to China today—they make us aware of how much the inside view differs from the external aspect of things. Even if we arrive at an intellectual insight into certain associations of ideas in the insider's view and can express them in words, what actually goes on in

the minds and experience of these people remains forever closed
to us. We are confined to the perspective of our own world of
experience, to our own environment, and the worlds in which
other beings live appear to us to be nothing more than fleeting
shadows. (I am thinking of Von Uexküll's book, *Nie geschaute
Welten. Die Umwelten meiner Freunde.*)* What thin films of
reality we hold in our hands when we summarize philosophical
systems, analyze developments of dogma intellectually, or explain the nature of the Platonic idea in a lecture! What lay
behind them in real, living existence remains beyond us. We
can never exchange our own existence for that of another being.
The cleverest animal psychologist, who can foresee certain
reactions with great precision, nevertheless will never know
how a monkey feels. The mystery begins at the horizon of our
existence, and the tiny speck of the self is imprisoned in the
center of that existence.

How curious it is that reactions here on shipboard are precisely the same as in ordinary life. As soon as people learn
that you are a minister, they come with all kinds of problems
of life and love and also the problem of the meaning of life.
Almost every evening when I am with the seamen on watch,
or chat with one or another of them who is off duty, the conversation somehow comes around to these questions. To be
sure, this happens only when I am alone with them. When you
see how they work all day, doggedly and industriously cleaning
and painting, painting and cleaning, when you share with them
their tales of life in port and hear them tell of their experiences
with expressive expletives and gestures, the external view (there
it is again!) can mislead you into thinking that they are completely witless, animal beings. Naturally, such types are here
too, and I have already made some comments about them. But
I am still amazed at how many of them are thinking and are

* For an exposition of Von Uexküll's thought in English see *Existence,
A New Dimension in Psychiatry and Psychology,* ed. Rollo May et al.,
N. Y., Basic Books, Inc., pp. 195-199. (Trans.)

troubled by their thoughts. Recently one of them told me that once when he was in a desperate situation he ran into a Catholic church and prayed. "Afterwards I said to myself, Man, what the devil is the matter with you?" he added apologetically and somewhat shamefacedly. But I noted that he clearly wanted to talk with me about it.

In the evening when the stars are above, a light is blinking in the distance perhaps, the breeze is blowing lightly, and we glide through the twilight, tongues are loosened and the soul begins to breathe. These are the finest hours. I rejoice in the fact that Christians and the office of the ministry enjoy a strong confidence even among those who do not actively avail themselves of the benefits of faith. Almost all of them would like to touch the horns of the altar with at least one finger and, down in some ultimate recess of their hearts, to count on this place of refuge. I have the feeling that they are glad to have among them somebody who ministers at that place and to be able to talk with him in the evening breeze.

July 26

Afternoon. In the Suez Canal. For an hour the ship has been lying to in a passing place to allow a convoy of about seventy ships to pass in the opposite direction. A hot, parching desert wind sweeps over endless fields of sand on either side. We are glad not to be in a dead calm. As it is, we perspire from every pore, and the sun beats down upon the ship. Even the cold-water tap yields only hot water, which must be left standing in the basin for a while to cool off.

The captain, who is always paternally concerned for our welfare, has come up with a fantastic idea: a swimming pool made of sailcloth. Today the carpenter work for it is being done. A ten by twelve foot frame is being erected; it will be fitted with sailcloth. Though the work on the red-hot deck is a beastly job, everybody works like a demon for the alluring prospect of getting cooled off gives wings to his spirit.

How the world has changed for us in twenty-four hours!

Yesterday evening after supper we were still sitting comfortably with the captain, listening to stories of Japan and China and looking out of the window of the smoking saloon at a sea that glowed with color and then grew ever grayer and darker. Later, as I was taking a walk around the deck, I came upon a group of seamen and machinists sitting on a hatchway. They were going to spend the night there under an awning, because their quarters had become unbearably hot. (In addition to the heat of the climate, some of them are subjected to additional heat radiated by the boilers, and thus are doubly in need of cooling.) I fell to telling them stories. At one point, two of them laughed so hard that they fell out of their chairs.

At half-past four in the morning we were wakened: the lights of Port Said had come into view. After days at sea it was a treat to see land and the regular lights of a city again. In the half-light I climbed up to the bridge. The Egyptian pilot, whose physiognomy was the first greeting from a foreign land and therefore one that interested me, was dressed in dazzling white. The harbor was very quiet, and we asked ourselves whether this was owing to the political situation.

Hardly had we made fast to a buoy offshore when a genuine oriental spectacle began to unfold around us and the scenes in our childhood story and picture books suddenly came to life before our eyes. Along with the physician (who was first to come aboard, to take some stitches in an engineer who had been injured) and a troop of officials, we played host to a teeming horde of traders who came on board. To see the approach of their colorful boats decked out like shops was like seeing a film in technicolor. They settled like a swarm of flies around every incoming ship. In no time at all this fantastic mob had spilled over the whole quarter-deck and set up their wares in picturesque fashion: rugs, shoes, trunks, trinkets and souvenirs of every kind and degree of trashiness, postcards, photo albums, and a few good pieces of handicraft.

At first I kept aloof, because I was somewhat shy of being pushed about and did not trust myself to cope with these bargainers. So I stood for a while on the upper deck quietly watching these characters. Some of them had rather insolent, rascally faces. One unusually fat Egyptian, who seemed to have authority over the others, impressed us with the red-lacquered toenails that adorned his warty little toes.

Finally I could no longer stand being a mere spectator, and joined in with the seamen. The enthusiastic, exciting, dramatic, gesticulating sport of haggling and chaffering, which provided great fun for both parties, drew me into its spell.

The captain was the best at handling these people. Being an old hand in the East, he doubtless had had more practice than the rest. He put on his act just like the Egyptians, exhibiting a tremendous range of acting ability, making parrying, pleading, temporizing gestures with his hands, building up dramatic and delaying moments, holding his ear to hear the trader's whispers ("Don't tell anybody how cheap I'm letting you have it") and himself whispering trade secrets into their ears. It was a spectacle to make you laugh till the tears came.

Through the telescope I was able to watch the life and activity on the fishing boats off shore. Large groups of men of all ages, who seemed to have met by arrangement, were holding palavers. Mrs. V. pointed out to me how different life on these harbor boats was from that on Chinese junks, which shelter entire families and in which work goes on as constantly as in an ant heap. Here only men were to be seen—not a single woman in sight—and they appeared to have a lot of time on their hands.

Also in the barracks-like structures on shore, which were open on one side like dollhouses, the traders and fishermen were huddled together, sitting on their hams. Beyond them on a drill ground Egyptian soldiers were practicing marching. The little company produced the curious effect of making propaganda against militarism. They seemed to do more resting than marching, and I wondered how they were able to squat and lie down in the blazing sun. It seemed not to bother them at all.

At this point the world outside attracted us less than what was happening on the ship itself. Among the hucksters on board there were some interesting characters who might have come out of the Arabian Nights. If you bought nothing from them, they were never sullen or resentful but remained cheerful, like children who knew that soon other playmates would turn up with whom they could carry on the game. They would even perform conjuring tricks for nothing and were delighted to be tossed a cigarette for their pains.

A photographer came on board, carrying a huge ancient camera, as large as a television camera, and a mighty tripod. With great ceremony he set up his apparatus and began to take group pictures. He took them directly upon photographic paper without using film or plates. He then used the paper as a negative which he had to re-photograph to produce a normal picture. Nevertheless, it was ready to take away in a relatively short time.

As the man reached under a black cloth that constituted his portable darkroom and went through the manipulations inside the box to develop and fix the picture, our crew watched him spellbound. This primitive method, which I saw years ago at a country fair in Estonia when I was a four-year-old boy, is a far more impressive demonstration of the wonder of photography than the perfected processes of a modern laboratory. The later, more sophisticated stages in the art of photography have lost their connection with its beginnings, which used to give a sense of stepping into a newly discovered world. I watched very closely, with never a sophisticated smile, but only a thrilled amazement at how the original fascination was preserved and even heightened by the magician-like appearance of the oriental photographer, the way in which photography still appeared, not as something taken for granted, but as a real feat of magic.

Suddenly these people noticed my camera—for, naturally, I could not let this chance for a picture escape me. They eyed the long tube of the telescopic lens with obvious respect, and all of them begged to be photographed. So, just as they had been pulling the wool over *our* eyes, I fooled some of them too and went through the motions of taking pictures, snapping a little lever that sounds like a snapshot. They took a childlike, never-ending delight in being photographed, striking fine, ornamental poses, arranging themselves in symmetrical groups, and each time expressing their thanks with a courteous bow.

One of them kept raising his hand and saying "Heil Hitler!", thinking in this way to break down our sales resistance. "Hitler and Nasser," they shouted, making respectful gestures. Our crewmen went along with it for the joke, and I realized how unreal the specter of the past had become for the younger generation.

Our convoy having been made up, we put out into the canal about ten o'clock in the morning. With the telescope I was able to get a grand view of everything on both sides of the canal, which ran in an almost straight line. I saw people on their prayer rugs performing their devotions, just as were the several Egyptian dockers who had been taken on board our ship with their boats. Though I had often heard the ritual and seen it in pictures, and thus was familiar with the gestures, I was nevertheless moved by it at that moment, when I realized that those people were really in earnest. Here was somebody who really believed in Allah and spread his prayer rug on the burning sands beneath the broiling sun. We could see that religion was still an integral part of their lives, as we noted the complete naturalness with which our Egyptians passed from conversation or roaring laughter to their ceremony of prayer.

But the great thrill that this passage through the Suez gave us was the sight of the work on the widening of the canal. I was able to secure some facts about this undertaking. Twenty-five thousand fellahin are employed upon this gigantic earth-moving, or rather, sand-moving, operation. They receive 66 milliemes for moving a cubic meter of sand, which is about a day's work—that means they work for 70 cents a day in this murderous heat. The canal is to be widened by 163 feet and excavated to a depth of 50 feet so that ships of 46,000 gross tonnage can pass through. The whole enterprise is a part of the Nasser Plan to deal with unemployment.

What these dry statistics say we now see with our own eyes: thousands of swarming, crawling human beings massed together at several places and recognizable even a long distance away by the great profusion of tents. As we pass very close to them we are able to observe them near at hand: they are shoveling the sand into baskets, carrying it high up along beaten paths, and dumping it. The only thing I can think of is the labor of ants; even the heaped-up mounds and the organized confusion remind me of this. Suddenly the question how the pyramids were erected is no longer a problem to me. An inexhaustible reservoir of human beings (thus, fabulously cheap labor) apparently is still able to compete with modern machinery. The gigantic dredges of the Canal Company were sunk and destroyed during the Suez crisis. Now the work is simply done by hand, just as the peasants on the other side of the canal farm by hand without any machinery whatever—as their ancestors did in the times of the pharaohs. Here the millenniums stand still.

When I look at these people, especially those whom we were able to observe at close quarters in the harbor, I think I can understand a little why the French and the English still do not want to give up colonizing and still do not take these peoples— I do not mean the Asiatics—very seriously as political powers. Of course, it is wrong to think this way, but at least I understand how they have come to think as they do. The people you see in the ports and on the banks of the canal often impress you as beasts of burden or merely as children. Naturally, I am aware that I may very soon have to correct this limited first impression. After all, a port never presents the optimal aspect of a country! And yet . . .

July 27

Sunday. Continued passage through the Suez Canal during the night. I went up to the station in the bow where the searchlight is operated. There the stillness was perfect. We no longer heard the engines, and there was not the slightest vibration. It was like a moonlight ride in a sailboat; soundlessly we glided past bizarre sand formations in the desert, military stations, tents with campfires and flitting figures around them, and palms sharply silhouetted against the nocturnal sky. The pale, shimmering light of the moon made the desert shine like a snowy landscape. Our eyes were so weirdly beguiled that we expected to see a skier come rushing by at any moment. Every one of us was carried away by that enchantment, and we were a silent company. Finally, when somebody began to speak it was not long until the entrancement of that silent gliding through the night opened up hearts and caused people to utter things that otherwise would never have been expressed. I noted that several had been deeply impressed by the naturalness with which the Egyptian wharfmen and dockers had performed their devotions on board. In our conversation this began to radiate into our own situation. I was glad of it, for throughout the day I had noted—though only among a few of the "primitives," the cruder sort—a completely uncomprehending amusement over the gymnastic aspect of these cultic exercises. Even when some of the sailors had tried to disturb them, the Egyptians had never faltered in the least. They seemed to be quite accustomed to these attitudes on the part of "Christian" people. When I spoke to our "primitives" about this, they simply shrugged their shoulders in annoyance. On this point they appear to be completely callous.

Meanwhile, we have long since entered the Red Sea. The hot breath of the desert is blowing upon us. It bears no resemblance whatever to the wind of the sea. But just now, as the heights of Sinai emerge from the mist to larboard, even the heat cannot prevent a cold chill from running down my back.

I read the Gospel for the day in order to observe the day with the worshiping fellowship at home. The difference in clock time somewhat disturbs this effort of imagination, for at home people are still in morning slumber. Even the decent summer suit, into which I struggled in order to mark the Sunday break for my own benefit, I soon took off again in order to meet the great events of the afternoon with a mind less depressed by heavy clothes. For this Sunday afternoon brought us a real treat.

Our swimming pool is finished, filled with fresh sea water and decorated with flags. A loudspeaker provides the appropriate background noise. Mr. N., who was condemned to give the dedicatory speech, has brought it to birth with obvious labor pains. Now everyone gathers around the pool, from the captain on down to the busboy—at least everyone who is off duty.

The sailors sit on the hatch right beside the pool. When the captain declares the season open, the two young ladies dive into the water first. The sailors follow these proceedings with adoring looks. They are obviously so fascinated by these two mermaids that they have been struck speechless, though normally they do not suffer from excessive shyness. When all the passengers are finally in the water, the captain challenges the silent crew to jump in too. But neither vigorous challenge nor fatherly persuasion can coax them in, even though all of them are panting for this chance to get into the pool.

These hard-boiled seamen, who have weathered many a storm on land and sea and in any case are quite devoid of the vice of prudery, are simply too embarrassed to step into the same water with these nice, gentle, well-bred creatures.

All of us grabbed hold of one or another of them with whom we had become acquainted and tried to persuade them to get into the pool; eventually, it became a kind of game to make these weather-tested men blush and find new excuses for not getting in. When Mrs. V., the mother of the two girls, joined in and challenged a young man who is normally a very lively fellow and who already had on his swimming trunks, he bashfully replied, "My mother told me never to swim after eating." Not until we were all in the dining room at the smorgasbord

31

which had been promised us for this evening did the news reach us that the men were leaping into the water in droves, and then we heard their shouting.

The smorgasbord topped off the day in festive style. The cook and steward in gleaming whites flanked the huge counter, whose culinary compositions would have been worthy of a color photograph. The talk of food continued in long, jovial conversations. Never for a moment did we passengers have the feeling that we were being provided with a "service." The captain and first officer, with their social imagination and cordiality, had the knack of generating something like a family atmosphere, and we fancied that they themselves enjoyed these hours of conversation.

July 29

It is only by reading the daily Scripture passages in the Moravian Brethren devotions that I know what date it is. Otherwise I would drop completely into timelessness. Everything, even time, seems to dissolve in this heat. Even the writing of my diary demands considerable effort, and correcting the proofs for my *Ethics,* which were sent to me at the harbor to be added to the large packet I had already received, is actually a hardship. The railings of some of the stairs are so hot that we cannot hold them. The temperature of our swimming pool is about ninety degrees, but still it is a relief. Even in the short time we have been exposed to the sun I have acquired a terrific sunburn.

Last night all the passengers slept on the reclining chairs on deck. The sailors set up a shakedown on one of the hatchways. Though I lay in the breeze, dressed in shorts, I was plenty warm.

First thing in the morning we had a bit of an alarm. The twenty-one tons of water that filled our swimming pool ripped a hole in the canvas. We saw all our Lido-dreams trickling away—but the whole thing has been rebuilt more securely.

This evening, as I sat with the carpenter, the electrician, and the cook—three very lively and open-minded men—we grew so terribly hot with our storytelling and laughing that, late as it was, we leaped into our renovated pool and continued our stories in the water. My guess is that the passengers on a luxury boat with a tiled swimming pool do not have as much fun as we do with this miniature ocean constructed with materials found on board the ship. If all goes well, I shall be able to report later without lying that I have swum in the Red Sea, the Indian Ocean, and the China Sea. After all, one must have swum in the waters of various countries in order to know them; we always have the genuine water on board.

During the afternoon it suddenly grew hazy despite the blazing, dry heat. Since, with my layman's understanding, I could not account for fog in these latitudes, I asked the captain about it. He explained that it is not a real fog, but is caused by sand —or rather a microscopically fine dust—from the surrounding deserts that is spread about by storms in the atmosphere and often settles down upon the water in long yellow stripes. We had already seen a large number of these stripes in the morning.

Indian Ocean

July 30

We have just sailed from Aden and are moving toward the Indian Ocean. I shall probably always remember Aden as one of the dreariest holes I have ever seen. Last night, which I spent on the radio deck after one of the hottest days ever— even the oldest seamen and the "oriental experts" on board said so—was refreshing. The elevated radio deck gave free access to the breeze caused by the movement of the ship. Besides, it had actually become a trace cooler. About seven o'clock in the morning, as we were passing by the steep, jagged, bizarre-looking foothills of Aden, I jumped into the swimming pool, in which the temperature of the water had gone down from ninety-three to eighty-four degrees during the night. One learns to appreciate and enjoy even that little difference in temperature.

After breakfast we entered the harbor, a sparkling expanse of water in the midst of towering mountains, alive with innumerable ships. But then the close-up view of Aden was very disenchanting, thus proving again that romance is a matter of distance.

We made fast right behind the stern of a big British aircraft carrier, so we were able to observe the activity on the vast top deck of the ship. Men of the crew, in shorts, were walking about or lying around in groups talking. Commands boomed out from tremendous loudspeakers. At brief intervals one of the two helicopters would rise to make a practice flight. Whenever it rose and returned, some crewmen would jump to get under its vanes in order to get the benefit of the prop-wash.

We had been quite apprehensive of the heat in Aden, since it is surrounded by mountains and therefore is generally without any wind at all. However, a lively and refreshing breeze blew all day, which made the stay on the motionless ship quite tolerable. We were able to enjoy the panorama and observe the many English and American warships that were concentrated there—probably because of the political crisis in Iraq. Judging from the activity on the ships, however, the crisis had grown less severe, for we observed a great deal of visiting back and forth. Boats filled with white-clad sailors were constantly arriving and leaving.

The city itself, part of which we were able to see, was enclosed by steep, barren, heat-furrowed mountains. We could see European business houses and residences that looked just as bleak and stony as the surrounding hills, and a large number of tiny stone huts occupied by the Arabs which looked like abandoned emergency quarters of the first inhabitants of the moon. In spite of the warning of experienced men of the ship's company, who cautioned that no good would come of it, N. and I could not resist the temptation to make a visit onshore. We had hardly stepped out of the cutter when we were set upon by a whole pack of Arabs, young and old, offering to conduct us through the city, get us a taxi or drive us in a taxi, and proffering all kinds of services and objects. We wanted only to ramble through the city, however, and search out what we could see for ourselves. As long as we so much as murmured a refusal to the babble of voices coming from the teeming, gesticulating swarm that surrounded us, they would not leave off. They seemed to interpret even our refusals as a welcome contact. Not until the two of us had come to an understanding, after a brief colloquy in our own language, that we would ignore them altogether and simply push our way through those human waves like the unfeeling bow of a ship did they gradually leave us. To continue the metaphor, one after another they gradually fell overboard. (This rather cynical, contemptuous conduct toward human beings took some effort on the part of one who had just received the galley proofs of his book on Christian ethics.) The begging children, who kept shouting "Baksheesh," were so charming that we certainly would have handed out all our coins if we had not been condemned to stinginess by the fact that we had nothing but larger bills.

35

In the narrow, fetid streets we learned to know what heat really was. The Red Sea was child's-play by comparison. I said to N., "If we should happen to lose sight of each other and you see a puddle in the street, it's me!" Through the unimaginable smells, past veiled women—how they can ever stand it, I don't know—through the midst of a herd of goats searching for paltry tufts of grass in front of the dirty cafes on the main street, through cordons of innumerable vendors, standing before their hot, open stores and trying to palm off on us their fountain pens, typewriters, cameras, and colored scarves, we pushed our way to the center of the city and into some of the side streets, taking a number of pictures under the suspicious and watchful eyes of the Arabs.

As we were taking the pictures, a nice young Englishman dressed in white flannels passed us. After going on a few steps, he turned back and spoke to us. He warned us not to photograph a veiled woman, or an Arab might well run a knife into us—it would not be the first time it had happened, he said.

As a matter of fact, the longer we fussed around with our cameras the more hostile became the attitude of the people. Even on shipboard I had noticed how the pilot of one of the auxiliary boats kept holding his cap in front of him whenever he saw me with my camera. Even though this defensive gesture hindered him considerably in doing his work, he was determined not to be snapped. Others again were coquettish and assumed poses without being asked.

Everything we saw in this blazing hot city, which assails the nose and ears alike, was confusing and wretched. Suddenly we were overcome by such a gross feeling of desolation, and the murderous heat became so oppressive, that we quite spontaneously turned around to get back to our homelike ship as soon as possible.

But it was no simple matter to get a ferryboat, even though we had already purchased our return tickets. One boat after another left us standing in the glaring heat, presumably because our tickets were not valid for it or because it was going somewhere else. Finally we decided that heavy tipping would do the trick, and suddenly everything went smoothly. The ladies, who had gone off in another direction, had to fork out even more.

When we finally (it was, after all, only a few hours!) set foot on our gangway, to be greeted with loud halloos by the crewmen, who were already grinning at us maliciously, it was like a happy homecoming after a long odyssey. All the experts, however, warned us against thinking that Aden was *the* Orient. This, they said, was just scum.

I find little material here to help me solve my question whether the peoples of the Near East are historically mature, or whether the former colonial masters are right in denying that they are mature. At most I ask myself whether the problem might be stated the other way around: Did colonialism itself produce certain symptoms of decay, or was it at least partly to blame for them? I note that my questions always arise from the impressions I get of the human beings I see. But these are the very questions which can be answered only by knowing people through a means just the opposite of the tourist's, namely, through many years of contact, not through more or less fleeting impressions. It becomes clear to me that this journey will provide me with more material for problems than for solutions of problems. In any case, all this brings up nothing but topics of conversation to which I must return when I meet my informed friends who reside in various ports.

July 31

We left the Gulf of Aden a good hour ago, and we are gliding out into the Indian Ocean. The crossing of the boundary between these waters is very important for our state of mind and body, for while the day began with a tail wind that neutralized the head wind and thus subjected us to a sultry calm, a fresh breeze is now blowing from the southwest. At lunch time muggy, oppressive air made the dining room and smoking saloon places of silence to be avoided, where the stale air was scarcely moved by the fecklessly revolving fans; now they are transformed: the tablecloths are flying off the tables, and the little table flags are fluttering in the breeze. You try to walk through the room, and soon you find yourself dancing a jig to keep your balance. The ocean seems to be breathing, and the ship quietly rises and falls with it. The bosom of infinite nature, of which the romantics spoke, has drawn us into its heaving motion.

It is incredible that a change in the atmosphere should immediately affect a man's mood. One knows weather and human life are interrelated, but only when the change of temperature and pressure is so sudden does he begin to realize how strong is the connection. (Just yesterday I was reading Goethe's "Thoughts on the Weather" in his account of his Italian journey.) How narrow is the range of temperature within which man must remain in order to achieve an optimum of well-being and efficiency! Instead of definitions like "Man is a tool-fabricating animal" or "Man is a *zoön politikon* [social being]," one might say, "Man is a weather-conditioned being."

In the paralysis of the dead calm of a tropical noon one suddenly feels very close to the ideas of Indian philosophy. And even though this may be no more than a peripheral and romantic notion, one feels nevertheless that, at least for a few moments, one has caught a glimpse of the way that leads to the idea of Nirvana. I begin to see that sweltering heat, with its accompanying floods of light and sunshine, is an integral part of the ontology of the Greeks and the ancient church. For me it has always been a somewhat distressing thought that it is so difficult to conceive of Calvin's doctrine of predestination or Luther's doctrine of the two kingdoms while basking in the blazing, sumptuous light of Sicily. The thought is distressing because the logical consequence would be something in the nature of a "geo-theology" and thus a kind of climatic or meteorological relativism. After all, it would be horrible to be compelled to make a confession tantamount to saying, "Tell me what the prevailing temperatures are where you live, and I will tell you the course of church history among you—or even what your religion is."

True, it is part of the incarnation, part of Word becoming flesh, that God's dealings with us should make use of the elements in which we live, but we shall never be able to define the relation between the truth and the prism which refracts its rays. The earthly medium into which the eternal truths enter remains for us an impenetrable mystery. The Greeks would never have understood why they should have had an intellectual constitution which made the Gospel appear to them to be "foolishness." Likewise, the Jews had no comprehension of why the same Gospel must inevitably be a "stumbling block." Here is one of the points over which we puzzle in vain, like that other unfathomable point at which our free will flows into the higher Necessity. Neither Luther with his metaphor of the God who "chops the rotten wood and rides the lame horse" nor Fichte with his doctrine concerning genius nor Hegel with his notion of the "strategy of the Idea" was able to fix this point geometrically; each was only able to describe it in mythological terms.

In any case, I observe one thing: Fascinating and at the same time appalling as it is for me to acquire a dim understanding of an alien way of thinking and believing through a change in climate and weather, and to note how suddenly a person's existence can be touched by something that before was only dead textbook knowledge about an alien way of thought, nevertheless in the midst of the change one thing remains constant. The Word of the Bible, which I read daily, does not recede farther and farther from me as I traverse the longitudes and latitudes of the globe—as do many things that already lie far behind me even now—but rather it follows me as does the light of the sun or moon that shines at home and everywhere. True, it glows with colors different from those I see when I read it as part of my work back home. Here in nature it affects one differently, and I find myself involuntarily turning to other texts (thus whole new aspects of the Psalms of creation or the Book of Job are opened up to me). This Word, it is true, shimmers in ever new refractions of that one Light, but it does shine now as it has always shone and, regardless of time and place, it is always relevant. It invades every medium: it comes to Jews and Greeks; it enters deserts and shadowed forests; it stirs men's hearts beneath the evening star and also beneath the Southern Cross. This Word goes "into the flesh," and thus it also enters into the geographical latitudes and into the temperatures. The diverse media into which it enters subtract nothing from this Word. Rather they become means for its infinite unfolding; they release the wealth of diversity in its store of light.

I must stop writing, for the paper is fluttering and flapping and will not stay still. Besides, I got a fresh sunburn today in the swimming pool, though I kept just my nose above the surface of the water. It would seem that the water above the shoulders acted as a burning glass.

August 2

Yesterday I could not write—all of us were "kayoed." The southwest monsoon was blowing at force 8, and the ship rolled heavily. Despite the wind, the air was so oppressive that we all had headaches and felt numb and paralyzed. The work on my proofs, which must be finished by the time we get to the next port if the printing process is not to be held up at home, was almost too much of an effort. I could not do this work very well on deck because the papers blew away or got into an impossible mess, and inside, with the windows shut fast on account of the spray, the air became unbearably stuffy. All the chairs were chained down, and the tablecloths were dampened in order to check the maniacal dancing of the chinaware.

Day before yesterday we passed the island of Sokotra, which lies at the threshold of the Indian Ocean. Repeated attempts have been made to establish a light there, but the natives have torn down the lighthouses and devoured the white Lynceus.*

* The tower watchman in Goethe's *Faust*. (Trans.)

In sailors' language it is still called Cannibal Island. The captain says there are many islands in this ocean which no European has ever set foot upon.

Again I am occupied with political questions. Is it possible that peoples who live in certain climatic regions can never play a great role in history? Will not work, for example, always be considered a curse, the business of slaves, in these areas? Can there ever be the same alertness, agility, and vital energy here as is found in the inhabitants of cooler zones? If Europe is ever deprived of its historical role (which is, after all, not impossible), it certainly will never be the peoples of *these* climatic latitudes who seize the reins. I'm not sure whether it was a thought or merely a thought-shaped groan over the heat that caused me to write this down.

At supper the captain told us about an old lady he knew in Singapore. She said to him once, "I have only one wish before I die: just for once I'd like to have cold feet!" I find that this statement expresses in concentrated, intense form the feeling about life which apparently will always dominate the European in tropical countries: he can never forget completely that there is a certain lack in his environment. The saying resembles in its striking symbolism another comment which I heard in America. This time it was a woman who spoke of a similar feeling that something was lacking. She said, "In America there is no twilight hour."

August 4

Approaching Ceylon. The southwest monsoon swept all the water out of our swimming pool, but the heavy swells made bathing impossible anyhow. Now our pool is filled again, and tomorrow before breakfast and at the close of the day we shall be celebrating our raptures of delight. The morning dip especially is a refreshment, because overnight the head wind always lowers the temperature of the water a bit.

Yesterday, Sunday, was very pleasant. Except for times when

I was occupied with talking, I spent it in a deck chair that I had placed in the shade of a lifeboat, the only place a bit of breeze could be felt. The result was the right mood for meditation. I made the most of this inclination for wisdom literature by turning to the Proverbs of Solomon, along with the magnificent essays of Gerhard von Rad on Israelite wisdom and the *Westöstlicher Diwan*.* When else could I ever find the time to savor these priceless, heavily freighted words and let them sink in? In this restful peace, one begins to feel that other organs of perception besides that of purely intellectual apprehension are stimulated and stirred into delightful movement.

Leaning on the railing with one's elbows and gazing into the water is a marvelous stimulus to conversation. So after supper I had two conversations that still stick in my mind.

First I met our old storekeeper on the starboard gangway that goes past the crew's quarters. It is still evident that these old tattoo-studded arms once had the strength of a bear. Now he sits peacefully on a chair in front of his cabin, drinks his liquor with gusto, enjoys the evening air, and dreams about something or other.

He really does dream and think, and therefore I like to talk with him. He is a genuine and kindly fellow. I tell him that young Henry has just come up from the engine room completely done in by the heat. But the old fellow only laughs to think that young men today should find the work in the engine room a hardship. When I tell him that I too would consider this work a beastly, infernal thing in these torrid zones, he says it is pure comfort compared with what *he* used to go through as stoker. He had to shovel coal for eighteen cents an hour in the Red Sea, and there was no pay for overtime in those days. He goes on to relate that he was a devil of a fellow in those days. Two hundred twenty pounds live weight, and he hardly ever used a block and tackle. Whenever he lifted a really heavy weight, the boatswain would say, "Man, man, what a man, what a

* A collection of lyrics by Goethe in the nature of apothegms, suggested by a German translation of the Persian poet Hafiz. (Trans.)

man you are!" "That's what he always said to me." He was known in every saloon in St. Pauli. They were all afraid of him there, and nobody dared lay a hand on him. Who would ever dare to pick a fight with him? Now in his old age, he says, he always dresses up fine, but in those days people thought he was a criminal.

I enjoy this charming braggadocio, which is doubtless no yarning at all. I find it rather engaging—it reminds me somewhat of Homer's hero stories—that the men on board should think so much of physical strength and swashbuckling. When they talk about a brawl, their eyes begin to shine, and one can hardly wait until the other is finished to overtrump him with his own story. Raw physical strength is the only level on which I could compete in the storytelling—people like us, though, can never summon up the naivete to brag about such accomplishments; we cannot get away from being somewhat ironical about ourselves. But this is no cause for being pharisaical. Vanity and inferiority feelings are very close together in people like us, except that they lie in *other* cracks and crevices.

I asked the old storekeeper whether he has a family. No, he said, he forgot all about marrying; there wasn't any room for it in his life. "My life has been a full life!" He went on to sum up his philosophy of life, which certainly must have been arrived at after long reflection. I did not respond to it at once (Was this right? After all, we will be traveling together for a long time . . .) but simply let it make its impression upon me. Although I know theoretically that there are people who lead such an existence, it still gives one a bit of a shock suddenly to hear it expressed as a real confession, and I had to cope with the shock first. What the storekeeper said was this: "I've enjoyed my life, and I never let anything burn me. Now at least I can crack my bottle every day. My pumper may still last for five years. Then: After me the deluge. But I have lived."

After a while I strolled on. First I walked for a bit around the bow and thought about this conversation. Slowly I ambled past the lighted cabins toward the stern. The sky was dark and moonless, a really dark night. Only the water above the screw swirled up in phosphorescent light. A young machinist-apprentice, a refugee from the East Zone, was taking his evening stroll and joined me.

Walter, who has a boyish charm, is only eighteen and slightly built. He is making his first voyage and has an unusually strenuous job in the engine room. "If I can only hold out," he said, more to himself than to me. I spoke a few fatherly words about that being the way it is in life, saying there are hard jobs on land and outside of the engine room, too. He has a risky flight behind him, and during his first months in West Germany he had a number of experiences that made him mistrustful of people. At home, he said, his mother always took care of him, and now suddenly he is all alone. He also has to struggle with seasickness on this first voyage (this he did not mention, but I have noticed it).

I asked him how he had gotten through his difficult time in West Germany and whether he had had anything to hold on to. "Yes," he said, "I had something. When I went away my mother gave me some memory verses. They are printed on a postcard. I didn't want it at first, and I said to her, 'What can I do with that anyhow?' But she insisted that I take it and said, 'You'll need it sometime.' And later this card helped me tremendously. I never would have thought it would." I asked him to recite it for me. He did so, declaiming like a child with a pause after each stanza. It was a series of verses which were unfamiliar to me.

I tried to explain to him that words can have a power, that they have been provided for us by a higher hand as guardians and companions, and I illustrated this with the saying, "Do not be anxious about tomorrow." I asked him whether he knew who had said this.

This evening—as I write this, it is quite late—a couple of stokers who were sitting on deck invited me to have a drink. To me it is very interesting simply to be with them when they sit and talk. It is amazing how many things exist side by side in these hearts without apparent conflict and how the ethical alternatives are certainly there (I am surprised and delighted at how decent and loyal they are in their way), but how completely differently they assess things from the way we do in our stratum of society. The way they can talk about their families and about their geishas in Kobe in the same breath, the way they can be tenderhearted in a really touching manner in the one area of life and completely unfeeling in the other, all this poses one question after another for me.

As a theoretician in ethics I am sometimes inclined to make this diagnosis. They live in a state of complete ethical schizophrenia. Some of them save and sacrifice for their families—here there is love and innermost engagement; at the same time they "play it loose" without feeling that there is the slightest thing wrong with it. But somehow there is something wrong with this diagnosis. Nowhere does one hear the click of a lever, so to speak, that is turned as the transition is made from one realm to the other; there is no switching over to another track. On the contrary, it always seems to be the same track.

I ask myself in all seriousness whether we are confronted here with a different structure of humanity which has been conditioned by society and style of life—in this case by life at sea. They have (at least the older ones among them) one room in their life in which the mind-body totality of sexuality remains intact: this is their home, their marriage, or their "best girl friend." They have another room in which the merely physiological hormone processes take place in much the same way as the digestive processes.

Sometimes it is still more complicated. They have steady girl friends in various ports, and, from the tone and substance of their descriptions, these encounters are sometimes more than merely momentary physical contacts. It is as if the geographical distance and the isolating effect of the ocean insulates these men and prevents the problem of rival affections, of "polygamy," from coming up at all, as if the question of loyalty and fidelity were a completely different matter here. Because I am very careful not to interrupt with moral objections — which would only block the frank telling of the stories and my own impartial listening to them—I try to insert my questions as cautiously as possible. For example: "If these various girls all have a place beside each other in your broad sailors' hearts, what does this look like from the *girls'* point of view? If they are so 'first-class,' as you say they are, if they are lovable and thoughtful and if they love you, do you think it would make no difference to one of them to find out that she is only one among several or even many?" And their answer is: "Naturally, they must not know about each other. What you don't know won't hurt you. And, after all, it's always such a long time in between that when we are in port we give all our time to them and they're satisfied."

The conversation goes on quite naturally, but occasionally there is an awkward silence. Then, as if everything that made them stop and think for a moment had only taken place in some quickly traversed anteroom, they suddenly go on talking, naively and unconcernedly. The phonograph needle slips into its groove again; it was only interrupted for a moment.

I cannot take a superior, doctrinaire attitude toward this; I must take seriously the question that it poses. Here a man writes fat tomes about ethics, tries to get a rest from these labors by taking a sea voyage, and then on that very trip, with its completely different aims, these fundamental and new problems affecting this very ethics suddenly crop up. Perhaps my project will have to include a whole new chapter that might be called "Ethics and Types" or "Refractions of the Norms of Good and Evil in Various Media of Life." It is only in situations like this that one realizes how relatively homogeneous is the type of human being we normally deal with in our jobs, even though, as in my own case, we may move in many very different circles. But how terribly we lack insight into completely different life-situations (the army life that could provide such experiences has long since passed . . .).

Nor does one get this inside view simply by talking now and then with mailmen, janitors, and workmen. For this kind of penetration—and even then at one single point—what is needed is the long breathing spell of an ocean voyage. What it takes is standing for hours in the evening with the man on watch or treating a stoker to a beer in your stateroom and letting the man's tongue gradually loosen in the presence of this guest from the remote world of the passengers. I never have the feeling of spying or of conducting a disinterested investigation, however. I like these fellows with their ingenuous frankness, and I think they sense it. I want to understand them, nor am I an enigma to them; I tell them what I think.

August 5

Saw the lights of Ceylon last night about ten o'clock. It was a moonless and starless night, with a darkness unknown to us at home. Toward midnight, after long conversations with a number of sailors, I plunged into the dark cube of the swimming pool. At first it was like swimming in a weird abyss, but it was wonderfully invigorating.

The conversation that took place on the bench on the lower deck—accompanied with beer and cigarettes—was set off by the question whether a person could be an idealist. A young Hessian denied it vehemently. When one of the others contradicted him and demanded that instead of yelling he should give some reasons for his view, he proceeded to tell some anecdotes from his own life. It came out that he was at odds with his old man and had skipped out from under the constant surveillance at home. His father was a businessman, he said, and dealt in products in the sale of which he saw no future for himself. It was evident from the way he substantiated this assertion that he was a thoroughly independent and stubborn fellow who knew how to think soberly. "My father built up the business, and he hangs on to it," he finally said somewhat resignedly. "And I can understand this. But only sentimentally. What I'm interested in is what it pays." "But after all, a man has to have a few ideals," said one of the others. Before he could say what he meant by this, the Hessian sailor barged in and fell all over himself to assure us how much it meant to him to rake in a maximum of cash with a minimum of effort, and that ultimately this was the only thing that counted in life.

As chance would have it I went on talking with him the whole evening, listening to what he had to say. In the course of our talk, I again discovered something that I had not expected after the preceding conversation—that is, how considerate and good-hearted he is with those who are really close to him and whom he likes, and how respectful, even chivalrous, he is with the colored stevedores, concerning whom he tells me a lot of things. He takes them along with him on walks and talks with them in order to make them feel less inferior. Naturally, he has a lot of things to tell about his acquaintance with certain establishments in various parts of the earth which are rather shocking to the respectable mind, but in this life of his there are also certain corners and recesses that contain some soundly structured values—there is love and loyalty. Like most of the rest of his comrades, he does not feel that his illicit conduct is a violation of this latter set of values. It is something that takes place, as it were, only in the foreground of the self and is a part of his physical life. "You have to have something like this," he said. "Otherwise, after these monotonous weeks at sea there would be even more sexual crimes. As it is, there are too many already. I don't know what I'd be capable of doing myself."

I try my best to remain receptive and—hard as it is for me to do so—to subordinate even my most stable opinions in this whole area as possible prejudices which may require some correction. I ask myself seriously what is Christian and what is bourgeois in these firm opinions of mine. Never before, even during the time when I was a soldier, has this question been put to me so radically as here. I note how difficult it is to strip myself of everything that is doctrinaire and simply to listen —to listen and leave every question open.

If I am honest, I must admit that at present I am not clear about many things and that I still do not know what the chapter on sex will look like in the next volume of my *Ethics*. If I only knew clearly what to do! At the moment, the problem of these simple, vital chaps is almost insoluble, unless they are granted the grace of faith and thus a special kind of support. Some of them have a hard and exhausting kind of work to do, when I think of the 120 to 140 and more degrees of temperature in the engine room—a job that calls for compensation by softness and a different kind of warmth. I also consider that seafaring itself exerts a kind of selective process with respect to vitality and physical strength. Above all, I take into account the fact that these healthy, simple-minded fellows, unlike educated persons in other classes of society, do not have opportunities for sublimation and do not know the adventures of the mind and spirit, the feast of books and ideas, aesthetic satisfactions, the delights of conversation. A certain crudeness of mind is matched by a crudeness of perception and experience, and the vacuum in the realm of experience brought about by the monotony of life at sea cries out to be filled.

I still do not rightly know how I should speak with them. Will I be a legalist if I destroy for them this naive, ingenuous way of experiencing life? Is the "anti" way the right way at all to reach their souls? Does not the Law exercise a killing function here too? Might it not be best to begin with the positive things in their life, perhaps with what they have experienced of real love on the part of a mother or a girl? Or perhaps also with the real shocks that they sometimes tell about: the sinking of the "Pamir" (one of them took part in the rescue operations), the flight from the East Zone, the loneliness of knocking about on their own?

It becomes depressingly clear to me how little I know about the people who normally listen to me—in church, primarily, but also in the lecture room—and therefore how often I talk over their heads and miss them altogether. And all the while I have always thought I knew them wonderfully well, because more than a few come to me and give me glimpses into their intimate lives. How many letters I read every week in which people's innermost secrets are bared! Here, however, as a listener to simple, unaffected conversations over a period of weeks, in discussions which, under the influence of alcohol and the tropical night, are uninhibited and expansive in a way that never happens normally, here I note how the very *situation* of pastoral care itself constitutes a strainer which filters out many things that would otherwise enter. The very presence of the pastor unconsciously checks, refines, and therefore alters the statements that are made—quite apart from the fact that, in itself, resort to a pastor for help is something that represents a break with ordinary habit that is unnatural and alien to some persons who by nature are more crude and unsophisticated.

Remarkable how this ocean voyage has produced effects for me which are totally different from what I expected; everything I have seen so far recedes behind this attack upon certain premises in my anthropology that I have taken for granted. I am becoming more and more absorbed in the world of the ship, whose inhabitants compel me constantly to exercise my mind, and force me to make severe revisions. What curious fellows they are! These young bears who root about in every honeypot in the world are bashful and frightened when our two girls step into the swimming pool. They still refuse to go in when the girls are there. They exhibit something that is almost a pious timidity, and all of a sudden they are small boys again.

In my Bible reading I note how gentle and lenient Jesus Christ is with the sins of the senses, but how harshly and relentlessly he judges greed and pride and lovelessness. Among his Christians it is usually the other way around.

August 6

The days string out like lovely, matched pearls. At the moment we are traversing the longest stretch of ocean on our voyage. Curiously enough I do not share the general and repeatedly expressed longing for meadows, trees, and houses.

If it were up to me, we could go on for a long time sailing through the water. Its diversity is just as great as the variations of a trip by land, except that it is more magnificent, since it employs only light, color, and rhythm.

Yesterday the sky, which has been slightly overcast, turned to utter blue and lent its color to the sea. It was as if Thetis were cleaning house and had opened her heavenly window to air out the whole globe. A fresh wind began to blow, almost at once the oppressive heaviness disappeared, and suddenly the atmosphere had the effect of a charm; it seemed to have more oxygen and more tingle. Instinctively, slack bodies tautened; the urge to be up and doing returned.

I notice the effect of the change in the weather on my reading. The cheap novels to which I had been reduced in the last few weary days suddenly tasted flat. I had to return to the *Westöstlicher Diwan* and *Maxims and Reflections* in order to get a sense of specific gravity. Many of these sayings are like smooth stones which a David might hurl at hostile giants. In this quiet restfulness the capacity for intellectual enjoyment is quickened, sometimes to the edge of intoxication. With sharpened senses you feel the noble stuff going in, passing into your blood, and beginning to circulate. Some of these sayings give the feeling that they are flowing into the uttermost extremities, as if the mind had ceased to be a separate, delimited region of the self. The terminus of this line would be that of pure sublimation; the body would be nourished and assuaged with intellectual food.

But when I jump into the swimming pool, I find that the physical has its glories nevertheless and that it refuses to live by even the noblest imports from Weimar. It is curious that I cannot read Søren Kierkegaard here at sea, even though he lived and thought in the environment of the ocean. I brought with me several volumes of the new edition—particularly the ones that caught my interest in my student days—but it was in vain. The "spell of the pathological" that hovers between the lines has no effect in these surroundings.

Before I go to sleep at night and during the noonday siesta I have been reading the books of Han Suyin, the Eurasian, most recently *A Many-splendored Thing,* in order to prepare myself for Hong Kong. On the human side the book is stylistically sparkling froth, and of course (as has turned out to be the case) good movie material. But when one has Homer and Goethe in his luggage, he is likely to be aware, as Goethe said, of a "large amount of water in the ink." However, the book captures the atmosphere of the city.

It is a curious thing to be approaching a city which has been the center of most of our conversations for weeks, the social conditions, the colors and lights, the buildings and people of which we think we know, and which now is soon to appear before us "in person." The ship's company of Hong Kong experts is playing a dramatic trick upon me similar to that employed by Schiller in *Wallenstein:* the hero himself does not make his appearance until late in the play. At first we meet him only as he is mirrored by the people and his soldiers. We catch glimpses of his figure only in the reflection which it produces in other minds. We recognize its light only in the many refractions it undergoes as it strikes the medium of various types and characters. And finally, after all these geometrical lines have been drawn to one point, our receptiveness to the exciting point of light itself has been intensified to the limit. So I look forward to Hong Kong somewhat feverishly.

Today there is a steady downpour and wonderful coolness, a real treat after the hot days. The ocean has altered its familiar appearance, has taken on an undefinable, deceptive color, and is roughened by the squall. The rain, of course, does not wash the ship clean, but rather bespatters it with dissolving rust and yellow streaks. The crew seems to have vanished. When it rains, the navigation appears to be conducted from indoors. They have all set out their flowerpots with their skimpy, rachitic little plants on the hatchways to catch a bit of heavenly nectar. The plants, which are ill-disposed to the ocean air, are like the denizens of the Berlin tenements and basements whom Zille's pictures have made familiar, reaching out of the shadows for the meager sunshine. So these under- privileged greens, which have been fluttering in the ocean winds, parched by the sun, or pining away in the staterooms, are now exposed to the longed-for moisture.

If you sleep outside despite the rain, as I did today at noon, you grow a bit cold. What a pleasure goose pimples can be! "In Hamburg you would be even colder," said the old store- keeper; "the blood has gotten thin now." Right, we now have summer oil in our engines. With a little pang of homesickness I suddenly think of the car standing alone in the garage at home.

August 7

Today little Henry of the engine room, who can look at one so cheerfully with his gray slit-eyes peering out of an oil- smeared face, is observing his eighteenth birthday. I cadged some coffee cakes from the steward and the passengers, and fortunately was able to add a little book to the present.

The morning began with a heavy tropical rain, brought by the southwest monsoon, and a heavy swell. During the night the spray caught my Brazilian cigars, even though they were well inside the cabin. But soaking in salt seems to do them good. It probably agrees with their nature.

After breakfast, just as we were approaching the islands off Sumatra, it cleared up. The captain was quite happy about it, for he had planned the time schedule so as to be able to give us a ride fairly close to shore. We had all been trembling lest his kindly plan should be spoiled by rain and fog. While we were sitting at breakfast, still paralyzed by the humidity of the air and feeling dull, listless, and disinclined to talk, we were galvanized when, after more than a week, land came into view again and we then coasted along for hours beside the primeval evergreen forests. Now that our eyes were confronted with green, we drank in all of the familiar color we could hold. (I recall returns from island vacations through the lush meadows of East Friesland; we actually envied the cows greedily eating their way through the succulent green.) Every once in a while enchanting green fields and idyllic glades appeared between the impenetrable thickets of forest, and occasionally in this mostly uninhabited immensity we would see huts, rising smoke, and gigantic felled trees. The telescope brought it all into intimate proximity. Finally we met fishing boats at close range. Man was no longer far away. The stories of missionaries and cannibals we had heard in our youth came alive again.

At six o'clock tomorrow morning we are to be in Penang. We all look forward to getting mail from home.

For the first time I have become aware of the dramatic element in the *Odyssey,* the ingenious combination of drive and inertia, forward movement and retarding forces. I read it now with a naive suspense which I should not have thought possible for me after years of reading it as a schoolboy and occasional later encounters—and this gives me great pleasure. I approach each new canto with a certain curiosity, like that you feel when meeting again old friends whose progress you have followed for years from afar but who will be both the same and yet quite different from what they seemed the last time you met them. When we meet with things that are unquestionably great, we note that we ourselves have changed and grown. What has certainly grown in me—and this is precisely what is becoming clear to me as I reread the book—is the sense of the oneness of life in Homer, the absolute opposite of the schizophrenia of modern life: the togetherness of gods and men, Olympia and everyday life, swineherd and hero, landscape and life. Everything is both human and divine, and Eumaens is actually called the *dios hyphorbos,* the "divine swineherd." Once we enter into the midst of the Homeric world, everything which at first struck us as an excess of glorification, as over-opulent ornamentation with glittering, unrealistic adjectives, loses its alien quality, and the *ens realissimum* ["essential being"] of this world emerges.

Malay Peninsula

In Penang. This day in Penang was undoubtedly the high point of the trip so far. If the sea through which we are now passing were not shining with a deep, rich emerald green and thus producing a concentrating effect upon my mind, I could scarcely hope to reconstruct in any orderly way the rich profusion of all we experienced.

Even the approach to Penang was a feast for our eyes, for we never grew weary of looking at the green of the tropical forest that bordered the shores of the islands (especially Sumatra). After nine days of voyaging, one acquires a furious appetite for green and chlorophyll.

At a safe distance we were not troubled by the fact that the primeval forest is really a sinister place. Not until we went ashore were we told by our friends everything that is at large in the forest: snakes, and tigers—only a few weeks ago a child was mangled near Port Swettenham — but above all Communist partisans who have maintained their pockets of resistance there since 1948 and who are all but impregnable so far as the military is concerned. For the soldiers this service must be terrible. Much worse than the partisans, whom most often they cannot find anyhow, are the treacheries of the primeval forest, especially the leeches that get into their shoes, to say nothing of the desolation of this trackless jungle.

In today's brutal heat it became clear to me that two songs have no prospect of becoming popular even in the best translation into Malayan: "Who made thee, lovely forest, so high above," and "Walking is the miller's pleasure." When the glorious natural beauty of Penang enticed us to get out of the car and walk for a while, we soon gave up, for we threatened to melt like snowmen in a south wind. There will never be a hiker's club here!

But I have gotten ahead of myself. As the ship was being made fast, the very friendly agent of the Hamburg-America Line came on board and invited me to tour the island of Penang. I took my fellow passenger N. along with me. An expert butterfly collector, who has his equipment with him, he wanted to go hunting in this classic land of butterflies. Ashore I found waiting for me a representative of a well-known Far East firm whose chief had notified him of my arrival and who proved a pleasant guide in every respect. This young German, Mr. St., has been living here for more than five years and till recently was the only German here. Apart from his business interests, he has immersed himself deeply in Malayan culture. He is exceedingly well versed in the political situation of the country, particularly the complicated problems of transition from a British colonial status to that of independence. It is immediately apparent that he lives among Malays and Chinese and that his information is firsthand. That he has a great gift of empathy I discovered by the way he immediately divined my own wishes and interests.

As we drove through the city we were charmed by the crowds of people and the cleanly, colorful street shops. All this is in pleasing contrast with the Arabian port of Aden where the hot, odor-soaked streets and the press of ragged people was simply shocking. The tricycle taxis present a varying picture at different times of the day: in the morning mostly people with serious, business-like faces and later, the closer evening comes, families with small children and radiantly happy pairs of lovers enjoying the cool of the evening. I made use of the opportunity, while we were in the city, to buy a belt, having left this important instrument at home. At first I had discovered in the dictionary the wrong word for this, a word which is applicable only in the feminine world. After this misunderstanding was cleared up to everybody's amusement, the salesman discovered that his entire stock of belts had been made for the slender figures of the Malayans. The whole store crowded about to gaze at me like a prodigy of nature whose anatomical proportions shattered all ordinary conceptions. They had their childlike fun over it, and I can only surmise the meaning of their amused winks and twittering talk.

The "snake-temple" was the first sensation we encountered: a colorful Buddhist structure with a terrace. It was not easy to reach, for a whole swarm of beggars surrounded us, holding dirty caps under our noses. It must be said, however, that these were the only beggars we encountered today. Despite my experience in Aden I still have to harden myself to the fury with which one must thrust off these onslaughts if he is not simply to be trampled under foot.

The temple immediately enveloped us with a mystical fascination, less perhaps because of its dusky light, which contrasts sharply with the glare outside, than because of the multitude of incense burners that pour out a stupefying aroma and so narcotize the 238 snakes that even the poisonous ones become harmless fellows and (allegedly!) can be hung about the neck without risk. Wherever one turns, he sees snakes; they curl around the lamps, all the way up to the ceiling, around every candlestick and every table leg, sluggish and obviously transported into the serpents' Nirvana. Although one is clearly conscious of the ulterior commercial motives, designed to catch the tourist trade, the cultic area itself nevertheless has a religious effect. Not until we began to understand the devices which are used to ward off evil spirits (and later encountered them in many hints and allusions in everyday life); not until the rituals for telling fortunes and producing good luck were explained to us, did we begin to realize the welter of fear that lies behind the stage-set of this paradise.

We then drove through the neighboring fishing villages, where the houses are almost all pile dwellings, probably a reminiscence of the threat of snakes and beasts of prey which continues to exert its influence in this atavistic architecture. It may be, however, that they have also proved practical in the tropical climate, for the families sit underneath them to escape the blazing sun.

This trip paid off for our butterfly collector, too. Again and again we got out of the car while he raced off to bring back gorgeous black Papilios with luminous white and red spots, yellow-red Delias, and Catopsilias. This was not only fine for us, since we could see these colorful marvels close up, but it also had the incidental effect of bringing the Malayan children out in crowds to stare entranced at this immortal sport of children. Not only the children pursued Mr. N., however, but also sometimes dogs, when he pushed his way too far into the gardens. For the children this two-front war on butterflies and dogs was an indescribable delight.

August 10

Port Swettenham. I had to take advantage of a quiet hour in this port to finish writing the diary entry for Penang. Our tour around the island took us over an excellent strategic road which is about twenty-six miles long and repeatedly affords—from varying elevations—gorgeously colorful views of the sea. The sails of the fishing boats and junks are like colored dots reflected in the water. The road took us past children playing and bathing, and through vegetation that revels in its own luxuriance, and extends its fruits right into your mouth. As if nature were trying to demonstrate the superabundance of its germinal, flourishing, and infinitely procreative power, innumerable trees are laden with a profusion of parasites, so that each has the effect of being a small botanical garden. The trees seem almost to be vaunting their excess power, as if they were saying, "We produce this stuff on the side, and it bothers us not at all."

Above us and on the horizon we saw great mountains of clouds, towering up beyond all dimension in fantastically sculptured shapes. Here everything is enormous and excessive, except for the dainty, slender human beings and their childlike gaiety. "What is it really like," I asked my guide, "to live in this eternal summer, without the rhythm of the seasons, without the winter sabbath of nature, without nature's parable of death and resurrection, Good Friday and Easter?" "It's hard to say," he answered. "You know that tomorrow morning the sun will surely shine, but you're not so happy about it as you are when it's a fine day in Germany."

It is a mystery to me how a person can bear a life without the systole and diastole of warmth and cold, rain and sunshine, growth and decay. To me, there is something upsetting about the constant presence of perfection.

What the rhythm of life means became clear to me within the very next hour when, exhausted by the plethora of all we had experienced and by the heat, we stopped at a summer resort restaurant called the Lone Pine. From the restaurant a lawn led down to the ocean, shadowed by a dense cover of leaves through which a mild breeze blew, and this was indescribably refreshing. Even more pleasant was the complete silence, which was only slightly disturbed by the lapping of the water on the shore. When the "boy" served us with fresh, ice-cold orange juice, I was overcome with an almost unreal sense of delight and comfort. Here we are in the atmosphere of an inn and therefore in an area that has been civilized. But how much more soft and gentle are man's footsteps here! In Germany the loveliest spots in the landscape are spoiled for us by the excesses of the tourist trade. We human beings seem always to destroy what we love. For no sooner do we discover something beautiful than we rush upon it like a wild mob and distort it beyond recognition. But here the atmosphere is still hospitable and human. We are in the safety of human care and yet surrounded by an unspoiled paradise, a piece of nature that is left as it was before.

At noon, we were in the Eastern and Oriental Hotel, famous throughout South Asia, which again is situated right on the ocean, so that the sea breeze blows through its shadowed rooms. It is a large, old-fashioned but altogether comfortable hotel in the colonial gentleman's style. The menu reads like an epic with many cantos. Everything about it reflects a grand style of living. This hotel has in it the fabric for a novel dealing with the pioneers, the planters, the colonial officers, and the merchants.

At many of the tables one still sees the typical colonial gentlemen: men with energetic, vital faces and the bearing of "masters." But they doubtless give evidence more of the past than the future. In the room where we took our seats for lunch there hangs a much disputed portrait of Queen Elizabeth II. The Malayans were all for removing it when their state was declared independent last year. It was only the unanimous protest of the Englishmen, whose economic influence is still important, and their vigorous threat of a boycott, that finally led to a compromise: the portrait remains, but now a portrait of the Malayan royal couple occupies an equally prominent place. (The Malayan king is chosen from among the sultans every four years.) This curious iconomachy is a small but significant symptom of the fact that here everything is in transition and that the contours of the new Asiatic world are not yet clearly defined.

In the afternoon we took the funicular up to the 2,350-foot-high Penang Hill and enjoyed the indescribable view and the relief of the breeze on the heights. In the midst of swarming Chinese families I saw a magnificently dignified figure striding along. With his gleaming white, toga-like habit, his long black hair and well-groomed beard, he reminded me of Rabindranath Tagore, whom I once heard speak. In his fingers he held a golden chain. He was followed respectfully by two women, and a man who might have been his secretary. Everyone observed the stately appearance of this man with great awe, and I hardly dared photograph him. But I hoped at least to catch him from a distance with a telephoto lens. When he noticed my rather timid preparations to do so, however, he immediately assumed a photogenic pose. He knew his optical value. I ask myself why it is that his obvious vanity did not diminish the impression he made upon me. Vanity, Bismarck once said, is a mortgage. But very valuable objects can afford to have a few mortgages. Perhaps this man is such an object.

At evening we were all back on the ship for supper, exchanging impressions of the day. My mentor, Mr. St., was our guest.

The conversation came back to the problem of whether and to what extent the peoples of South Asia are capable of having a history. I put forth my thesis—less because I am sure of it than because I wanted to draw out my well-informed partner—that the capacity of a people to make history depends ultimately upon the climatic factor and that the Malayan heat and the tremendous munificence of the soil would certainly accord with a certain *laissez faire* characteristic of the lilies of the field which have no history. There is lacking what Toynbee says is the prerequisite of any people who are to be a power in history, namely, the correspondence of "challenge" and "response."

I even risked developing this thesis further and inserted a further bit of speculation into the discussion. It might be assumed, I said, that this absence of historical influence is intensified by the additional lack of changing seasons. What is lacking is an articulating rhythm which divides and apportions time, and in this way makes one conscious of it. Since the passive rest of winter and the creative outburst of blooming and ripening are lacking, time stands still, as it were, in one continuous, undifferentiated moment. Today is like yesterday and tomorrow. "All at once," so to speak, without any perceptible caesuras or breaks, the child becomes an adult and an old man. Apparently birth and death are not distinguished from one another with that absoluteness which is characteristic of our latitudes, where we are very conscious of the phenomenon of time, where we are constantly reminded of the process of becoming and passing away, where we keep moving and active because time is running out, because we are finite and everything we want to achieve is enclosed in the limited span between birth and death.

To my surprise, my Penang friend—for that is what he has become in this brief time—confirmed this little meditation to a

large extent. He did so primarily in terms of external manifestations. The Malays, he said, wanted political independence,
but are not really making proper use of their independence.
They drift along. They work just long enough to have sufficient
for the next two weeks and then stop. It is not necessary to
exert oneself beyond this minimum for an existence which
nature provides cheaply.

But our conversation penetrated even deeper into this tendency to be unaware of history. Mr. St. said that the Malayan
language contains no words for divisions of time. To me this
is a significant piece of information. In Malayan the past is
expressed simply by adding the word "finished" and the future
by adding "wait." If Mr. St. asks his "boy" when this or that
occurred, he is always perplexed (like the other Malays to
whom such a question is put) and slips into evasive, indefinite
statements: it was "once," or "some time or other," and it is
never clear whether it was yesterday or four years ago.

The same is true of the people's consciousness of history.
Beyond a span of fifty years all is gray, featureless antiquity;
there is no depth of historical perspective and therefore no
consciousness of history. A missionary has the greatest difficulty making clear to his people the idea of the future—there
is no such abstract noun in Malayan. Even he and his European friends, said Mr. St., were beginning to lose their sharp
sense of history; they were losing their sense of time. This is
particularly clear to them at Christmas and New Year. They
have to remind themselves what time of year it is by sheer
force of recourse to the calendar. (*Later note:* On the return
voyage I presented this problem to other seasoned Europeans,
especially in Singapore, and received confirmation of these
facts.)

Naturally, in this connection the question also arises whether
Communism is in a position to be able to force these peoples
"into history" by terror and coercion, whether it can inspire
in them the kind of activity which the earlier colonial masters
communicated through their other forms of pressure (although

no "historical" activity in the strict sense was achieved in this way).

In connection with this line of thought another bit of information emerged, which—after all I have heard so far—seems to me to be very characteristic of the Asiatic peoples' attitude toward Communism. (*Again a later note:* I made exactly the same observation later in Hong Kong, Japan, and the Philippines.) The really active bearers of trade and therefore of economic "history" in Malaya are the Chinese. In Penang I was struck by their castle-like villas, which were undoubtedly intended as conscious demonstrations of their position of leadership in society. "All the Chinese I know," said Mr. St., "and I know representatives of all levels in society, including Chinese academic men who have traveled extensively, admire Red China. I have not met a single exception to this rule. They are all dazzled by the success of the reconstruction, and their national feeling is flattered." I asked him why they did not go back to Red China, then, in order to enjoy the regime at first hand. "The fact is," he answered, "that nobody wants to live there. They say this quite frankly. They are quite aware of the oppression and joylessness there. And yet they all say quite consistently: For China there is no other way except this one."

These observations confirm for me a fact which could also be observed in the Third Reich: the external impression is always made by things that can be photographed and expressed in statistics—the newly built dams, the production of automobiles and jet fighters, the establishment of automatic telephone systems, the whole process of industrialization. It is only the items of economic and political achievement that make an impression outside the country. But people are hardly aware of the philosophy that underlies these achievements. The constant loss of freedom, the irrational atmosphere of pressure that paralyzes the person but stimulates his productivity, the hidden blight of ideological dictatorships which has fallen upon life— this cannot be projected to the outside, and does not appear either in pictures or in statistics. This may be the reason why the peoples of Asia look on spellbound at the miraculous works of Communism in Red China and thus become victims of an optical illusion.

In the last analysis we are confronted here with an acute theological problem—the question of what historical reality actually is. Does it consist in the objective *achievement* of a people, or does it consist in its deeper *condition?* Perhaps this question also should be addressed to the historians: What is the material that actually underlies your chronicles? Or better, in what dimension of existence do you look for this material? Do you look for it in the actual events or in the motivations that produced these events? The question addressed to Christ—By what authority, in whose power, and in whose name are you doing these things? (Matt. 21:23ff.)—points to this profoundest problem of historical reality.

Of all that we talked about this evening—especially the problem of Red China—there is one small statistical comment made by Mr. St. that stands out in my memory: In the year 2000, four human beings out of five will be Asiatics, and two of them will be Chinese. What will this biological pressure, intensified by the dynamics of Leninist ideology and implemented with planned power and impact, mean for mankind? With this somber prospect we come to the close of an idyllic day.

August 11

Between Port Swettenham and Singapore. My kind benefactor in Hamburg had also arranged for a helpful guide in Port Swettenham. Immediately after lunch we drove to the Malayan capital, Kuala Lumpur. The road took us through villages with the familiar motley of street life, through endless, miles-long rubber plantations, and also through modern settlements which are very elegant and well laid out. One senses the young state is beginning to stir.

In the city itself we visited the huge stadium, in which a

school festival was being conducted with music, speeches, flags, and all the bright colors of the children's blouses. The stadium was built to celebrate the declaration of independence of the state of Malaya, and everything was done to make it presentable. Its colossal concrete pylons carry loudspeakers and floodlights, and its architectural lines are excellent, combining magnitude and grace. I was told, however, that it was only half filled at the time of the declaration of independence. My astonished inquiry why this was so elicited this explanation: The people were very well off under English rule, and therefore independence represented no momentous change. Subsequently, as we drove on and I was told about all the English have provided in the way of schools, as well as other cultural and social institutions, this judgment struck me as quite plausible.

Suddenly, however, all driving and touring was stopped by a cloudburst which I can only say was as gigantic and violent as the Flood. In a moment everything was dark, the streets were flooded and emptied of people, the windshield-wipers were unequal to their task, and we had to go on at pedestrian's pace. Because of this furious onslaught of the forces of nature it was impossible for us to visit the great mosque. We were barely able to make out its lofty, serrated outlines. Even in the murky gray downpour it seemed to have something about it which was brilliantly imposing. We were just able to make it to the German embassy, where we had tea, regaled ourselves with all its fine accommodations—the master of the house was away on leave—and watched the natural spectacle of this tropical flood from the dimness of a cool room that looks out upon a magnificent terrace, enjoying the cool air that was coming in. A noiselessly flitting "boy" in snow-white dress seemed to divine our most secret thoughts, and anticipated our wishes before we had expressed them.*

---

* A humorous sequel to this adventure is revealed in a letter of the author to his friends and is worth including as a footnote. In the spring of 1959 Dean Thielicke was a lecturer in the Christian academies in the Union of South Africa. Here is his account:
"I spent a very jolly evening in the German embassy. During the

65

August 13

Between Singapore and Hong Kong. Last night we left Singapore shortly before midnight, our friends waving to us, and two hours later—during which we still shunned our beds, having to digest our experiences in further talk on the bridge—we reached the China Sea.

In the burning sun but with a fresh head wind we are now lolling in the comfort of deck chairs after the turbulent and impression-filled sojourn on land. We endeavor to digest mentally and reduce to a certain order the multiplicity of experiences we have had.

A Chinese family—parents and an eighteen-year-old son—now completes our passenger list. The young man is constantly alert to every motion his father makes. A slight gesture is sufficient for him to rearrange the deck chairs. He always places his close to his father's, and appears to treat him with tremendous respect. The one German word they all know and which they use at every opportunity contains the most profound and meaningful greeting that the language of Luther and Goethe has produced, namely, "Mahlzeit." *

opulent, many-course dinner something funny happened. The ambassador had just recently been transferred from Kuala Lumpur to the Union. When I had visited Kuala Lumpur scarcely nine months previously, I had taken refuge with my guide in the embassy on account of a tropical downpour. This companion, a young merchant who is a resident there, said to me, 'The ambassador is not here; the first embassy counsellor is a good friend of mine, but he too is away. The only one left is the Malayan servant, and he will do what I say.' So, like spongers, we ordered up the most sumptuous things in a private home. Though a gentleman should by no means do such a thing, the euphoria of the moment took away all our inhibitions. So when on this evening in Kapstadt I unsuspectingly remarked that I felt infinitely at home in the German embassy and that everything struck me as being so familiar that I felt as if I had been there before, this seemed somewhat queer to my host and he pressed me for further details. Then this shameful deed of my recent past suddenly came out. And only the good humor of the ambassador kept me from sliding under the table in embarrassment. Every time I have done something wrong it has always come out—and in this case even in another quarter of the globe, almost a year later. Schiller is right after all with respect to his idea of moral order in the world." (Trans.)

* This word conveys anything from "Hello!" and "Goodbye!" to "I hope you enjoy your meal." (Trans.)

How busy the two days in Singapore were! Again our friends in Hamburg had arranged contacts. We had hardly landed when the son of Mr. Sch., whose representatives in Penang and Port Swettenham had already helped me so kindly, together with another young man from Hamburg, Mr. R., who is to be a future Hapag department manager, came up the gangway and surprised me with a complete program for these two days.

After a jolly breakfast on board ship, at which our friends particularly enjoyed the German rye bread (afterwards we gave them several loaves), Mr. R. drove me through the city and its outskirts. I was surprised to see the large number of gaudy posters, banners, and tremendous signs, which reminded me somewhat unpleasantly of the propaganda practices of totalitarian states. In reply to my astonished question I learned that an anti-spitting campaign is being launched in Singapore with this heavy artillery fire of propaganda. Without having to ask for further explanations, after the first impressions I received during this journey to the south and east, I have some idea of what this means: in Asia every man appears to be a kind of reincarnation of the llama. In these parts spitting is an elementary expression of life, as are certain sounds produced in the throat with fantastic variations and piercing loudness. Spitting is indulged in as a simple necessity of life, so to speak, and also with a sporting passion, the missile being emitted in far-ranging ballistic curves, quite precipitately, without any perceptible preparation. I hardly believe that a campaign against breathing would be less successful.

In order that Mr. R. should not get the idea from my photographic equipment that he was expected to show me nothing but monuments and the "sights of the town," I made it clear to him at the outset that I am the most "untouristical" man in the world and that I am only secondarily interested in the extraordinary. My first concern is the ordinary everyday life. I told him that I wanted above all to know something about normal life in the Chinese quarter.

The colorfulness of the strange and to me illegible signs

exerts upon me the charm of the exotic. And the faces of the people fascinate me, too. Whereas at first they all seemed equally yellow and equally slant-eyed, and even their age was more difficult to determine than it is for one of our own race, I think that more and more I can see them as individuals.

When I stop to consider what it is in these physiognomical studies that is so attractive to me, I think it is this: I am intensely inspired by the certainty that all these people—with their desires and doubts, their hopes and fears—are just like me. I have the feeling, however, that these identical concerns of the human soul differ in goals and objects. It is true, their fear is the same fear we have, but what *causes* them to fear is something different—or at least something that conceals itself behind different cyphers. This subject has all the fascination of a riddle and it is constantly gripping my mind. True, these other people are human beings like you and me. And yet I keep asking myself: Who are you really? You are one who loves—but *whom* do you love and how do you *live* your love?

I ponder the fact that up to now I have actually known only Christian Asiatics. With them this question never troubled me nearly so much as it does here. To me their faces appeared open and familiar. The strangeness was, so to speak, reduced to the small element of biological differences. But this strangeness was not opaque; it allowed a brotherliness and sisterliness to shine through it, and this was expressed not only through the medium of words but also in their faces, which we were able to interpret. They looked more relaxed and liberated—perhaps they looked more "redeemed." * But here a spell seems to lie upon these faces, the shadow of the unredeemed creation. What will it be like when I can speak, as I hope to do, to Buddhist priests and monks in Japan, that is, to people who have risen above rude, primitive dullness and achieved a higher rank? Will it still be possible to detect this unredeemed char-

* The allusion is to Nietzsche's comment that Christians would have to look more "redeemed" (*erlöst*) before he would believe in their Redeemer (*Erlöser*). (Trans.)

acter there? In any case, I am resisting all the obvious prejudices which obtrude especially upon a theologian, and I dare
not allow my sense of self-criticism to fall asleep.

The photographing of people, who are, after all, my primary
interest, is a rather exciting business. Since the Chinese are
very shy about having their pictures taken, my companion
went up to various ones whose faces were particularly characteristic and politely persuaded them, with the help of tips
and American cigarettes, to submit—thus we avoided any
trouble. But the pictures we obtained did not amount to anything, even when we did succeed in cajoling a few of them to
serve as subjects. For they either assumed a pose or screwed
up their faces as if they were at the dentist's, since they were
evidently struggling with the feeling that something weird and
uncanny was being perpetrated upon them. So we finally gave
it up and tried another tactic. We drove through the streets at
pedestrian's speed, and every time I discovered a subject I
jumped out of the car. Mr. R. remained at the wheel and kept
watch in order to give me a whistle when it was time for me
to jump back into the car and move on as quickly as possible.

Actually we were repeatedly met with hostile glances, which
was not exactly pleasant in a neighborhood where we were the
only Europeans. A little boy shouted after us, "Red devil!"
(Mr. R. knew the word.) Nevertheless, the children were
much interested in my paraphernalia and came running in
flocks to watch me when I was photographing distant scenes.
Naturally, I was also anxious to get the children themselves
into the picture. So I surreptitiously set the distance lever and
then suddenly turned the camera on the troop of children. I
can hardly describe how precipitately the scene changed. With
earsplitting shrieks they scurried off in all directions, one tum-
bling over the other; it looked as if a hand grenade had
exploded in the midst of them. Unfortunately, the poor light
in this narrow street would have made a longer exposure necessary to catch this small panic on film.

I keep asking my friends what the reason for this fear of being photographed might be and what these timid spirits are thinking of when they run away at the sight of my camera as if it were a cocked machine gun, taking their young under their wings like startled hens. The answer is always one short word: "Superstition."

And yet this answer is probably much too general. Beneath the mask of superstition may there not be a genuine awareness of the mystery of images? In any case, I cannot believe that it is only the flash bulbs and the strange technique that shocks them. I remember an old Chinese proverb, "He who sees himself does not shine." Obviously, this means that we shine only when we are unconscious of ourselves, in any case at certain levels. As soon as we know ourselves too precisely, we are spoiled by reflection and lose a fundamental naivete. Then we know what effect we are producing and thus also strive to produce certain effects.

In his essay on the marionette theater, Kleist describes how a young dancer quite suddenly loses his unconscious grace as he practices a certain pose before a mirror. The moment he splits himself into both subject and object, into the actor and the spectator, aesthetic innocence vanishes. Then one sees intent in every one of his movements, and one is put off by it. Once paradise has been lost, says Kleist, one must travel around the whole world in order to re-enter the lost paradise from the other side, through a small back door. Then, in order to reach the freedom of a new childlikeness—a naivete once removed, so to speak—one must break through the "sound barrier" of reflection which becomes increasingly less permeable and therefore more threatening.

Have not all of us felt the curse of this becoming conscious of ourselves? How often we look into a mirror (even if it is only while shaving), how many pictures of ourselves we have gazed at, and, if we have anything to do with the radio, how often we have heard our own voices! We actually make use of this experience as a kind of self-training in forming our own personalities (and sometimes in our academic seminars we turn it into a method of instruction). We reflect upon ourselves in order to improve a gesture, refine our enunciation, eliminate an accent, or cultivate a particular kind of articulation or intonation. But is all this really an improvement, or, more precisely, is it *only* an improvement? Is it not at the same time a "Fall" into reflection that destroys the self, and are we not glad when we are so carried away with some idea or some passion that we throw off these shackles, to be transported for a few moments at least into the paradise of pure and unconscious rapture? May not this insight of Chinese wisdom have something to do with the fear that these street urchins have of the camera? Or is that too farfetched; am I reading something into it?

This is quite possible. There may be quite a different mystery behind this aversion to having one's picture taken. Sartre is fond of saying that "the others"—other people—are our enemies because they "regard" us, and "fixate" us by looking at us. The word "fixate" has a meaning that hovers between "to regard" and "to pin down." When we are observed by others, we are laid hold of and, so to speak, nailed down by the claims and demands that these others make upon us. We are "fixed" by certain value-concepts with which our environment confronts us and measures us—for example, fashion. Even if we should have a desire to walk down Main Street on a hot summer day in bathing trunks, we still do not do so, because "people" don't do such things. The passers-by on Main Street compel us by their "fixations" to wear the kind of clothes that "people" wish to see here.

Is not photography an intensified form of fixation? One not only "regards" a person but "catches his image." The Queen of England dare not yawn or sneeze outside her private chambers lest she be immortalized in the press as a yawner or a sneezer.

When one realizes the role that charms and spellbinding play in Eastern religions, it is easy to understand the Chinese fear

71

of being photographed. Why is Israel forbidden to make any graven image or likeness of Jahweh? Because this would be to "fix" God and thus place limits upon the illimitable. This is sacrilege. And why dare his name not be uttered? Because even the knowledge and utterance of the Name is something like an act of binding. Even our fairy stories show us that he who knows the formula "Open sesame!" possesses magic power to burst bars and unlock doors, and that he has control over whatever he thus calls by name.

So I can well imagine that something like this may be going on in the mind of the Chinese: The white devil wants to "catch" me in his camera (isn't this exactly the way we express it in German?); he is trying to bind me by putting me into the little box. He wants to seize me and reduce me to a picture, "fix" me upon film.

The fact that we can express all these fears in symbol-charged words of our own language shows perhaps that here a kind of human knowledge may exist that is stored up and preserved in the cellars, the threshold levels of our collective consciousness.

Thus it may be that an ancient wisdom is actually seeking expression through the medium of superstition. And now that I realize this, I have a bad conscience when I photograph these people. For I must honor the ancient wisdom. My passion for hunting photographic specimens is at odds with my respect for this knowledge. The solution that technological man finds in a delicate situation like this consists in . . . screwing a telescopic lens onto his camera. This is the degenerate form of respect that technology pays to the numinous!

The hustle and bustle in the narrow streets is only a meager foretaste of the turbulence in the market place. The eye can scarcely follow the medley of colors, movement, people, flowers, and fish. But is the eye actually the most important organ of perception? This question forces itself upon me, since this hustle and bustle strikes me as something that is happening on another planet. And yet I have seen it all many times—in illustrated travel books and documentary films. Why is it, then, that I can hardly recognize it? Why is it that these scenes, which are in themselves so familiar, turn out to be unfamiliar, and that everything is so strangely new to me?

All at once I know why it is so. It is because the pictures cannot reproduce the odors and the noise, in any case not this encompassing, *total* clamor that comes crashing down upon one from every side. Now I begin to see the difference between photographs and the pictures of great masters. Painters and poets of high rank not only let us see; they also help us to hear, taste, and smell. They give us the totality of life in *all* its dimensions. I am reminded of a saying of Wilhelm Raabe, which I read today in Hermann Pong's biography of Raabe. The highest praise that can come to a poet, according to Raabe, is that it be said, "His productions always thrust themselves upon us as a whole, so that he who has any taste for such descriptions of the world is compelled to see, hear, smell, feel, perceive, and think the way the author wants him to from the first to the last page of his book."

A photograph cannot do this. It remains flat and sketchy, even if it is reproduced stereoscopically and thrown on a wide screen.

Is there such a thing as a psychology of smell? I believe the nose is the organ of the unconscious. Odors we have smelled preserve memories far better than the impressions received through the eye. I still know the odor of my grandmother's kitchen, and I am sure that a wave of homesickness will come over me whenever I happen to meet this odor. When Hitler refused ever again to enter a Catholic church, despite his love of architecture, it was doubtless because he was an altar boy in his youth and the odor of incense would have brought him into secret conflict with the impressions of his youth.

It is doubtless this polyphony, or sometimes, cacophony—these chords and atonalities of the olfactory waves—that is overwhelming me here in this Chinese market place far more than anything I see. For what assails the nose here is so massive and penetrating that it not only invades the unconscious but also assaults the conscious mind with such vehemence that one is forced to hold one's nose.

After all this, we were so exhausted that we simply had to escape the heat and the stupefying reek and find some place to cool off. Mr. R. knew the whereabouts of an air-conditioned bar, and no sooner had the decision been made than we headed toward it with *élan*. Before we reached the goal, however, we still had to go through an inferno. That is to say, we could not find a parking place in the choked, traffic-filled streets. Since we were soaked to the skin with perspiration, every stop of the car, no matter how short, that kept the breeze from blowing upon us and allowed the sun to beat down on the top of the car was a torture. Compared with this a sauna is like a visit to the North Pole.

Finally we found a small space which was just sufficient for our car. But it took some maneuvering to slip into it. This repeated backing and filling and constant turning of the steering wheel made the sweat spurt out of my companion's pores, and I myself thought I would dissolve into a puddle on the seat cushion just from looking at him.

But when we entered the cool, air-conditioned room and drank an ice-cold orangeade, we felt as if we had been elevated to the bliss of the Olympian gods. Suddenly the mental paralysis vanished, and we talked and discussed things in a state of heightened consciousness which I think I have never experienced before. We talked of our memories of school days in the Gymnasium—Mr. R. is a "St. John's boy" from Hamburg—and about the ancient Greeks. We found that we shared a common love for Homer, the Greek text of which he too carries about with him in Singapore. A little philosophy of the enjoyment of life emerged from this hour of blessed cooling off: Could we ever have enjoyed the delight of recreation so much, and would we ever have experienced with such pleasure the psycho-physical indivisibility of man, if we had not previously perspired so freely and been reduced to an almost liquid state? Pleasure always lies in contrast—just as humor does. One who lives in a continual state of comfort and is spared the rhythm of suffering and release from suffering deprives himself of the possibility of joy, and lapses into the torment of boredom. A perfect standard of living condemns itself. We cannot visualize either hell or heaven because the very continuousness of "the same thing" robs us of the power of feeling and experience. A heaven which is not a matter of faith but merely something conceptualized or visualized is not happiness at all, and a hell conceptualized ceases to be a damnation. A somewhat perverse poetic fancy keeps repeating the notion that heaven is a never-ending torment of boredom, while hell represents a (somewhat macabre) hangover from amusement; for the pinching and burning and torments of hell are never *merely* torture, but are still thought of as being a welcome, relieving change. Well, even the transition from tropical heat to an air-conditioned room can give us a lesson on believing and seeing.

After this rest we were relaxed enough to drive to the shore and look at the junks. We hired a boat and were rowed about through the old-fashioned flotilla by an ancient Chinaman with a fluttering goatee and a picture-book straw hat. We were delighted with these fat-bellied wooden houseboats.

Then we met Mr. and Mrs. Sch. on an airy, shady hotel terrace right next to the sea. We ate our chicken—quite Homerically—with our hands. "And after we had driven away the desire for food and drink," as it says so often in the *Odyssey,* we went off for a siesta in the Sch. family's comfortable home, which stands alone on a hill with open terraces and windows, surrounded by Chinese villas. As the car climbed up the hill we could feel the atmosphere growing less heavy. It was especially pleasant to watch the two blonde children with their Chinese playmates and listen to their mixed lingo of German, English, and Chinese.

August 14

I still have a lot of things to add from Singapore. The sea is now as smooth as glass, and not a breath of air is moving except the head wind. Above the horizon hang brilliant clouds which look like snow-covered mountains. As I write this I am constantly being interrupted. Almost everybody stops and talks for a while. The glorious weather and the fresh head wind perks us up, and the anticipation of Hong Kong raises our spirits.

The hospitality in the Sch. family and the other homes! At first I had some hesitation about taking advantage of it in this way. But my friends explained that hospitality can be quite different here from what it is at home. There are plenty of servants and there is no need to worry about preparation of meals—the European housewife here would actually "lose face" if she were to work in the kitchen. The Chinese cook must be paid the honor of taking over sole responsibility, even though on state occasions he may borrow the tableware from other houses with the help of his relatives. So my hosts were free to give me many hours and to drive me around.

We spent the afternoon and the following morning sightseeing. We visited the largest mosque. Since it is situated outside the city in Malayan territory, we had to pass through two police check points. We were questioned very carefully whether we had any foodstuffs in the car. When Mrs. Sch. translated the question for me, I wondered why the police should be particularly interested in food. I learned that in Malaya the transportation of even small quantities of food is strictly prohibited and that control stations have been set up at all the local boundary lines. After failing to destroy the Communistic partisans who have escaped into the jungle, they are now trying to starve them out. Since the partisans live on provisions they secure by highjacking automobiles and other transport, it is hoped that they will be struck at their weakest point if not a single unguarded transport or private car is permitted to carry even so much as a piece of bread. A gentleman whom I met in the evening at the consulate, who was going to Penang by car the next day, told me that he must plan his trip in such a way as to avoid hunger, arriving at stopping places at the right time. Furthermore, motoring through the countryside is allowed only between sunrise and sundown.

When we arrived at the towering, snow-white mosque, majestically enthroned upon a hill, the guards were not to be persuaded with money, cigarettes, or kind words to allow me to enter, because I was wearing shorts and, stupidly, had not foreseen any difficulty. Even the fact that I was a German— which often works like a charm here—did not help, and I put my shoes, which I had already taken off, back on.

We had hardly gotten back into the car when we were startled by the terrific, throbbing scream of a siren, which reminded us of the air-raid alarms during the last war. I stepped out, as Mrs. Sch. smiled knowingly, and discovered at once that it was the call to prayer which was being sent out over the countryside from gigantic loudspeakers on the four towers of the mosque. This hideous wail, now moaning, now bellowing, now sustained, now tremulant, is utterly impossible to describe. Compared with it, an air-raid alert is like Mozart's *Kleine Nachtmusik,* and I actually believe that this bold comparison is hardly exaggerated.

We then strolled through the botanical gardens, where I was struck by how few flowers there were. On the other hand, I could scarcely take in the innumerable varieties of palms to be found here. Likewise, the term "orchid" here covers an unheard-of multitude of species.

Especially amusing are the antics of the monkeys, who perform gymnastics all over the place. Even for the Malayans, who are quite accustomed to them, they seem to be an inexhaustible source of amusement and drollery. For the first time I saw mother monkeys carrying their young (who cling to the fur on their mothers' bodies), and despite this burden making the most hazardous leaps from branch to branch.

The old comparison between Zen-Buddhism and Amida-

77

Buddhism occurred to me. The doctrine of grace in Zen-Buddhism is symbolized in the baby monkey. Grace bestows security like the mother monkey, but like the baby monkey we must do something in order to participate in this grace. We must cling to it, and thus it requires a certain co-operation. The concept of grace in Amida-Buddhism, on the other hand, chooses for its illustration the picture of the mother cat and her young: she simply carries her young in her mouth. The kitten does nothing whatever. It does not even need to hold on. Grace is total and effectual by itself. The difference between the Catholic and the Reformation concept of grace, which is strikingly analogous to these nuances of Buddhism, might be explained to a European catechumen by means of this exotic example.

What a delight it would be to roam through such country if it were in Europe! But here after a few hundred yards of weary plodding one is totally spent and yearns for the breeze that comes from riding in a car.

The most fantastic sight of the day was the sprawling Tiger Palm Garden. It was built by a millionaire Chinese who made a fortune on a headache remedy and other medicines. It is said that a fortune-teller told him that he would live as long as he continued to build. The main project he chose for the prolongation of his life is a veritable monster of an exhibition park that extends for hundreds of yards and presents a tremendous mass of huge, luridly painted stone figures and scenes. Everything from bloody, sadistic scenes of hell and other representations of Chinese mythology and history to modern traffic accidents, from figures of Buddha to legendary beasts, all the rubbish that has settled in the cellars of the Chinese psyche is given shape in the monstrous concrete sculptures of this panopticon; at the same time they are a portrayal of the humanitarian fancies dreamed up by a kindly old Chinese millionaire with time on his hands.

I should think that for a cultured Chinese all this is nothing more than conglobulated *Kitsch* ["gingerbread"]. But in any case it is the most enormous *Kitsch* that I have ever seen. It is curious that the instinct of such an ancient civilized people becomes confused and unsure as soon as it abandons its genuine traditions and allies itself with alien values and influences, in this case with a questionable form of Americanism. This park is a mine for the psychoanalysts.

The evening of this full day was a great, relaxing pleasure for me. The consul general arranged a dinner for me at his home to which he invited many guests of various nationalities, and it was extremely instructive and fascinating to speak with them. In the course of the evening it turned out that immediately after the war the consul had been interned in the same Ludwigsburg camp where the Americans had given me permission to speak to the prisoners. Later he was in Tübingen and there heard a number of my lectures. For a moment we had a vivid realization of the gracious providence manifested in this path of life marked by the names of Ludwigsburg, Tübingen, and Singapore. If anybody had told us in the starvation camp of Ludwigsburg, where thousands of men—mostly university men—were gathered together indiscriminately and without cause, that we would see each other on a festive evening in Singapore! *O quae mutatio rerum!* The thought of God's goodness kept recurring as we talked of all this.

The consul's gracious wife is a superb hostess, and she understood how to give style and form to the evening. The beautiful, spacious rooms are furnished with costly Indian and Chinese furniture, carved chests, and ancient tapestries. Before the dinner, which proceeded with oriental sumptuousness in six or eight courses, served on beautiful china by mute Chinese servants, we listened for about an hour to music played on an excellent instrument. After such a long interval in which I had heard no music—unfortunately, our instrument on board ship does not function—I drank in the sounds like a man parched with thirst. While the music was being played, we sat in the surrounding rooms, all of which open upon the central hall. The house was darkened, so that each person felt quite alone. A gentle wind was blowing in, and the ceiling fans provided further cooling. So we listened with complete concentration to Veracini's *Flute Sonata,* and Bach's *Violin Concerto No. 2,* played by Oistrakh.

During the meal itself, the hostess, who is a marvellously deft interpreter, helped me so skillfully that I hardly felt that I was contending with other languages.

There is one phase of the conversation that I must note for my *Ethics.* Among other things, the talk came around to the situation of the young unmarried Europeans, who as a rule have Chinese mistresses. The reasons given for their not being able to get along without these "temporary marriages" are first, the stimulating effect of the tropical climate, and second, certain irrational factors. As far as these latter could be explained to me, they are probably to be seen in the fact that the absence of all accustomed ties—not only separation from one's family and from the conditions of life at home, but also from a completely different order of nature (one which is determined by the change of seasons, for example)—causes a person to seek that more intimate assimilation and empathy which he hopes to find in the realm of the erotic. Besides, there is a certain fascination exercised by the Asiatic woman just by reason of the fact that she is completely different from the Western woman. She lives wholly and solely for her man. She still understands what it means to serve a man by giving him love. This too helps a young man to bridge the gap between the two worlds. And finally, it was explained to me, these Chinese women are for the most part of high culture and fine quality; they live with a man as unselfish companions.

Various observations I had already made with respect to this problem prompted me to ask whether the result would not inevitably be complications and unhappiness when such a relationship was later dissolved and the European married a Western wife (for marriages between Westerners and Chinese are still rare exceptions). This complication was admitted, but it is mitigated, it was said, at least as far as the man is concerned (though, after all, his situation constitutes only *one* side of the problem!), by the fact that the Chinese and also the Japanese woman, if she is not the mother of a family, thinks of her relationship to the man as being exclusively erotic. If he should wish to discuss with her a question that troubles him or to allow her to share in his business concerns, she would hardly be able to keep up with him on this level. Rather she would then devote all the feminine art of love to caressing away the lines of care from his brow. But at times like these the European man seeks for something else. He wants a companion and some real sense of affinity, at least if his erotic sense is still intact and has not been completely reduced to the physical. Here, they said, lies the limitation of such liaisons, unless this limitation is partially removed by the establishment of a family, and the relationship thus given a broader *human* outlook.

This conversation rounded off, in a way which is very important to me, a number of isolated observations and fragmentary remarks that had caught my attention earlier. I realized again how impossible it is to subject these things to a rigid system of morals. I remember again that the Gospel is far more than morals, and I ask myself how it can help in a situation like this—without becoming a deadening law and an oppressive burden—and how one would have to speak to a person in such a situation. In any case, the worst thing would be for me to jump in with ready solutions merely in order to appear faithful to my vocation as a theologian. I must simply persevere during my momentary helplessness and also bear the humiliation of the fact that I, a professional writer on ethics, should have nothing to say on a question like this. If solutions are given to a man, they are given to him only as he works his way through these phases of vacuum and does not evade them by stuffing them with doctrinaire straw.

As I looked over the group gathered for this lively evening of discussion, I was struck here, as elsewhere, by the cheerful composure of the Europeans. Some of them—particularly the clergymen, of whom a number were present—went through grievous imprisonment by the Japanese during the last war or even in prisons in Red China. But the German businessmen here did not have an easy time of it either, some having lost everything twice in their lives. Nor do they know how long that which they are now doggedly and calmly rebuilding will endure, for everything is in flux. This year Singapore is still a British crown colony. Next year it will be independent as to internal affairs, but will remain bound to the British Empire in so far as foreign policy is concerned. Whether Singapore will eventually be politically united with Malaya is still altogether uncertain. The Malayans themselves appear not to be particularly desirous of this because they fear that then the ascendancy of the Chinese may become too great. These apprehensions are based not only upon the size of the Chinese population, but above all upon the fact that all of the economic power is concentrated in the hands of the Chinese.

The shadow of the Red Titan with its emanations is perceptible everywhere. There is never a discussion in which its presence is not felt. It is the strongest, even though unknown, factor in every calculation. And even if these latitudes are not Bolshevistic—except for the Red partisans, who are "hibernating" in the jungles, and the fifth column, which has established itself in industry—all the colored people are at one in their rejection of the white man. What is going on behind the masks of their friendly faces can only be surmised.

Of our second day in Singapore I shall mention only the evening, for which the representative of the Hamburg-America Line invited me to a Mohammedan restaurant. Immediately upon entering, we were overwhelmed by an unimaginable swarm of munching people, scurrying waiters, odors, and noise. I was horrified when I saw the quantities my host was ordering for us. Actually it was almost everything on the long menu. An almost endless caravan of waiters brought on the multitude of courses, all of which looked gray-brown or gray-green, and none of which I could identify—except a few chicken legs.

When I remarked to my host that it seemed to me that he was buying out the whole restaurant, he explained, "Here you can order as much as you want; you pay later only for what you have actually eaten." An innocent European is naturally somewhat flabbergasted by such business arrangements, and I did not dare ask how often the remainders would appear on the plates of other guests. I confess that I did not fall to with any great enthusiasm and that the taste was also very strange to me. But the nausea which threatened to overcome me at first soon passed away. The strong taste of curry and the other hot seasonings that bring tears to the eyes creates the illusion that you are eating some kind of corrosive disinfectant and that any possible bacteria have long since been burned to a crisp before they disappear into your mouth.

This hygienic illusion also helps one to cope, at least partly, with the aesthetic situation. The bones and other scraps are cheerfully thrown on the table (some throw them on the floor), and it was not long until the heap towered on our table. Before the pile grew too high an Indian cleared away the garbage. But naturally he could not prevent its leaving a monument to gluttony in the form of big grease spots.

The restaurant is located in a quarter occupied by Chinese, Indians, and Arabians. So when we left, the stroll through the streets with their still open shops offered us a feast for the eyes. With the smart of the caustic condiments still lingering in our throats, we felt even more a part of our surroundings.

Then a furious drive in the car brought me back to the ship. It had been waiting for me for some time. The captain and the passengers were on the bridge, and they clapped their hands as we arrived to let us know in a very decent and kindly way that we were late. The ship's family was glad to be together again, for there is something very stimulating about reliving one's experiences in the telling of them as the ship glides slowly past the strings of light in the harbor into the darkness of the sea.

Hong Kong

I have already mentioned the fact that since Singapore we have had a small part of a Chinese family on board—father, mother, and a grown son. It is really only a fragment, for it turned out that the young man has six brothers and sisters and that a further increase is on the way. In addition, the father probably has one or two other wives. So now even the ship reminds us of the prolification of the Chinese. However, we can hardly get acquainted with them, since the parents speak only Chinese and the son knows only a few scraps of English. The simple laws of physical circumstance dictate that the solids in the human stomach are heavier than air and thus give rise to sudden changes in the atmosphere, sometimes producing sounds (internationally familiar) during and after meals. All three of them are unassuming, altogether friendly and smiling, and we are glad to see them.

At the moment the father is sitting in a deck chair a few yards away from me, staring at the sky, the water, or nothing at all. In spirit I try to place myself in his mind, and I discover how remote we are from a man of this kind and how little we are able to understand him. The distance between us is certainly not—or at least not primarily—due to lack of verbal communication between us. It has deeper causes. I imagine certain analogies between what I think and dream as I lie here dozing in a deck chair and what is going on in the mind of this yellow-skinned man.

I find that I can state these analogies only in the most generalized and abstract form, but by no means directly and concretely. I imagine that he thinks about his home, just as I do, and his garden, and his other children playing, perhaps, with the dog, or the older ones taking care of the younger ones. Very well—we are human beings whom the good Lord created in his image, and surely it is because of this ultimate community which binds our existence together that the basic figures of our life are the same. But does not the analogy stop right there? I am troubled again by the same question that has been puzzling me for some time: Even though the basic figure of father-child love appears in both cases, *how* does this Chinese man, who sits near me dreaming, look upon his children? My children are blonde, but his have coal-black hair. I find the little Chinese children charming, and I can never see enough of them. They seem like exotic dolls to me. I always have the impulse to play with them. But when I make the attempt, I sense that this tall white man is somewhat strange to them. Now what for me is "exotically" attractive in these children is for my Chinese neighbor "familiar." He will see their black hair and slanted eyes quite differently from the way I see them. Very likely for him the faces of white people look like contourless wheyfaces. Our features may appear to him like physiognomic porridge, while here among his countrymen and his children he sees clear lines and contrasting colors. The faces which are impenetrable for us are for him eloquently expressive, and for him their stereotyped smiles are full of nuances.

Can I really have any conception of what is going on within him as he sits there dreaming in his deck chair? The Platonic idea of love may bind us together, but it is transcendent, like all Platonic ideas. Love in its concrete shape is different in his mind from what it is in mine because its objects are different. (Only when I see the Chinese mothers, dandling their babies on the junks, is the immediacy present. The "realm of the mother" exists in a stratum which seems to lie beneath all the differences.) His fears, too, are different. For him they come creeping out of the realm of evil spirits, but for me they come from "the morrow," which generates cares, or from the assaults of Nothingness.

And yet I ask myself whether these differences are fundamental, whether they divide mankind with insurmountable barriers. After all, the miracle of faith which produces fellowship does occur, and it makes no difference that one person pictures God as a white man and the other as a yellow man, that one person pictures the angels' Gloria as being blown upon trumpets and the other upon jade flutes. God embraces all his children in one glance. And we catch a reflection of that glance whenever the miracle of brotherhood occurs among us or whenever we suddenly see the image of man in another person.

Last night I slept on the radio deck again. Towards morning I woke up because of the cold and then covered myself up. Half asleep, I was happy for being a little bit cold, and remembered the story of the old lady with cold feet.

August 16

Today—no, already I must say *yesterday*—late in the morning we sailed slowly through the maze of islands around Hong Kong into the harbor. From a distance, as always when one sails into a harbor, the rough outline of the landscape appears first, and then as one comes closer the human element begins to register. When one traverses broad oceans, man becomes a microscopically small creature; one must come close or use a telescope to discover his traces.

First, then, we observed the magnificent chain of mountains around Hong Kong. The city itself seemed to lie hidden and enchanted behind the protection of many island guards. Only secret mariner's paths lead through the labyrinth to this jewel of a city, and the presence of a pilot at this point is really symbolic.

Every minute as we came closer the panorama changed. We rushed from starboard to larboard and from bow to stern. My camera was obliged to take on a supplementary task and give permanence to all the fleeting impressions, for this abundance was too much for the eye to take in. When these pictures are shown on the screen at home they will not only be recollections of what has actually been seen, but will allow me to see many things for the first time and lend permanence to the all too brief moments of the original encounter.

Now the villas on the slopes emerged clearly in the noonday light, the skyscrapers shone in the sun, and gradually the telescope also picked up the muddy slopes which are covered with the miserable hovels of the poor. Hundreds and thousands of them cling to the steep inclines like ragged birds' nests. Sometimes they are washed away by the tropical rainfalls, drowning some of the poverty and the poor themselves. Below, there was something we could not make out from the sea but did see later when we looked down from the heights. Thousands upon thousands of refugees have erected corrugated iron huts, wooden boxes, and tentlike shelters on the roofs of other dwelling and commercial buildings, where they spend their lives in the pitiless heat of the sun. Seen from the heights, the poor look like lice in the perukes of the citizens, or scabs on the scalp of society.

The landing maneuvers turned out to be very difficult here, since the approach to the "parking place" at the pier is too narrow. Suddenly there was a great hullaballoo at the stern as one of the junks, which were already beginning to swarm about our ship, brushed against the screw for a moment and capsized. Father, mother, and children were swimming about in the water, already grabbing at pots and other utensils that had toppled into the water with them. We felt that the situation was rather dangerous and quickly computed the damage it might cause this poor family. But with incredible adroitness, without a single outcry, and as matter-of-factly as if it were an everyday occurrence, they righted the junk with the help of those on other houseboats—the comradeship among these junk-dwellers is always impressive—secured the utensils, changed their clothes, and a few minutes later were already busy cleaning up and drying things out as if nothing had happened.

These people seem to be like animals in the sense of being confined to the experience of the moment. They proceed to do what needs to be done in complete concentration upon the immediate task. It reminds me of a cow when a thunderclap strikes in her immediate vicinity: she looks up for a moment in mild amazement and goes on eating; she has no fear of the lightning, and the memory of what has just happened no longer troubles her. In the higher stages of consciousness every experience is multiplied by three: it is present first as the factor of expectant concern, then as that which is actually experienced, and then as a echoing memory. Perhaps the reduction of experience to the moment, as we find it in animals, children, and primitives, is one of the strongest limitations placed upon our capacity for empathy.

We anchored at the pier of Kowloon, on the other side of the bay from the island city of Hong Kong. Kowloon, which is part of the mainland, has been leased by the British for a term of thirty years. In later talks with friends in Hong Kong there came up again and again the anxious question of what will happen after this period and whether there is any use at all in making long-term investments. The transitional character of living conditions throughout Southeast Asia can actually be dated, here in Hong Kong. Nevertheless, at least as far as this respite of three decades is concerned, the people here regard the situation with relative equanimity. For Red China, Hong Kong is a good source of foreign exchange, a market, and a distribution center. The colony capitalizes on this opportunity.

But I have already gotten ahead of myself in my account of this day. While we were still in the midst of the docking maneuvers, the ship suffered another slight dent in the side, in addition to the collision with the junk. All the noise that accompanied these maneuvers—the shouted commands, whistles, sirens, and other signals—was drowned out by ear-splitting hammering aboard a neighboring British ship. This hammering, I learned, will move over to our ship tomorrow and then to other ships. This attack upon the eardrums originates from some three hundred Chinese who are knocking away rust and renewing the paint. One has the feeling that by some miracle of technology an ant heap is giving forth sounds and transmitting, through acoustical signals, the secret processes which are going on within it. Only careful searching with the telescope revealed the myriad sources of the hammering: human termites balancing on the ventilators, scrambling about on the hoists, standing and squatting on enormously long planks hung along the sides of the ship, which look like telegraph wires lined with innumerable starlings. Through their pounding off thousands of particles of rust and paint and applying countless brush strokes, within a few hours a mighty ship acquires a fresh coat of color. And all this is done for a ridiculously low price, for labor is fabulously cheap here and men are available in almost unlimited numbers. These coolies have only three days off in a year, and they work twelve hours a day. If they stay away for a day, they are docked two days' wages.

These observations and reports are extremely disquieting. One begins to realize what a bridgehead this social misery constitutes for the onslaught of the Red Titan, though for the moment—at least here—it appears to be accepted without resistance and with a certain fatalistic *laissez faire*. But woe betide us if these dull and mechanically functioning coolie brains—at least that's the way it looks; but this may only be the superficial impression of a passer-by—woe betide us if these brains are ever roused to conscious awareness; if someone comes along and galvanizes them into action with some kind of dynamic.

During the docking maneuvers we saw two gentlemen and a lady standing on the pier in the burning sun. As it turned out later, they were there to meet me. They were Mr. J., the head of an old East Asia firm—he had been kindly informed from Hamburg of my coming—and Consul Dr. P. and his young wife. They presented me with a cordial letter of welcome and invitation from the consul general. To my pleasure it turned out that Mrs. P., when she was a student, had once missed the bus in Stuttgart which was to take her to Tübingen and when she thumbed a ride it was my car that picked her up. So we rode together for a while, never suspecting how and where we would later meet again. Later she also attended some of my classes. Immediately, therefore, a fine human contact was established. These three people who were waiting for me there on the pier made my day in Hong Kong unforgettably full and pleasant. They had talked over how to pack as much as possible into this brief time. Since I would be able to rest to my heart's content later, on the ship, I thoroughly agreed with their rigorous program.

First Mrs. P. helped me to make those cheap purchases every visitor to Hong Kong makes, which, apart from their actual purpose, also provide many glimpses into Chinese business life: tiny, stifling shops where one must bargain to make a purchase, and larger ones in which everything is conducted as seriously as in German stores, where cash registers ring and proper bills are made out.

In contrast to the Egyptian and Arabian tradesmen, it was pleasant to note that the Chinese are courteously assiduous and untiring in bringing out and showing their wares but they never press them upon the customer. Sulky faces and disappointed countenances, which one sometimes meets with in the stores at home, are not to be found here despite the murderous heat. Often one gets the impression that the point of the transaction is not the outcome of their efforts to make a sale, that is, the profit, but simply the business of displaying the goods, impressing the customer, and parrying his objections, no matter whether he buys or not. The game that goes on between the demands of the buyer and the offers or recommendations of the seller, the play of attack and defense and pretended disinterest and temporizing resistance, always strikes me as being a kind of "play" in which it is not so much a matter of who wins and how it comes out, but rather of something which is done for its own sake. This is obviously more a matter of sport and play than work and downright seriousness. To be sure, this is possible only among nations and races in which men are traders and charismatic speculators almost by nature, as the Chinese are. They not only make a living by the profits of their business; their whole life is their business.

Far more fascinating than the stores are the streets themselves—this flood and whirl of crowds which is like the surge of waves in the ocean. They produce crests and splashes—repeatedly individuals and groups move off the sidewalks into the streets, and again and again they nip straight across the path of the cars that choke the streets. The constant streams of traffic right and left are constantly spraying drops on all sides. The Chinese women wear high-necked dresses, but their skirts are slit to above the knee on the side. Fantastically large, precariously balanced sun hats in many shapes go floating past in the flood. The advertisements on the stores and banners strung across the street present a shimmering, impressionistic diversity. Despite their colorfulness, even though one is surrounded by them on every side, their effect is not at all blatant or penetrating; they look more like colorful holiday decorations and almost appear to serve an ornamental purpose. But this is probably only an optical illusion brought about by the fact that I cannot read the Chinese characters; these signs do not engage my attention in the sense that I am compelled to heed their message—except when an all-too-familiar trademark of an internationally known beverage company or gasoline company leaps into view. (These trademarks seem to be the one thing the whole non-Communist world holds in common unreservedly; they have at least partly overcome the Babylonian confusion of tongues.) Advertising stripped of its real purpose and transformed into a surrealist's palette of colors—this is a new and very charming phenomenon.

The abundant colors and figures, which at first strike one as an inchoate mass, gradually sort themselves out into clearly contoured images: bank buildings the size of skyscrapers tower over the Victorian business center from which narrow, brooding, hot streets filled with human ants branch on all sides at almost every horizontal and vertical angle. The Europeans are a small minority. Although the Chinese element is by far the majority, the multiplicity of Asiatic races crowded together in this city of millions—which is not only a city but also a safety valve and a catalyst—is impressive.

If I make a conscious effort to fix my first impression, if I close my eyes for a moment in this swarming throng and then determine which shapes and shadows remain the longest on the radar screen of my psyche, I must say it is children—children, children, and more children. In every entrance and in the middle of the sidewalk they sit and play. The larger ones carry the little ones around, perched astride their hips. The mothers carry the smallest on their backs in a cloth sling like a rucksack, especially while they are at such work as street construction (where many women are seen) or while they are doing their housework. The infant swings gently to the rhythm of the mother's movements. The lower part of the child's head is held fast with a handkerchief so that it does not flop backwards or sidewards. Again and again one comes upon children lying on their stomachs, sides, or backs in the middle of the sidewalk, fast asleep. One carefully steps over them. Only rarely does it happen that, as a child lies there in a particularly comical position, the brief tender glance of a passing woman falls upon it.

This multitude of children and young people naturally brings to mind the phrase "yellow peril." It implies the possibility of being overwhelmed by a biological avalanche. It produces the impression of tremendous potential, though still dormant, energy. The indescribable industry of the Chinese—the running and scurrying, the pulling and tugging—further enhances the impression of an inexhaustible dynamic. If, despite all this, our feeling of menace remains within bounds, it is surely because of the friendliness of these people, their completely unaggressive behavior.

But one hardly dares to carry the thought further. What would happen if this potential energy were awakened and mobilized, if it were changed into kinetic energy by the hand of a dictator? Might not this very capacity for passive endurance be transformed into extreme activity? Could it not become a compliant submission to some dynamic and militant intelligence? I am not much comforted when the China experts assure me that the individual Chinese has no talent whatever for historical activity, that on the contrary—so far as politics are concerned — he is definitely an onlooker, tends to avoid decisions, and lets things go their way. This seems to me to be a wrong calculation. Here again, psychological categories are inadequate. Creatively gifted and intelligent beings do not *need* to be purposeful, strong-willed men in order to be politically effective. They need only fall into the hands of such a willful man in order to become, as instruments that carry out his will, eminently capable of creating history. If they are by nature (and therefore psychologically) inclined to be passive and indifferent, they will remain coolies and fellahin as long as they are left to themselves and their own lack of initiative. But they will become mobilized historically to the highest degree once this passive willingness to be pushed around becomes subservient to the will of a superior, ideologically motivated dictator. Then they will provide such a dictator with an open psychic field in which he can operate without let or hindrance.

On their own initiative the Chinese, looked upon as a whole, will certainly *not* conquer the world. Nor will they resist the one who conquers them with the proper means. From a political point of view they will perhaps always remain passive objects. But if they become objects of their own dictators they may constitute compliant material by means of which these dictators may then conquer the world—especially if this material keeps on increasing in geometric progression from year to year through excess of births over deaths, with the devastating effect of a population explosion. In obedience to a superior guiding will, which may proceed to multiply their biological power as a people many millions of times, they may very well become the masters of our planet.

However, all these are reflections which emerged later as these impressions were being written down. What shocked me right there on the streets, and not merely on the basis of later reflection, were the rickshas. These too I knew from the picture books. But now that I see them in reality, with my own eyes, I realize that I knew nothing about them before. In this murderous heat the coolies run along between the shafts of small two-wheeled vehicles. They do not walk, but actually run, even the old and the worn-out ones. Whereas people like us creep along like snails, yet soaked with perspiration, trying to take advantage of every shadow and yearning for a shower and a change of clothes as soon as possible, they keep running at a trot and pull a load besides. Because the pictures cannot show the heat, they can give no idea of what these rickshas mean. Naturally, these people are accustomed to the climate, and, naturally, they are more competent and certainly tougher than we are. But it shocks me nonetheless, particularly when I am informed that they do not even own these little carts themselves. The rickshas are the property of some rich Chinese who rents them out at a usurious rate. And not until a coolie has run long enough to make up this rental do his paltry earnings begin. In Red China the rickshas are prohibited. There, it is said, they have been put into the museums as a reminder of the epoch of exploitation.

What should be said about this? It occupies me, torments me constantly; we talked about it a number of times. One person says that there are far worse forms of drudgery than these rickshas. Are the coolies in the harbor any better off? Or the people who come flooding into Hong Kong every day among the masses of refugees, camping anywhere on the streets, joining the hundreds of thousands of unregistered persons? Or are the people in Red China any better off, tormented with quite different and more refined tortures—brainwashing, terror, and other excesses of the dictatorship?

From the rational point of view, all these objections are naturally quite correct. Being a ricksha-coolie is certainly not the worst of the dubious morsels which this old earth has handed out in the past and in the present. So why do I get excited about it?

94

But it is curious that all these arguments do not help me get over the shock it gave me—perhaps because it is hardly possible to comprehend this impression rationally. For the crucial point, it seems to me, is a certain symbolical implication: here one human being pulls another through the streets. The one who pulls is obliged to run and tug like a draft horse or a motor—like an animal, therefore, or a thing. The one who is being pulled, however, lies back comfortably on the cushion. The one endures the heat in a far more intensified form in order that the other may feel it less and rest quietly beneath the sunshade.

All this is to be found in hundreds of other areas of life. For "some are in the dark and others are in the light." (Curious that this particular verse from Bert Brecht's *Threepenny Opera* should occur to me just now!) But in those other areas of life this "order" of things is usually less strongly symbolical; it does not make itself felt so immediately and demonstratively. There it is hidden in the apparatus and mechanisms; there it is submerged, as it were, in the large-scale structure of society.

The rickshas *betray* this cunningly concealed secret of upper and lower, of "light" and "dark." They are like a sketch plan of life that has been exposed and betrayed. They seem to be whispering, with their quiet rubber wheels: If I did not keep whistling my life away, you perhaps would not even take notice of it.

In any case, I can understand why Einstein refused to get into one of these rickshas, thus upsetting a procession which was to be formed in his honor. Certainly the corresponding vehicles seen in Malaya and Singapore are not much less hard on the coolie, even though there he sits on a bicycle seat and propels the ricksha with pedals (which is also said to be the sole amelioration that Red China has brought to this problem.) But the very comparison of these two similar vehicles only makes the significance of their symbolism more certain. The fact that the coolie is in a sitting position, like the passenger— even though he performs hard labor while he is sitting—takes something of the sting out of the offensive parallel with the draft animal, for at least he sits on the same staircase as the fellow human being he is propelling, even though it be on a lower step. Here the symbol appears to preserve something of human solidarity.

When one returns to these streets late at night they are almost as busy as during the day. There seems to be hardly any difference here between day and night, or between weekday and Sunday. Where the stores are closed in the evening — though most of the open-front stores exhibit only a symbolic form of closing—some of the Chinese sleep in their stores, on or under the counters, or in a corner somewhere. Only the more well-to-do business people have living quarters above the store. The wealthy Chinese, however, occupy castle-like villas on the heights, and even from the outside the extravagant splendor and comfort that prevails inside can be surmised.

Before I returned to the ship late in the afternoon we refreshed ourselves, after our sudorific purchasing expedition, in a large hotel whose Victorian rooms are even more reminiscent of colonial days than those of the E. & O. Hotel in Penang. Here what struck me back home as being exotic becomes merely an example of the extravagance of many Europeans. I note a number of women whose dyed hair and hairdos are so fantastic that it looks as if some rare vegetation were growing out of their heads and the heads themselves were modeled by a surrealist painter. A significant whisper floated about the tables as a dignified matron with peroxide-blond hair sailed through the room: "That was Hong Kong's beauty queen of 1907." I wonder if back then, a year before I was born, they played "Dolly, you are the apple of my eye" when she was crowned. Anyhow, that's the oldest popular song from my earliest youth I can think of. But even more I am reminded of the old soldier's song, "Ah, the roses fade, every one." Not only do the roses, both botanical and human, fade and wither away, but also historical epochs, and for a moment I catch the musty odor of an herbarium. Despite the excellent service,

I was glad to get outside of the place. When a person is troubled by the question of the future, anachronisms are painful.

In the evening there was to be a large gathering in the home of Mr. von H., and I had been asked to speak about the intellectual and spiritual situation in Europe. The attempt to regenerate myself under the shower in my cabin and make myself fit to slip into some decent clothes was only moderately successful. Even before I had put on my necktie, I was in a state just as bad as before. And, as I had to walk down the full length of the pier in the blazing sun in order to take the ferry to Hong Kong proper and the car that was waiting for me, I felt as if I would melt and be resolved into all my component parts. For anyone who always prepares very carefully for an address this in itself would be a very painful thing; in this heat I had not been able to muster the strength to prepare. By this time I no longer cared. But this also saved me from being nervous. So now I realize that nervousness is *also* a sign of surplus strength. A person has to have some strength left even to be nervous. But at the moment I could not manage it.

The head wind on the ferry and later the fast BMW car brought me the first relief, so that I was able to drink in the majestic color of a splendid sunset. And when I entered Mr. von H.'s house all my physical tiredness vanished. The pleasant coolness of the house immediately gave me the alertness necessary to appreciate the culture of its splendid, spacious rooms. But the view from the terrace left me breathless and speechless. The house is built halfway up the height on a cliff. Immediately to the left is the great hospital which I know from reading Han Suyin's *A Many-splendored Thing,* and beneath is the broad expanse of the sea and the islands. In the distance, shimmering in the twilight and already dark below, are the mountains. The colors of departing day glowed all around us like flickering flames. As the tropic night fell swiftly, covering the depths beneath us with a thin veil of mist, the warm yellow lights of countless junks began to send up their twinkling gleams. Mute Chinese servants offered drinks, hors d'oeuvres, and cigars. While the host chatted with Mr. J., who had driven me up — the other guests had not yet arrived — I had to subject my soul to a bit of discipline in order to cope with the tremendous view outside and the lonely interior. For courtesy's sake and in order to make conversation I listened to an explanation of the "environs" (how banal a word for the "many-splendored thing" that shone up here and on every side!). "Those heights over there are in Red China, and that one over there is the old Portuguese colony of Macao. Our firm has its annual picnic there." But what are geographical and political concepts here! All human additions to this panorama are too small to assert themselves at a time like this.

Gradually the company assembled—the consul general and his staff and their wives, many business people, and quite a number of young people. It is an uncomfortable thing for a speaker not to know his listeners and their mentality. But I saw at once that these were lively, sophisticated, open-minded people—a type quite different from what one occasionally finds among Germans abroad who, despite their efficiency, are not infrequently quite plebeian and limited in their interests.

I was delighted by the cordial welcome I received, and then spoke on my subject. The lively discussion, which finally resolved into smaller groups, went on until almost two o'clock in the morning. We stood or sat about on the huge terrace as the increasing coolness gradually refreshed us and the lights twinkled in the distance. The gratitude these people expressed that for once it was possible to strike up a different theme in the midst of the usual business talk was honest and spontaneous, and I have the impression that the discussion will continue to stir and perhaps go on for a long time.

Again and again the problem of Red China cropped up in the conversations. There were a good many gentlemen present who had lived in China for decades, including some who have been there recently and are returning in the near future. Moreover, they receive excellent information through their firm representatives. Though we did not enter into a discussion of any possible ideological differences between Russia and China in their understanding of Marxism and Leninism, in listening to these accounts of personal experiences I was struck by something that does not agree with my previous opinions. While we at home generally tend to speak of the two Red power blocs as one, here, where the situation is seen close up, there would seem to be many differences between the two. Thus Chinese Communism is considered to be essentially more radical than the Russian. In Russia, eyewitnesses tell me, any opposition to the system is punished with iron severity, but the authorities are rather tolerant toward opponents who keep quiet and are at least ready to do their work in loyal cooperation. In China, however, they demand positive professions of faith and cultivate not only guidance but also control of the unconscious. Thus their approach is far more radical. Besides, the contemplative and meditative nature of the Chinese in itself tends to make them more submissive to disciplines for the inculcation of ideas, and allows ideological demands to infiltrate more deeply. Actually, such pseudo-religious disciplines, the purpose of which is to promote the recognition, repentance, and correction of ideological deviations, as well as civic consciousness, are being practiced increasingly. There are actually Communist houses of discipline set up in monastic form for this purpose.

In this connection I have repeatedly encountered the conjecture that this historically and typologically conditioned difference in the way Russians and Chinese accept Communism may eventually produce various "trends," schools, and sects of Communism and increase the tensions within the Bolshevistic power bloc. But above all, the much-publicized growth of population in China means a pressure upon Russia which even now is certainly greater than the pressure of America and Western armament and which has already created a hissing safety valve for itself in the direction of Siberia.

In view of this impression, I am obliged to ask myself

whether my critical attitude toward America's China policy can be upheld as simply as before. Hitherto—like many Americans with whom I have spoken—I could never rightly understand why the Americans continued to ignore the fact of Red China and dissociated themselves from it. I felt that the pressure America was exerting on both Russia and China, without making any distinction between them, was only welding the two Red giants together more closely and forcing them into a closer fellowship. This policy seemed to overlook the old strategic rule *divide et impera* ("divide and conquer"), whereas a certain understanding with China might perhaps begin to melt the Communist "ice-bloc" and break it down somewhat. I was of the opinion that here psychological factors are at work: the Americans, it might be speculated, are unable to forget their abortive Chiang Kai-shek policy, their partial responsibility for the Bolshevization of Asia, and the death of their soldiers in Korea.

Must I not revise this view of the situation? I ask this very seriously. May it not also be conceivable—this is a thought I cannot get away from after this evening's discussion—that America wishes to let the two Red dictatorships stew in the juice of their internal tensions, and is simply waiting for the outcome of this power conflict? But who would know the answer to that question?

There is another problem we discussed for which nobody could give me an adequate answer. I asked the experts who still remembered the old China how it could be possible for abstract Bolshevist collectivism to make such deep inroads upon a family-conscious people that it has been able to grind up the "natural stone" into molecules and then fuse it together again into the "artificial stone" of the collective.

The conjectures as to how this was possible were widely divergent, especially since in actuality a whole complex of causes and conditions have influenced the situation. The most important factor, certainly, was that the Chiang Kai-shek system was so terribly corrupt. That is why the neatness and the incorruptibility of the Red troops and the new administrators were welcomed at first with a sigh of relief, and inspired such great trust. Then, too, it may have been a factor that the lowest classes, such as the coolies, most certainly experienced some easement of their lot. Now people are no longer seen collapsing on the street from hunger or dying forsaken in the gutters. More than one person with whom I spoke this evening had seen these shameful things with their own eyes. It is also a disgrace to the Europeans who took things easy when they were the colonial masters, and the beneficiaries of the social misery. The abused and exceedingly numerous lower class is now definitely better off. And since its members have *always* been enslaved and the objects of terror and exploitation, the pressure of the totalitarian system is not a new or strongly felt burden.

But, after all, much more important than the question of the causes of this penetration into the traditional structure is the problem of how deeply it has entered. Is this a genuine victory over a millenniums-old tradition, or is it only an accommodation of the passive, elastic soul of the Chinese to a new pressure—after the pressure is released will they quickly go back to the place where they started and rediscover their ancient entelechy? Naturally, even the knowledge of experts is insufficient to answer this decisive question.

Such a regeneration would not need to be "reactionary" at all. For it is as clear as day that China has been awakened, that its return to itself would therefore never mean a return to its previous historical position—in other words, that any possible colonial ambitions on the part of the white man would be nothing but impotent desires. But what makes me hesitate to put any credence in a regeneration of this refined character is that same glance at the rapid increase of the Chinese people and the relative shortness of their normal life expectancy. In a few decades, if Mao Tse-tung succeeds in winning the younger generation, China will be composed of entirely new people. And in an even shorter time the overwhelming majority of the younger people will throw the relics of the older generation out the window.

What is actually happening and what will happen in the future is therefore hardly to be described. Moreover, any analysis of the ideology, and thus any attempt to derive any idea of the determinative trends of development from Bolshevism's understanding of itself, leads one into an impenetrable thicket.

For example, in recent years, when Mao Tse-tung inaugurated his policy of "Let all the flowers bloom" and suddenly announced what was actually an unheard-of liberality, he stated some definite theoretical reasons for doing so. He referred—in contrast, incidentally, to the doctrine of Moscow—to the "antagonism" between the proletariat and the administration which, according to Marxist teaching, must inevitably result from the fact that the former is stamped and molded by such tools as the plow and the machine, whereas the latter receives its stamp from such tools as the desk, filing cabinet, and typewriter. Since man is molded and determined by his tools, opposing instruments must necessarily produce antagonisms between the corresponding groups—in this case, between administration and proletariat. In view of this antagonism, argued Mao Tse-tung, safety valves must be opened up from time to time to release the dammed-up pressure and effect something like a self-purification and a balance of the latent antagonisms. At the time all this was based upon theory, and, as we learned, it led to a vehement controversy with the Kremlin, whose rulers interpreted the doctrine in a different way.

But now, after these conversations in Hong Kong, I ask myself whether an examination of such controversies gets us anywhere at all and whether the doctrine can be used at all as a survey map by which to orient ourselves. For the policy "Let all the flowers bloom" was dropped; the reason given was that now the opponent had been lured out of his hiding place by loosening the reins and opening the vents, and they knew where they stood with him. And the flowers which had ventured to bloom all too trustingly and brashly had their heads cut off. So none of it was theory, it was all pure tactics, and the whole thing reminds one, not of philosophy, but of tricky peasant cunning. Who would presume to be an interpreter of this confusion?

Mao certainly has achieved *one* success. From now on he can grant any measure of freedom; indeed, he can actually pose as an apostle of freedom. And many in the West will listen to his statements with fascination and find them grist for their mill that keeps grinding out the same old message: Communism isn't so bad after all. But no Chinese, nobody who has been "burnt," will ever believe him again; nobody will ever fall for this bloody, diabolical game of deception again. Uttermost tyranny will sail under the flag of a philosophy of freedom. The flower beds of these lovely words will be laid out in the foreground of a gigantic barbed-wire camp—for the complaisant self-deception of the passers-by and those who examine the terrain from afar with their telescopes. Many Western and Far-Eastern eyes will be delighted by the wealth of color and overlook the barbed wire behind it. But there are no flowers growing behind the wire any more.

As I left the cool air of the heights to go back to the ship, my mind still occupied with various thoughts stimulated by these weighty conversations, the usual heat settled down again. Even now, in the middle of the night, a shower bath produces only feeble relief, especially since the water is no longer cold but only moderately cool.

Though the ship was full of coolies who continued unloading throughout the night, and though glaring lamps illuminated all the decks, I tried to force myself to fall asleep on the radio deck. But this time the exciting impressions of the day and the reverberations of the discussions, along with the noise and the light, combined to banish sleep. So I sat up and utilized the over-stimulated wakefulness of this night to work on my notes. As day began to dawn and gradually asserted itself against the brightness of the lamps, I stopped to read the Sunday Gospel and think of the people who would gather to hear it many hours later. For at home it is hardly midnight Saturday.

August 17

Sunday. After it grew light—I will be honest and admit even in indicating the date that the new day has long since begun—I strolled about the deck between sessions of writing my diary and looked at the junks that cluster around the ship like algae. Only a small part of these barges is taken up by the living quarters of the families. I saw some of them still asleep. They lay—parents and children together—for the most part on the open deck, under clean, colorful covers, gently rocked by the waves. Most of them, however, were already up and at work. The mothers, carrying their little ones on their backs, were cooking and mending. The men were loading and unloading, and a number of them were stirring the steaming rice kettles which stood in coal fires. An old man right below me was obviously taking pleasure in feeding his little granddaughter. Thus they live their whole life in this constricted place on the planks. Here they are born, and here they die. Great-grandparents and great-grandchildren constitute a close community of life.

To the outsider it looks as if all the families on the junks are related to each other. Everybody seems to be leaping back and forth between the boats. They help each other, and there seems to be no shirking and no withholding of property from others. A hidden family grouping binds them all together, and I have the impression that in their way they are happy, that they feel something like the security and warmth provided by a nest, and that the fat-bellied boats with their fine portly shapes furnish them with a place that to them is home. Watching all the polishing and scrubbing going on, I felt that they have a love for it. Sometimes it looks as if they were caressing and fondling their utensils.

But in the midst of this idyl there are more somber and

104

dismal scenes which immediately put a damper on any incipient romanticism. Yesterday we saw a small child tied up—perhaps because he had been naughty. His hands and feet were bound together so that he could not straighten himself but lay in a crouched position. Even more dreadful than the torture, however, was the resigned, uncomplaining look on the child's face.

August 18

At sea again. Between Hong Kong and Yokohama. I have some further account to give of Hong Kong. Late yesterday morning Consul P. and his wife fetched me for a little drive in the surrounding country. To supplement my observations of the previous day we sought out a number of places where junks are massed by the hundreds. The junks themselves and the streets on shore are filled with swarming activity. But this is neither strolling nor aimless walking about; everybody has a purpose, and everybody is doing something; everybody is pulling or hammering, buying or selling, working or trading. The Chinese seem to be filled with an almost uncontrollable voracity for work—and again I was seized by the thought of what might not be done with such a people if they were directed according to a plan.

This time we also drove and walked through the slum quarter. How luxurious by comparison are the quarters of our refugees in the transit-camp in Wentorf! (I was there for several weeks in the spring with my students.) How comfortable in retrospect are the dormitories, which then seemed so degrading and depressing, compared with the miserable board shacks and the utter exposure of the homeless in the streets that I saw here.

And yet I wonder whether such comparisons are proper. If one were really to arrive at any trustworthy conclusions, would it not be necessary to measure not merely the external conditions but the degree of subjective suffering that obtains here? In any case, it was conceivable that the Chinese who is here delivered over to the utmost of miserable destitution may possibly suffer from it less—or in any case no more—than the refugee from the East Zone whose camp quarters appear almost palatial by comparison. The Chinese has not come from an incomparably better standard of living, his frugal nature also allows him to bear many things more easily, and finally the climate is in his favor. Our refugees at home suffer as "individualists"—for this is after all what they are compared with the Chinese, who are conditioned to living in families and groups—they suffer incomparably more from not having a corner of their own and from not being able to plan their future, whereas the Chinese who live timelessly do not so much "plan" a future as simply allow themselves to be pushed into it.

By this I do not mean to minimize the misery of the situation of the Chinese, but merely want to point out how difficult it is to compare forms of misery, since the diversity of subjective experience robs one of almost every criterion. These reflections are important to me because when we were working in the refugee camp in Wentorf my students and I were constantly being confronted with this comparison with Hong Kong, and it always left us somewhat defenseless.

For lunch we drove to the residence of the consul general. If it is possible to speak of any greater beauty than I have already seen, it is to be found here. This magnificent residence, which is the property of the Federal Republic of Germany, is situated on the top of a peak, high above Hong Kong. The German flag fluttering in the breeze on a high mast gave me the feeling of home. We Germans have little liking for flags any more; but here it is a welcome greeting that stirs one's heart.

We stopped our cars before we arrived—Mr. J. had joined us in the meantime—in order to remove the evidences of our forced march in the heat; in other words, we put on our neckties, rolled down our sleeves, and reluctantly crept back into our jackets. In the midst of this hypocritical business, however, we were caught by our host, who had seen our car approaching and had come to meet us. Then we were kindly ordered to reverse the whole procedure, and rolled up our sleeves again.

As I was admiring art treasures and the furnishings, overwhelmed by the view from this height to the sea and the blue distance, I was somewhat sobered to learn that this fairy-tale house has some less pleasant aspects just because of its altitude. Sometimes it is covered with clouds for weeks, so that rugs, tapestries, and pictures become covered with mold. So even this view and this refreshing coolness are not to be had without cost!

Our hosts, who surrounded us with kindness and cordial warmth, had prepared for us a grand Chinese meal, which we ate, quite properly, with chopsticks. The many courses with their delicate savoriness were so enchanting that I suffered less than at first I expected from having to manipulate these strange instruments. For when I succeeded after the second or third attempt in hooking a tidbit—the rice falling hopelessly between the sticks—the morsel which was caught and conveyed in perilous balance to the mouth was so exquisite that I was glad to pay the price of many a futile stroke. In any case, it would have offended my honor to have accepted the kindly offer to allow me to eat with a knife and fork. The servants watched me with an impassive courteousness. But surely they were amused by my clumsiness. And quite certainly that day they achieved a pinnacle of their culinary art.

I was particularly delighted with the rice wine, which was served in small porcelain cups and refilled from a small tankard. It tastes like hot sherry. Each time the tiny cup is emptied one holds it—very much as a German corps-student did in times past—somewhere in the vicinity of the third vest button from the top and looks at the host in salutation. The fact that the open end is held outward is undoubtedly meant not only to demonstrate that the cup is empty, indicating that it hit the spot, but probably also to convey a silent entreaty for a refill. A noble Rhine wine with dessert we felt to be not an incongruous thing but rather a refined supplement: the great phenomena of life salute each other and are intimately related. The host told of his experiences as a diplomat in Tiflis, and we reveled in our common love for anecdotes. This man's noblesse of mind and manner and the kindness and naturalness with which our hostess filled these shining hours gave us all an unforgettably warm feeling. And I am delighted to see how the Germans in Hong Kong are attached to this couple, who represent the fatherland. I took leave in the hope of seeing them again on my return voyage.

I then drove to the shore with Mr. J. for a swim. The fairly cool water was tremendously refreshing, and we never grew weary of romping in the surf. Mr. J. told me the story of his family as we were driving—it is a part of the history of German pioneers in East Asia. He and his brother and cousin are re-building their firm for the third time because he feels an obligation to the heritage. As we drove by he pointed out the place where his parents and grandparents had lived. By his dynamic intelligence and vitality it can be perceived that the ancient energies of his family are still at work in him. At the same time, he is far more than a mere tradesman. He is equally vitally rooted in the two cultures which determine his life and that of his family.

When he had finally brought me back to the ship and waved to me from the pier as we sailed out into the falling twilight, I stood on the bridge for a long time with the captain, the first officer, the radio operator, and my fellow passengers. In long nocturnal conversations the rich experiences of our days in Hong Kong were evoked once more, as for the first time the air grew somewhat cooler and we blissfully enjoyed the caress of the night breeze.

This city, which is so fascinating in its contrasts, fills my memory to the bursting point. And just *because* I cannot reduce all this to a formula—the culture and the misery, the continuing influence of the past and the uncertain future, the rickshas and the limousines, the villas and the barracks—it will not let me go and sucks me into a vortex of infinite images and thought. It is a slice of extremely concentrated life; it is like a poem. But what a poem! It is a ballad and a romance in one. Here, too, there is no name that would be comprehensive enough.

Midnight. Today we passed Formosa, which appeared in the mist to port with the sun going down in flames above it. The captain had the top deck painted with the German colors and illuminated in order that we might be clearly recognized by Chiang Kai-shek's air patrols. Some American planes also thundered close above us and photographed the ship. We were glad to leave this crisis area behind us.

All of us greatly miss our three ladies, who disembarked at Hong Kong. It is amazing how the tone and atmosphere has changed since we have become a ship's company made up only of men.

In the evening I sat in the forecastle with a young sailor. With his clear, open sailor's face, he has caught my attention from the beginning. The general exchange of certain sailors' adventures in Hong Kong, which always takes place among the crew after a stop in port, probably prompted him to discuss this number one topic with an older person.

He is an exceedingly thoughtful and serious young fellow who does his own thinking. He is quite sure—and says so in simpler and more circumstantial terms than those I set down here in abbreviated form — that sexual experience finds its optimal possibilities only when it includes both body *and* soul. But, he says, for those young fellows who finally get ashore after a long, monotonous turn at sea and search for the radiation of feminine warmth, there are some forms which are preliminary and emergency forms of sex. In his graphic, natural speech he said to me, "I imagine that a good marriage is like butter. Once you know that taste, margarine no longer tastes good at all. But for the time being we young fellows have to eat margarine. What else is there for us?"

Obviously this is a very real predicament from which these young people can hardly extricate themselves by their own strength and for which even proper education and the supporting factor of a good family provides only a limited safeguard. (But how many of them do not have even this!) On these long voyages the force of these insistent physical energies appears to be almost overwhelming. But might not some of the men be better helped if they were offered something else in the ports and were helped to sublimate these elemental needs a bit? I must discuss this sometime with the first officer, who seems to me to be the right man for it.

August 19

It is odd that yesterday's conversation was continued this evening. I do not know whether it was I who touched it off again or whether the others brought the conversation around to it. When the mind is much occupied with a question, it suddenly makes its appearance, as if at some secret call.

After supper, as I was chatting briefly through the galley window with our incredibly well-versed and ambitious young cook, a sailor named Günther almost ran me down. He was rushing to the washroom to clean up for his evening off. When it turned out that tomorrow he will be twenty years old—I had thought him considerably older because of his bushy beard—we made an appointment for this evening. I like him very much —not only because he is a seaman body and soul, but also because, quite touchingly, he provides for his parents and brothers and sisters, who are not well off financially. In addition he is saving money for his seaman's schooling.

A half-hour later we joined two of his comrades on a bench on the quarter-deck, and I treated all of them to a beer. Nobody has written to Günther for his birthday and he is quite sad about it. Tomorrow he celebrates the fifth of his birthdays at sea.

They asked me to tell them something of what I had seen in Singapore and Hong Kong. When I had done so, Günther said, "Yes, fellows like us see nothing but the same old harbor saloons and a few other things. It's like seeing Hamburg only from the elevated. And all the time those at home think how wonderful it is to have seen the world, and they admire and envy us."

I asked him why he and his comrades were so stupid. I said I could understand why they would seek some kind of outlet for their energies after such a long turn at sea. But the way they generally did this must, after all, be pretty monotonous, boring, and even disgusting for such decent fellows as they were. I could not really understand why they should say when they came into port, "Now we're going to have some 'life.' " Could this really be "life" at all, when they always knew beforehand just *what* it would be and it was always the same thing no matter whether they were in Europe or Asia or Australia?

All three admitted I was right; but I noted again how easy it is to be right in the negative. For immediately they went on to ask, "But what else can we do? After all, you are a professor and you know what is to be seen in a city. Fellows like us don't know this. Once we went to a fair in Tokyo. That was very interesting. But then we went back to the harbor again anyhow. There you know your way around." I asked them, "Is it really a matter of seeing 'sights' and unusual things? I find it very interesting just to walk through a Chinese market and watch the people."

Günther, who is especially open-minded and has his own ideas about life, agreed with me, but the others did not. "Shucks, that's almost the same as the fishmarket in Hamburg," said one of them, "except there are other faces and more racket. I don't see anything in that."

In that moment I realized that it requires a certain degree of culture to be able to see significance in normal things. More primitive natures need something out of the ordinary to engage their attention. These are fine, decent fellows and when I use the term "primitive" I do not mean to suggest any criticism

111

whatsoever. I know how far superior they are in other respects to people like us. But the lot of these young seamen troubles me, and I keep thinking of how I might arrange a sensible shore leave for them which would not be merely a brief explosion of their dammed-up instincts.

They spoke of several seamen's homes and missions with great appreciation, but others they criticized and even expressed contempt for. Obviously it is very difficult to find the right note and the right style in this matter. They have no use for being preached at or for moralizing and hypocrisy. "The Law kills—it may show the way, but it has no strength in its legs." This utterance of Luther based on the New Testament was again drastically confirmed by what these men said. It is quite apparent that the Gospel can reach them only through Christians who demonstrate a new kind of fellowship in their own lives, a definite style of life and sociability, and draw them into it.

Without exception they are all—including the others, officers and crew alike, with whom I have talked—enthusiastic about an Australian seamen's pastor who invites them to the mission every time they come to port. True, he speaks the Word to them and never fails to read from the Bible, but he does so in an atmosphere he has previously created as a man who has *himself* been under the Word. He brings the sailors in from the streets, mercifully and wisely warding off much that tends to make them give vent to elemental passions and that thus exposes them to the filth of the gutters. He invites them to decent and well-kept rooms where they can play and read. Young people of their own age are there who take an interest in them and invite them to their homes or show them the city. In the evenings young women from good homes are invited for dancing. At the close of the evening the pastor speaks a brief word of farewell in various languages, and when he says, "Now it's time to go home," he adds with a smile, "Ladies first!" The young men then stay for a half hour longer.

So here they endure what elsewhere would seem to them

112

abstinence, and accept it without grumbling and even happily. True, this may not be so of all of them, yet I am amazed at how many on this ship have told me about this same seamen's mission and how warmly they speak of it in retrospect. They will not disappoint this man in whom they sense an unselfish, understanding, and empathetic love. For a brief time he restores their standards and opens up for them areas of life for which their basically unspoiled souls are yearning.

What is true of these young seamen seems to me important elsewhere, except that for some strange reason Christendom seems hardly to be aware of it. Obviously it is not primarily the *spoken* Word, but rather the Word that has found form and structure in life, that touches them, at least at the first encounter. Why is it, I ask myself, that generally the adherents of the splinter sects prove to be the firmest confessors of their faith and that they are so successful in keeping their people "in line"? It is inconceivable that they should achieve this by means of their peculiar dogmatic notions, which are often extremely odd. It is difficult to believe that the eccentric element in their teaching is capable of creating such ties. Rather, the binding and impressive strength in the sects stems from the fact that as relatively small groups they are capable of creating an integrated style of life—a definite, very intense atmosphere of togetherness—and that their preaching, which has assumed the concrete shape of the fellowship itself, sustains these people. In this respect at least, the sects constitute a very significant symptom of the sickness of Christendom; they are a scurvy on the body of the church which indicates a definite lack of vitamins. The sects show us, often enough in perverted form, that the Word is always striving to incarnate itself, that it is constantly seeking to become a body, a fellowship, a way of life, and that it seeks to be found not only *behind* these structures but seeks to find its *own* structures behind these forms of life.

But beyond this I ask myself—and I must talk to the ship's officers about it—whether the agencies of the shipping companies could not also do something in this matter. Wouldn't it help if they arranged bus tours for the crew, in some of the ports? Even showing these young fellows points of interest would be a little better than blindly leaving them to their own helpless initiative? If only a few were helped, much would still have been gained. I am not suggesting some kind of a "strength through joy" project on the part of the shipping companies. But the helplessness of pure ignorance is hardly describable. One can ruin people by treating them as if they are mature when they are not. Many a democracy has been shipwrecked upon this superstition. In the small world of a ship all these problems show up as in a magnifying glass.

Above us, as we talked, were the unfamiliar constellations of the China Sea. Only the Milky Way, which extends like a white band across the firmament, is familiar to us. "Well, I guess I'd better hit the sack," said Günther. "I'm on watch at four in the morning. I'd like to sleep under the stars. When you look at the stars, you can really let your thoughts roam."

"I don't see anything in that," interrupted Uwe. "I'm too pooped to see anything." We did not argue with him. We had the feeling that perhaps he was trying to nip any sentimentality in the bud.

Günther stood up: "Well, good night." I called after him, "Now that you're going to sleep, even though you'll wake up on your birthday without having received any mail from home, think of all the good things you have experienced in these twenty years."

"And all the bad things too," he said, smiling; for perhaps he caught an unintended preachy undertone in what I said.

"But after all, you have been preserved and guided through it all. And you ought to be able to muster some gratitude for that."

"Yes, that's true," he nodded.

"And tonight think about God a few times. It won't hurt you."

There was a pause, and then he said, "No, it won't hurt."

114

It sounded like a shyly signalled Amen. The other two said nothing, and I did not know what they were thinking. But they said a very friendly "Good night."

August 20

Last night's talk keeps pursuing me today. Every day I see more clearly how good these people are at heart, how grateful they are for a word of encouragement, and how anxious they are that their lives should count for something. Time and again I hear them saying of old seamen they have known or of captains and officers, either "Some day I want to be like him" or "I don't want to be like him." Anybody meeting these young roughnecks on land would certainly not note anything of this kind. And among themselves they are also somewhat reserved. But when they meet someone who they feel means well toward them and who also has some time for them—as is now the case with me on this leisurely voyage—they come out with the thoughts they have been thinking while painting, standing watch, or steering the ship. Just because I see all this, it grieves me to think of the dull sameness of the amusements to which they are exposed in all the ports of the world, from Hamburg to Hong Kong, from New York to Colombo, from the west coast of South America to the east coast of Japan.

So after tea I went up to the bridge to talk this over with the first officer. He is young and energetic, very thoughtful, and altogether human. He is both loved and feared. I notice how the seamen involuntarily draw themselves up when they speak to him. There is nothing stiff or formal about this, but rather the breath of laughter and good comradeship. Everybody knows how devoted the "First" is to his wife and little boy—a fine, clean radiance comes from this relationship. The few words he finds now and again to say something human to his men have the ring of truth. The transparency of his nature speaks for itself and invites confidence in him.

How many evenings we have stood together on the bridge and talked of heavenly, earthly, and hellish things—and of *human* things too! I had told him beforehand that I wanted to talk with him about "my problem," and now he himself insisted upon it, for he was troubled by the same problem.

As with most professional people who know the particulars, he looks at the problem quite objectively and even with some resignation. (When a man like this, who is an idealist and not a skeptic, indicates that one must be resigned to a situation, we are likely to pay attention to what he says, for we are aware of his superior experience.)

For me everything he said was of vital interest even from a theoretical point of view, for he made it clear to me once more that almost none of the problems of ethics emerge in a vacuum, that there are no such things as abstract ethical decisions, but that all these questions are tied into the network of reality and set off a veritable chain-reaction of fresh questions.

For example, he declared quite simply that it is out of the question to think we can lift the "moral level" by exerting personal influence, by giving advice, or by coaxing. If the life of sailors in port is to be given another direction, some altogether external conditions must first be changed. There can be a meaningful, sensible stay in port only on *one* condition (and without this condition all persuasion and admonition is nothing but sterile hypocrisy): the sailors should not arrive on land at ten o'clock at night and dead tired. Increased speed and rapid transhipment have brought with them shortened stays in port, leaving the crew hardly any free hours. Even on a long voyage like ours some of the men never, or hardly ever, get off the ship at all. Therefore there cannot be any appreciable improvement in the leisure-time conditions unless, in addition to certain aids (of the kind which I myself had thought of), provision is made in some, though not all, ports for a reserve crew to take over the routine work in port and thus relieve the regular crew.

So this is the way things really are: the responsibilities we bear for the deeper needs of human beings are by no means merely a matter of attitude, of personal good will, or of being nice. Rather, in each specific situation what is required are some very real changes in the structure and organization of *things*. These cost money, however—quite simply, money. And again, what determines whether this expenditure will be made is not merely our own good will and willingness to be helpful; it is also a business calculation. Here the question of profit and loss comes into play.

This whole string of satellite problems, which group themselves about the central problem of how a vital question in young men's lives can be solved, certainly cannot be settled by our deliberations on the bridge. One can only implore all who are concerned to take the problem to heart. I also believe that there may be a willingness to rethink and re-examine the economic factor from the point of view of these human questions. The difficulty is that it is not easy for those who sit in the executives' offices to see these tasks which lie between the columns of figures.

August 21

Stifling heat. When I try to write the paper sticks fast to my arm. If it doesn't stick, it flies away with the wind. The whole ship is filled with anticipation of Japan. No other country exercises such fascination upon everybody—from the ordinary seamen all the way to the captain. We have some fourteen hours to go before we reach Yokohama.

This morning we passed a great formation of American warships, called forth no doubt by the Formosa crisis. A huge aircraft carrier was surrounded by submarines and destroyers. A swarm of planes buzzed about in the air, among them a number of helicopters. We watched the planes taking off and landing with great interest. They circled our ship in salute and we replied with a flag salute.

Later. After the terrific heat of the day the evening breeze is soothing and refreshing. The stars twinkle softly. "Quiet rest the stars above and beneath them the graves"—what may not be buried at the bottom of the sea! A little while ago I went up to the fore-deck where it was completely dark and quiet, and the ship seemed to glide like a silent canoe through the summer night. Have the children come back from their vacation? What are my students doing now? There is a little stab of pain that comes from the fact that twice a year the lecture hall community breaks up and is scattered to the four winds. When I get back home there will be all new faces again.

As I walked slowly back on the starboard side I saw my old storekeeper sitting on a chair in front of his cabin. There he sat again, quiet and alone, as he does almost every evening. Though I could see no sign of a glass, I knew that he was quietly tippling and gazing into the water of which he had never grown tired, even after forty-six years at sea.

He was very cheerful and peppy. He would not let me past, and insisted that I have a drink with him. "I like to talk with fine gentlemen who have gone to good schools," he said. "I too have read and seen much, and the gentlemen often ask me where I got it all." Who could resist a fellow like that?

"Whiskey is very good in the tropics," he said, and fetched two fresh glasses, which we set on the railing. "In the bad times I used to make it myself. Yes, I know a lot of things you wouldn't see to look at me. 'You're a great one,' the chief said when I gave him a drink of it, 'You're a great one.' But today there's no romance in seafaring any more. The young fellows aren't young any more. Ha, I was a great one," he chuckled.

When I asked him why the young fellows are no longer really young, he replied, "I'll let you in on that," and then very secretively, "Do you know what they do after they're through with work?" He waited to see whether I knew. And when I said I didn't, he leaned closer to my ear and whispered this grave secret: "They drink ice water!"

Gradually I realized that there was something else he wanted to say to me. He hemmed and hawed a while and had to take several drinks before he summoned up the necessary courage. "I'm not Catholic and not Evangelical. I'm a freethinker, and thirty years ago I withdrew from the church. But it wasn't because of the few coppers of church tax. I give that to the Red Cross and the Salvation Army. I've been wanting to tell you this, because, after all, you're . . . well, what is it you are? Let us be frank. You won't mind, will you?"

It was touching that even in his mild befuddlement he was still concerned that he might offend me or even hurt my feelings—touching that this rough old sea-dog, this former cattle drover, renowned as a hero of all the St. Pauli dives in Hamburg, should be so pathetically sensitive.

"But I too believe in a God, and in the evening when the sun goes down," he went on, "I always say to it, 'I hope you come up safely again.' That's my religion."

Again I was obliged to have another drink, though I didn't want it. I would have hurt his feelings if I had not acted as his guest. Naturally, we went on to talk about whether the sun is really a god and whether this would not be a very convenient God to have, a God who would allow one to do pretty much what one pleased. I indicated something of what the living God is in judgment and grace.

But in this enchanting tropical night he was already so tipsy that I was not at all sure he understood. What a confounded situation for a theologian! When the good fellow is slightly befuddled, his heart is open and receptive, but nothing you say gets to him. Sober, he doesn't discuss religion.

Then, in order to lodge at least one sharp barb that might hold, I said to him, "Since you read so many books, you ought to study the Bible too some time. Then you may learn something you never suspected before." He said rather bemusedly, "The Bible isn't a bad book, it's not a bad book at all." I said good night to him then—with the curious feeling of having achieved a minimum of missionary success with a maximum of alcohol consumption (at least for my capacity). But perhaps the good Lord in heaven smiled a bit over us. Perhaps he smiled a little at this good old sea-dog. I am prepared to believe that he did. After all, he is greater than our hearts, and what do we men really know about each other?

Japan

Tokyo. Shortly after six A.M. yesterday, as we were approaching Yokohama, the pilot came on board and gave me the message that I was expected to deliver a lecture at Union Theological Seminary in Tokyo at ten o'clock. The note contained no indication of the subject of the lecture or the language in which it was to be delivered. This was quite a blow for me. Some months previously, it is true, I had been asked to give several lectures here, but shortly before my departure I had begged to be excused, since I wanted to devote the few days in Japan exclusively to travel, sight-seeing, and discussions. The eight days in which I shall be able to travel about Japan until the ship picks me up again in Kobe are short enough as it is, even with careful planning of my time.

Now I had two hours to rummage through my papers in order to find something appropriate. I chose the theme of historicism and existentialism, which I had available in an English version. As I was "chewing over" my speech I did not notice that we had already docked, and was much surprised when representatives of the embassy, the Evangelical Academy, and the East Asia Mission, with my physicist friend, Tadasu Suzuki, entered my cabin and immediately took me off to Tokyo. It was especially heart-warming to see the young Japanese again. He had attended my lectures in Hamburg, and translated one of the two books of mine that have appeared in Japan.

About an hour's ride by automobile brought us to Tokyo. The closer we came, the more bewildering the traffic became. I have the impression that this motorized creeping and crawling along the streets exceeds even the conditions in America. Only shortly after the beginning of the trip did it occur to me that I was now for the first time in a truly foreign country, for while I often saw English signs on the streets in Penang, Singapore, and Hong Kong not a single Western letter is to be found here.

When I mentioned this to my friends, they all—except the Japanese, naturally—were full of stories of their adventures in trying to find a certain address or explaining to a taxi-driver where they wanted to go. I breathed a sigh of relief that I was in the care of dependable guides who knew the way.

We soon arrived at the Fujimo Church, where Union Seminary had scheduled the lecture, and I was amazed at the number of professors and students of various universities who were present despite the fact that this was a vacation period. On the way I had already learned to my relief that I could speak in German and that an excellent translator had been provided.

Actually, the fluency with which my colleague translated the by no means easy text into Japanese was astonishing. I noted during the discussion how accurate and expert his work must have been.

Because of the frightful heat, which was made even more oppressive by the formal clothes I was wearing, a fan was kept blowing upon me constantly, and out in the audience too fans were in constant motion.

In the course of the discussion I was amazed to discover how widely German theological works, including my own books, are known. A great many Japanese who cannot speak a word of German and can hardly understand spoken German are nevertheless capable of handling the language in print. It may be owing to the Japanese-Chinese ideograms, the "character" and content of which are not bound to the language itself, which therefore provide a greater possibility of understanding than does the spoken word, and that the Japanese comprehend the language from the written word in a way altogether different from ours.

As I was leaving to drive to the German embassy, I received a first impression of the Japanese capacity for expressing gratitude and clothing it in dramatic form. From the exit to the car, which stood some distance away, the students formed a line and bowed deeply as I passed by. As they did so they beamed with joy and cordiality.

The acting ambassador—the host himself being away on leave in Europe—received me like an old friend, and had also invited my Japanese friend. He showed me about the embassy building, explained the gallery of portraits of former ambassadors, and took me up to the steaming hot roof from which there is a good view of Tokyo.

We then drove with several gentlemen of the embassy to have lunch in a distinctively Japanese restaurant, the Tempura-an. They wished to give me a first glimpse of Japan that would show me this new world from the most characteristic angle.

At the entrance we were met by two pretty waitresses in geisha costume who were on their knees and who bowed repeatedly to the ground, offering us slippers to wear. One does not enter a Japanese house with his street shoes on. When they finally discovered that none of their dainty slippers would fit me, and I had to enter in my stocking feet, they were greatly amused and broke out into dainty, tinkling laughter.

Two dining spaces were reserved for us. Before we sat down, I looked around the spacious, graceful room. It was enclosed by sliding partitions made of paper and wooden latticework. The lovely simple lines of the room, which creates its own effect with almost no furniture, radiated a quiet, restful culture. When the sliding doors were opened to let in more air, we were suddenly sitting in the midst of one of the famous Japanese gardens that represent a landscape in miniature, with trees, tiny mountains, streams, and bridges. All around us was the rippling of water, conveying the suggestion of coolness.

Here for the first time I encountered what was to become more familiar day by day. One fancies that one can feel and hear the purling, sparkling stream of this new and strange culture flowing minute by minute into one's consciousness.

We sat on straw mats at a table elevated only a few inches

from the floor. The girls spoke to the gentlemen, who understood Japanese, in their soft, twittering tones and brought us damp towels in lovely bowls, with which we refreshed our faces. They renewed the towels repeatedly throughout the meal. They served the food in dainty vessels and cups, each time with formal ceremonial gestures and always on their knees and with innumerable bowings.

When I succeeded this time in eating somewhat more skillfully with the chopsticks, having had a little practice in Hong Kong, they clapped their hands enthusiastically and yet very daintily and broke into silvery laughter again. As the cook prepared the food before our eyes, cooking and mixing, sprinkling and pouring, ever new morsels and delicacies were served to us, and I was really amazed that the many kinds of raw fish, seaweed, and strong seasonings tasted so good to me.

Among other things there was *maki-zushi,* a rice cake with ginger mixed with vegetables and chopped eel, the whole wrapped in thin pieces of seaweed; Japanese radishes pickled with raisins and served in lacquered dishes, called *daiku;* and minced pork with carrots, bamboo sprouts, and taro roots in soy sauce. Among the specialities of these restaurants are crayfish which have been dipped in batter and baked in oil. They are called *tempura.* The serenity that delights the eye as one looks around the beautiful quiet room or out upon the toy world of the tiny garden, the ceremonial, the service and the cooking, and not least the relaxed friendliness of the people in this room, all certainly helped to transmogrify the alien taste of the food.

After the meal several Japanese came to get me in order to show me the sights of Tokyo. Though they had arrived at the place long before without our knowing that they had come, they did not announce themselves, but waited quietly and with touching consideration in another room until we rose of our own accord. On this very first day I was repeatedly impressed by the delicate tactfulness of the Japanese people.

Though the embassy had already devised a plan for showing

123

me around Tokyo, these Japanese friends insisted that they themselves must show me their city. Besides my friend Suzuki, there were Dr. Odagiri, a specialist in internal medicine; Dr. Watanabe, a political economist; and Mr. Sakaeda, a professor of theology. I was happy that they were familiar with German and had read most of my works—right from the beginning there were many topics of conversation that bound us together.

We visited chiefly a number of Shinto shrines in which famous Japanese are venerated as gods. I was especially impressed by the house of General Nogy (Nogy-jinjya), which had been made into a sanctuary. General Nogy committed hara-kiri upon the death of the great restoration emperor Meiji in 1867. A balcony-like footbridge, from which one can look through closed windows into the interior, runs around the entire house. We saw the bedrooms and living rooms, antique Japanese in style, and also the room in which the general and his wife committed the ritual suicide. The temple of the Emperor Meiji himself is situated in the middle of extensive, parklike, awe-inspiring grounds, where a veritable mass migration of people moves along the broad, well-tended walks. The Sengaku-ji shrine, which is a memorial to the forty-seven samurai who committed hara-kiri in 1867, is connected with a museum in which these knights are represented in fantastic and frightening wooden sculptures clothed in armor and costly robes, a superior form of panopticon which has been hallowed by tradition.

To reach these Shinto shrines, you pass through three lofty, widely separated gates, which are either constructed of tremendous wooden timbers or cast in bronze (as in the Emperor Meiji shrine), and then walk along broad avenues which in some unexplainable way immediately communicate the sense of the numinous. One has the feeling of being subjected to the radiance of the "holy."

Before you enter one of the shrines you come to a roofed water basin, where the people pour water over their hands with ladles to cleanse themselves ritually. I had the impression,

however, that the people performed the ritual not so much for
ceremonial reasons as because they wanted to cool off a bit
in the heat. Almost all those who bow before the shrine of
Emperor Meiji, clapping their hands at the beginning and
closing of their devotions, are older people. The great majority
pass by like museum visitors and exhibit only a historical
interest. The temples appear to have become less religious
shrines than nationalistic monuments to Japanese history, and
the tremendous crowds of visitors are perhaps to be explained
by the fact that here the Japanese is making a kind of cult of
his historical self-consciousness. The younger generation quite
obviously does not know what to make of a man who is venerated as a god, and seems to be baffled by the religious dimension of these cultic shrines.

I did notice a few youngsters who were imitating the ceremonial routines of the few older folks. But they were probably
doing this only as a joke, and seemed to get a great deal of
amusement from it. As they went through the motions they
kept looking at me with interest, cutting all kinds of capers and
obviously trying to find out whether the whole thing was giving
me anywhere near as much fun as it was them.

Secularization seems to have seized the whole world and
all religions. What has remained may be the category of the
religious itself, which keeps alive a certain yearning for the
psychic side-effects of religion and continues to attract the
people to the monumental simplicity of the Shinto grounds
with its effect of calm, composed contemplation. Even a person who no longer has any immediate contact with the religious
reality itself and who feels that he has been emancipated from
its "engagement" can hardly escape the awesome impact and
the inviting gesture of these sublime Shinto gates. Here the
indestructibility of the *numen tremendum et fascinosum** makes
itself felt.

* The quality of the "holy" as being terrifying and forbidding and
at the same time fascinating. The phrase was originated by Rudolf
Otto, the religious philosopher. (Trans.)

I was constantly being wrenched away from these somewhat depressing thoughts and conversations by the fact that passers-by were eyeing me as some Goliath from another planet and were terribly amused every time I had to stoop or bumped my head. My companions were visibly amused by this astonishment of the people, and they endured our mutual running of the gantlet (mutual, because they looked like little goblins attached to the giant to furnish a contrast) with good humor. "If you were a Japanese, you'd have to become a wrestler," they said.

We refreshed ourselves from the attrition of the terrible heat and the profusion of impressions in a towering, five-story restaurant called "The White Coach," where again I enjoyed the cooling restorative of the air conditioning. The tremendous building has no windows. The individual storeys are grouped about a central shaft, the top of which constitutes a vaulted ceiling of colorful, lighted mosaic, the bottom ending in a lighted pit in which many-colored birds flutter about and equally colorful fish play behind glass walls. When the Chinese synthesizes his culture with Americanism he seems to become uncertain, whereas the Japanese is more successful and knows how to mix in a dash of his own that fits into the alien conception without clashing with it. Perhaps this is because the Chinese are more original and therefore can assimilate only at the cost of losing their identity. (Will they also give up their own identity when they encounter the alien growth of communism, and yield to it?) By contrast, the Japanese are like sensitive photographic plates—they pick up impressions and ideas from the outside more receptively without distorting either themselves or the ideas in the process. Naturally, this is rather too generalized a statement, for certainly among the Japanese there are original elements and also distorted adaptations.

As we were talking about all of this—I could scarcely believe my ears!—the orchestra suddenly began to play Mozart's *Kleine Nachtmusik*. My friends smiled significantly. Their

126

smiles were only one of several circumstantial proofs that they had requested it for my benefit; but they did not say so. The delicacy of their hospitality delighted me even more than the familiar strains. They beamed when they saw that I was pleased. By the very refinement of their courtesy they made it impossible for me to thank them.

For supper they took me again to a distinctively Japanese restaurant. I marveled at how the Japanese art of entertainment succeeded in creating the impression that we were the sole guests and that the entire establishment existed solely for us. This guest house, the "Genghis Khan," is really not a house at all, but a small colony of tiny interconnected temples with pointed roofs, in each of which there is a large round table slightly raised above the floor. Here you are alone with your friends, and geisha waitresses are present who wait only upon your assembled party. At the open door stands the cook with his charcoal burner, and you see him working throughout the evening. It was a special relief to me this evening to find that I did not have to squat on a mat again (my limbs were still somewhat sore from having done so at noon). I was seated at a place which had obviously been constructed for Europeans. In front of my place and cleverly concealed beneath the table was a hole dug in the ground into which the legs could be extended. It would have been necessary to look very closely to discover that my seated position was any different from those of the Japanese, so cleverly was this convenience constructed.

My companions were Christians connected with the Ecclesia Movement. This movement has no strong confessional position. Under the influence of the powerful evangelist Kanzo Utshimura it has produced a number of groups which consist for the most part of academic people and practice a very simple, biblical, and almost primitive-Christian form of worship. Here there flourishes a free lay theology which is surprisingly vigorous by Western standards. I gained a very vivid impression of it this evening, for suddenly something like a small theological dispute emerged.

What happened was that Dr. Odagiri raised a question which struck me at first as being remarkably reminiscent of the history of dogma, and at first I hardly knew what to do with it. His question was whether it is not wrong to call Christ "God," whether he ought not rather to be called God's "Son." Inevitably I thought of certain controversial questions which were fought out between the Antiochians and the Alexandrines in the second century, and for a moment I surmised that young Japanese Christianity was in process of recapitulating the history of Christian doctrine in accelerated tempo. Although I was a bit ashamed to admit it, I was almost regretful that the conversation should take this turn, for it diverted me from the enchantingly unreal goings on around us which were claiming my whole attention. Was I going to be obliged, here of all places—in this dreamlike moment, in the midst of these fairytale ceremonies accompanying our meal—to conduct a colloquium which I might just as well conduct in Hamburg and which was a part of my routine work there? So at first it was only as an act of resigned courtesy that I asked Dr. Odagiri to explain his question more definitely.

As he did so, the faces of the others showed tremendous interest. Occasionally they supplemented what he said and defined it more precisely. I immediately gained the impression (which later turned out to be correct) that this was a very hot question and one much disputed in present-day Japanese Christendom. The lay theologians here assembled assured me that they were in violent controversy with the professors who have been schooled in Western theology.

And the fact is that the problem is far more exciting than I had supposed. For the question is: what happens to the Christian message when the Japanese, with his categories molded by Shintoism, seeks to understand it? If Christ is called "God," said my friends, then immediately the Shintoistic association presents itself and suggests that here a great, perhaps even unique, man is being deified and elevated to the dignity of the shrine. The Gospel, however, proclaims an event that proceeded in the opposite direction; it does not speak of the elevation of a man but rather of the condescension of God, and everything depends upon seeing to it that this point of the Gospel is not distorted by the Japanese categories.

Put in this way, the question began to interest me deeply. It only seems to be a doublet of the problem presented in the first Christian centuries. Here it comes out of an engagement with the *present*. Here it touches upon fundamental problems of missions as a whole, upon the dialectic between what is declared and the varying categories in the thinking of those who receive what is declared. Here it touches upon the fact that the Gospel enters a changing history and that it must maintain its identity even though its light may be refracted through different prisms.

The passionate discussion and the freshness of the "existential substance" of what my friends said made it immediately apparent how deeply concerned they are with this problem and that for them it is anything but a colorless theory or intellectual sparring.

My Japanese friends put me up in a Western style luxury hotel, which was by no means agreeable to me. I should have preferred to live in genuine Japanese style for once. They made it clear, however, that this week would be very strenuous for me and that therefore I would need the refreshment of a well-cooled hotel. And the fact is that the air conditioning and the luxury of a bath after this hot day acted as a fountain of youth. It was very late, or rather, very early, before I went to bed. The hot and cold bath so stimulated me that I enjoyed the coolness of the room for a long time as I wrote down the impressions of the day. When I looked out of my cool room into the street in the first light of dawn, I was surprised to see men wearing short-sleeved white shirts outside.

August 25

Kyoto. Early yesterday I had hardly recovered from the shock of the improbable hotel bill when Suzuki and his young wife came to fetch me. In our tour around Tokyo I had gathered from an incidental remark that he had only recently been married, and I said to him quite spontaneously, "I must get to know your young wife." At the moment I did not realize that such a wish is never expressed in Japan and that it must have embarrassed Suzuki. And yet back on shipboard, Mrs. V., in her effort to give me some instruction in Japanese manners and thus serve in the role of an East Asian Emily Post, had emphatically impressed it upon me that one does not inquire about the "lady of the house" when visiting in Japanese homes and that one should not be surprised if she does not put in an appearance at all—but that if in an exceptional case she does appear, she is not introduced and the guest is not introduced to *her*. She was, said my mentor, a *quantité négligeable*. One does not burden his guest with his own wife. Japan's society is emphatically masculine.

And now I had made this *faux pas* and obliged my friend Suzuki to do something so un-Japanese as to find a way to introduce his young wife to me! When I realized the impossibility of the situation it was already too late, and I had to let things run their course.

He came with me into my room where I was finishing my packing, and there occurred an amiably awkward scene for which obviously there were no directions in the protocol. I felt sorry for the young wife because I had subjected her to this embarrassment, which she, of course, was enduring with a touching charm. She is a teacher of the history of Japanese literature, but despite her academic degree she exhibits the same humble desire to serve men as all the rest of her Japanese sisters.

I was still too new to this country not to be a bit frightened by her exceedingly respectful courtesy. With a charming gesture she presented me with a gift of hospitality, an illustrated work on the Japanese gods which she had wrapped in lovely Japanese paper. She was obviously afflicted (but what was I to do?) by my allowing her to precede me, according to European custom, as we entered the elevator and passed through the other doors, and furthermore each time it sent my friend into an egg dance, because he was obliged willy-nilly to do the same and could not very well depart from the European custom. At that moment I had the feeling, which can be supported only with humor, that I was mixing up the two cultures with a rude and barbarous spoon. I felt that I was imposing myself upon these people by adhering to the chivalrous customs of the West, which are based upon deference to the gentle sex, and trampling about in the well-kept flower garden of Japanese manners.

But the situation grew really bad when the little lady attempted to carry my big suitcase and her husband reached for the other. What would it look like for me, a big strapping fellow, to walk empty-handed between these slender little people struggling along with my luggage? So I refused to permit it. Consequently, on the short walk straight across the street to the main railroad station, which was right next to the hotel, there occurred a little battle of politeness. They refused to be put off and insisted on at least helping me carry the suitcase. (And not a porter in sight who might have put a sudden end to all this distress!) Since, because of my stature, I carried the suitcase rather high, they were unable to help me to carry it with down-stretched arms but were obliged to keep holding it up with their elbows bent at an angle. This was naturally very strenuous, especially for the little lady. This I could not bear; I had to lift the bag *still* higher and thus carry it myself with bent arms, until finally it was so high that they were more hanging from my bag than lifting it.

Though heaven has bestowed upon me great physical strength, this turned out to be a berserk and sudorific transport, what with the heat that had already set in that morning. And then if it had only been a matter of getting across the street! But I have never yet seen such a huge station, with endless passages and corridors. And what is more, if it had only been the distance—but there were all the people flooding toward us from the suburban trains. Never have I seen so many people in a railroad station. In the great cities I have known elsewhere the great crowds of people seem to be divided into waves, and there is a certain ebb and flow after the arrival of a train. Here, there is a broad unceasing stream that fills the concourses and tunnels from left to right. People, people, and ever more people.

At first I did not realize what was strange about this scene. But a few moments later it became clear to me. It was the complete silence in which these tens of thousands of people moved along. Not one of them appeared to be speaking, and I even asked Suzuki whether speech was prohibited here—to which he responded with a laugh. Only the quiet shuffling of feet could be heard.

I was able to observe all this during the few moments we were purchasing our tickets. Immediately afterwards, the three of us resumed our painful *via crucis,* our transport of the luggage made all too difficult by politeness. Now the three of us abreast with the luggage jutting out on both sides—a really formidable broadside!—had to face the stream. Any bridge pier has it easier, because it is pointed or round and parts the waves. But we had to push against them with a broad front. We set ourselves against the tide, and though the Japanese who were approaching us were polite and did what they could to avoid us, in a crowd like that there are limits set upon even the best will in the world. And every once in a while the word "Gangway!" escaped me, though presumably nobody there understood what it meant.

But this trial too came to an end, and finally we arrived exhausted at our train, which was to take us to the ancient Japanese capital, the center of culture and temples, Kyoto. It had seats, reclining chairs, and sofas with dazzling white slipcovers, and was equipped with air-conditioning. A whole ensemble of stewardesses, porters, and other attendants was at our disposal.

Before we said goodby to Mrs. Suzuki we sat together for a

while until train time watching some Japanese farewell scenes. I would not have thought it possible that even aged people should bow so deeply and repeatedly. It is as if—by strange contrast with our world—everybody wanted to have, not the last word, but the last bow.

I estimated that this ceremonial included no fewer than eight bows—that is, sixteen on the part of both partners. This respect for the other person is certainly not merely a hypocritical and empty form. It corresponds to the Japanese teaching that every person is "a center." So the whole of life is filled with ceremonial; the whole of life is, as it were, elevated above the careless laxity of merely existing and letting oneself go, and is consciously given structure and form. It is filled with symbols as is Japanese writing.

Even taking up tickets on the train was a cabinet piece of chased and ornamented courtesy. The conductor appeared with the chief stewardess, walked a third of the way down the car, lifted his cap, bowed deeply, and announced the business that he was about to perform. Thereupon the stewardess—again with bows and smiles—took the tickets from each of the passengers, arranged them to be punched, then handed them to the conductor and back again to the passenger.

The train raced at tremendous speed through a rapidly changing, varied landscape of mountains and streams, lakes and broad rice fields, and through great long tunnels toward Kyoto. Fujiyama, which I had so looked forward to, was unfortunately not to be seen. Its crest was covered by clouds, but the massif visible to us below was enough to suggest its immensity.

In addition to the landscape, the life within the train offered plenty of variety. Frequently announcements were made over the loudspeaker. This was done in the same way I had observed the day before in other situations. First there was the sound of a few measures of a folk song on the flute, or sometimes bells, and then came the human voice. This is quite different from our custom; often we are startled out of a drowsy nap by a deafening crackling noise and then yelled at by an over-

133

loud human voice. I felt this gentle Japanese insinuation of siren sounds into the ear humanized technology.

As we walked to the dining car, we saw two younger men in dark blue suits seated in different cars. Their dress itself was noticeable, since everybody else sat in a white shirt without a jacket. One of them held a large photograph surrounded with white crepe, apparently a picture of his father. It was held out so that everyone who passed by could see it. The other sat in a reverent, extremely disciplined attitude, holding a casket-like urn draped with white cloths, decorated with Japanese characters, and covered with flowers.

In the dining car itself I was made aware of the populousness of Japan by the large staff of waiters which operated like a precision instrument. As we were eating I told Mr. Suzuki how much I appreciated his accompanying me. I was moving in a world of completely alien signs and sounds. I couldn't even read the timetables in the railroad stations. How could I ever have made it clear to a taxi-driver who knew nothing but Japanese that I wished to go to a train station?

One of the German gentlemen whom I met in Yokohama told me an amusing story about this. A taxi-driver utterly failed to understand that his fare wished to go to the train. The poor passenger in his despair began to make paddling motions with his arms and tried to imitate the rhythm and sound of a steam locomotive by saying "choo-choo." But even this seemed not to help, since the railroads in Japan are mostly electrified, and there is no more "choo-choo." Finally a gleam of understanding came into the taxi-driver's eyes, and he deposited his passenger at the gasworks, where a steam engine was in fact chugging away, blowing its clouds of steam into the air.

In Kyoto I am met by Professor Ito, a Japanese sociologist, and my old school friend J., who has been a missionary and teacher in Japan for more than twenty years. Even during our student days in Marburg I was fond of him because of a quality he had which may be best described as "curiosity about life." Though he had very definite talent as a theologian from the beginning, his outlook was never obstructed by the blinders of the doctrinaire, and he was able to pour himself into a philosophical system or a human attitude which was alien to him regardless of what it cost. He was not always ready with his "ifs and ands," nor was his primary interest to safeguard his own position. He was capable of looking at things steadily and calmly, observing and trying to understand them. It is certainly impossible to overestimate what it means to me that he is willing to take several days off for me. For through him and his intimate knowledge of Japanese life I shall be able to learn much that a Japanese cannot tell me, either because he may hesitate to do so or because he is too close to his own way of life to be able to see it as objectively as someone who has come from the outside and then penetrated deeply into it.

Mr. Ito speaks perfect German and is cheerful, humorous, and relaxed; he will be helpful to me as an interpreter in discussions. I sense at once that he will be a good, reliable companion.

I am living in the Myoko Hotel, with its ancient dignity and modern comfort. To my dismay I have again failed to get one of the Japanese rooms, and have to go on living in European style. However, the accommodations in the room are so tastefully comfortable and the service so exquisite and considerate that I will soon get over this minor disappointment.

More painful is the fact that I must now take leave of my friend Suzuki, who has rendered such faithful service as an adjutant. To enjoy the tactful discretion, the empathy, and the sensitive concern of a Japanese companion has been a new and happy experience for me. I am ashamed that I devoted so little time to him while he was in Hamburg. And yet, as he said repeatedly, he wished all this kindness and helpfulness to be understood as thanks for the bit of neighborly love I allegedly showed him when he was abroad. In any case, I now know what it can mean to have a Japanese friend.

From the windows and balconies of the hotel there is a captivatingly beautiful view of the mountain landscape, studded and crowned with many temples, in which this ancient capital and cultural center of Japan is set. Here everything seems to be permeated with an ancient sacral life.

The subject of our first conversation, when we met for tea, struck me as utterly un-Japanese. My two companions spoke of a Hilty Society here in Kyoto, as well as in other cities in Japan, which publishes the works of this great Swiss sage. I could not altogether suppress a somewhat conceited feeling of satisfaction at being able to join in the conversation and knowing all of Hilty's books. This man of the late nineteenth century is almost forgotten among us in Europe, and in the student generations of my academic life I have never met a student who knew him. Nor would I know him myself had my father not presented me with the books and contrived to get me to read them thoroughly.

Hilty wrote what might be called Christian wisdom literature. In a simple, paternal, and sometimes homespun way—with a faint aura of the Swiss upper class—he taught about the meaning of eating, drinking, reading, writing, listening to music, sleeping, etc., and on this basis went on to give instruction concerning a meaningful form of life. It is very remarkable that this philosophy of living should have been so largely forgotten among us, despite the widespread yearning for meaning in life and a balanced form of living. (How else are we to explain the demand for books by Krishnamurti or the simple techniques for living promoted by Moral Rearmament?)

However, the question that suggests itself to me now is why should this old Hilty, so long forgotten in Europe, have such a strange "comeback" in, of all places, Japan. To answer is to indicate the inner dimension of Japanese culture, which grows out of two root stems: Buddhism, with its art of meditation, which is turned inward and is indifferent to the external world; and the teachings of Confucius, which are definitely turned toward the ordering and shaping of the external world, toward

136

finding one's way about in the world, and thus toward the art of living. Confucianism is the counterweight, so to speak, for the ethical deficiency of Buddhism. The polarity of these two forms of wisdom appears to produce a high degree of tension in the Japanese character. Despite his mysticism, his love of symbolism, and his propensity for the hidden background of things, the Japanese—the "Prussian of the East"—is a man of action rooted in realism, a conquerer, organizer, and tradesman. The introvert in his nature is balanced by the urge to be an extravert, and contemplation, which by itself would lead to historical sterility, is balanced by the *vita activa,* which, without meditative anchorage, would result in futile activism.

The fact that, as far as I can see, the Japanese is preserved from both of these one-sided emphases, that much of what has become ruptured and fragmented for us still appears to remain whole and balanced in him (although old experts like my friend J. see many evidences of decline here too)—this he doubtless owes to these two intercommunicating vessels (Buddhism and Confucianism) in which his "life-substance" is contained. It is therefore the Confucian side of the Japanese nature that is making Hilty a recognized teacher of wisdom and preserving his influence. On the whole, a great deal of what has become strange to us in the West and has long since receded into the background appears to have been preserved and rediscovered here.

My two companions wished to make use of the evening to give me a general view of Kyoto by means of a sight-seeing tour. There is an organization that provides good services, but which did not have a car available for this evening. When the porter brought us this disappointing news, Professor Ito wordlessly disappeared into a telephone booth and a few minutes later returned with the information that he had secured a special car. When we asked him in astonishment how he had worked it, he replied, "I acted as a go-between for the head of the company when he was married. He was obligated to me." In feudal, patriarchal states like Japan connections appear to be everything.

Before we set out on the tour we strolled about the city for a while. Today was a great festival for children which concluded the annual festival for departed souls. Children were singing and dancing at many of the street corners and plazas and also in the houses, whose paper walls had been pushed aside, giving a view into the interiors. Their gay costumes and colored lampions form fairy-like pictures so charming that one feels oneself falling into a deep enchantment. Again and again we came upon children, sitting in smaller and larger groups on the street, listening with fascination to a man who was showing transparencies by holding them in front of a box in which a flashlight or carbide lamp was burning. He also regaled his tiny listeners with fairy stories. To me this simple chamber theater puts to shame the "perfection" of any children's hour on television.

First we drove to the Gion House, which has been assigned to the training of geisha dancers. We sat on mats inside wooden booths, each of which held about four persons. My friend J. and I were the only Europeans present. There were two Americans flashing and snapping pictures like mad. Otherwise we were completely surrounded by Japanese folk. The dancers wore magnificent ancient Japanese costumes and the elaborate, high-piled hairdos of the kind that we know from Japanese lithographs and woodcuts. They executed dances full of symbols, the presence of which one could sense without understanding the details. Persons like myself could therefore enjoy the incidental effect but not its real meaning. Only now and then is there a human gesture which is familiar despite being stylized, such as a scene depicting expectation, or a person adorning herself or showing fear. The faces are rigid and mask-like, without any personal expression or coquettishness, the movements ordered and imitative of great ancient patterns fixed by tradition.

This dance is the opposite of the kind of self-expression

familiar to our Western tradition—whether it be the tradition of the drama and dance that expresses conflicts and emotions, or the conventions of our films that turn out stereotyped neo-romantic heroes and heroines and budding stars who flaunt their masculinity or femininity. Here, however, the personality appears to be completely extinguished. It is completely absorbed by the statuesque character of the role, by the impersonal character of a rigidly prescribed convention.

These must be very poor souls who vegetate in this borderland of personhood, this no man's land between man and stereotype. And it was precisely my Japanese companion who as a sociologist opened up some whole new aspects of this phenomenon for me by pointing out that these dancers come from the poorest stratum of society.

From there we drove to the Buddhist Shorenin Temple, where a priest, after performing a brief devotion, told us the history of the temple. He had such an incredibly cunning, "this-worldly," sensual face that I might well have taken him for a cheap-Jack at some carnival who swindles people outrageously but does it with such amusing tricks that nobody is angry with him. He is probably more of a guide here, and the little cultic intermezzo is part of his job as spiritual emcee. After all, he has to illustrate the situation realistically! The effect he produces is painfully unconvincing. As a matter of fact, my friends confirmed my impression, saying that the Buddhist priesthood is partially dependent upon such sources of income. Hence the overtones of commercialism.

If I had to judge Buddhism and Shintoism by the priests and the temples I have seen so far, I could not document much more than signs of decline. But I am still hoping to discover some other aspects of the question right here in Kyoto. Thus, for example, my friends informed me that this temple, despite its sacral character, was not originally a sanctuary, but was built in temple style as a residence for wealthy priests and members of the imperial house. Hence its aristocratic design and its spaciousness.

Around the sanctuary itself are many sumptuous apartments furnished with magnificent sliding doors, ornamental framework, and richly carved beams. They in turn look out upon a garden which, with its glamorous floodlighting, really has the effect of a stage setting that depicts the world in miniature. Valleys, ravines, mountains, streams — everything is there, compressed and condensed into the smallest space, as if some "space-saver" had turned the cosmos into a chamber theater. Buddhism loves nearness, it seems to want to gather the world into itself. It therefore represents the world as a microcosm and makes it subservient to itself. What a contrast to the spaciousness of the gardens of Versailles! Here the horticultural structure seems rather to be intended to divide a tremendous expanse of space and, as it were, humanize it—not in order to enclose man in his world but rather to lure him out of himself and bring him into carefree contact with a world which is really a humanized landscape, a terrain which is congenial to him and not only flesh of his flesh, but spirit of his spirit. Two young women in colorful kimonos played upon large zither-like instruments as we were served exceedingly strong, thick tea in earthen cups by a young priest.

The tour then went on through narrow streets where, before public prostitution was prohibited, there used to be nothing but brothels, to an elegantly furnished house where a geisha put on the tea ceremony for us. As we entered and left, the geisha, this performer of a bit of history—though, of course, it is not to be regarded as merely *past* history!—made certain movements, enacting the gait of a prostitute in a manner that was so rigidly stylized as to appear almost grotesque and that barely showed traces of its origin in an over-conventionalization of a provocative feminine walk. Here again, what the sex bombs of our movies present naturalistically and directly is present only in the form of subtle and scarcely legible ciphers. Above her gorgeous costume, which must have weighed sixty pounds, there floated the same pathetic, masklike face we had seen before, a face without the trace of a smile or movement.

Even this area of life is incorporated into Zen Buddhism. Even the erotic is subjected to a ceremonial which makes its performance appear to be almost an impersonal ritual act and which, by means of the tea ceremony, creates delaying factors that dam up the elemental impulses until they finally discharge.

Our way home took us through the streets of this ancient city, still bustling with nocturnal traffic. We had a snack at a lunch counter adjoining a small temple. But this time, when there was no subtilizing culture to cast a softening veil over the preparation of the food, it did not taste good to me at all. To see the raw fish being prepared and spread with strong condiments like ginger is a rather gruesome sight. I had the feeling I was gargling prussic acid and soon gave up. To be sure, it took some pains to explain to my kind Japanese friends that this strange feeling toward the food implied no criticism.

August 26

Kyoto. We had planned for today a visit to the ancient temple city of Nara. When I woke up a heavy rain was pelting the window. It is a first harbinger of the typhoon forecast for tomorrow evening.

After an hour's train ride—the train flying at a murderous speed and we sitting in a veritable hurricane coming through the permanently open windows—we arrived in Nara, and fortunately the rain stopped for several hours. Nara was the Japanese capital in the time of Charlemagne. Whereas Tokyo is determined by Shintoism, here the prevailing influence is that of the Zen sect of Buddhism.

The architecture of the temple seems frugal, parsimonious, and archaic. As we looked at the ancient figures, particularly in the excellent, well-arranged museum, it struck me that even in the ninth and tenth centuries of our era the human figures—despite their stylization and the standardization of gestures, attitudes, and drapery—very often exhibited individualized features and personal coloration.

The tremendous pagoda, with its many classically curved

roofs piled one on top of another, combines the feeling of the gigantic with the sense of floating weightlessness that we know so well from the delicate Japanese wash drawings. And certainly even the miniature reproductions of it in porcelain do not represent a distortion.

The houses, streets, and shops of the city, with their medieval charm, could have been a Japanese edition of Rothenburg on the Tauber. Again and again our route led us past huge square buildings reinforced with beams which had no visible windows or entrances. Centuries-old treasure houses, they were built to be airtight, which probably explains the excellent preservation of the priceless wooden sculptures they contained.

Most important of all, we visited the gigantic temple of Buddha in which the prodigious, commandingly situated cultic image exerts, by its tremendous proportions alone, an overwhelming, almost numinous power. What we really have here is quantity transmitted into quality. The enormous size of the head not only creates the impression of nearness and omnipresence but also seems to obliterate the ego as if it were of no importance whatsoever.

Even that temple served more as a museum than a sanctuary. Though we sat for a long time at a spot with a good view, we saw only a very few who accorded cultic reverence to the Buddha. For the constantly moving troops of visitors who scour every corner it seemed to hold only an antiquarian interest. One gets the impression that Buddhism is no longer an elemental reality among the people. Here too the sanctuaries have become institutions of cultural education.

One party of travelers was actually committing a gross misdemeanor. A number of young fellows and middle-aged men were sticking shirts, hats, and socks on a sculptured tree with a bamboo staff; they thought it great fun to see how the botanical image was changed by these textile blooms and clusters. Nowhere had I heard among the Japanese, who normally conduct themselves in public with great restraint, such loud and repeated peals of laughter as here, of all places, in a temple.

Other groups too came up and joined in the fun. The amusement was therefore quite general and unmistakable.

I was happy to have my friend J. with me to provide a
commentary on the great profusion of new impressions, and
to correct my impressions. Various couples we observed,
among whom I was struck by the devoted attitude of the wife
—not toward Buddha, but toward her husband-god!—suggested the topic of Japanese marriage. J. confirmed what I had
already noticed and what had also cropped up in other conversations, namely, that Japan is a masculine society. It is the
land of laughter—for the men, although the women laugh too;
but for a woman it may often be mere pantomine covering
darker depths, something put on and part of her duty. Perhaps it may be only the "mask" of a smile. It is mainly the
women who bear the burdens of life, and even in the realm of
eros they are more servants than partners. True, they too have
their place in life where they can become sovereigns—that is,
as mothers of sons. But along with this eminence there goes a
position of terrible, broken mortification.

I must confess that these observations and accounts have not
brought me any closer to accepting the thesis of universal
"equality" of the sexes. On the contrary, apart from changes
in social structure which contain a trend in this direction, it
seems to me that this assertion of equality can be traced back
to the tacit admission of women that they can no longer achieve
equality *by way of* the man and therefore they keep pushing
themselves into the front rank. It was doubtless this admission
that a wise Frenchwoman had in mind when, looking back
from a position of achieved equality, she said, "In the past we
had more to say than we do now."

As we were talking about all this in a corner of the temple,
J. told me this thought-provoking anecdote. A woman acquaintance of his wanted to marry off a young Japanese girl.
She emphatically recommended that the girl marry a *Christian*
man. In response to the girl's somewhat astonished question
of why she should do this, she replied, "He has more inhibi-

tions!" I must confess that up to this point I did not find the story very edifying, because at first I misunderstood and thought that the woman was saying that Christianity furnishes a person with complexes. But J. interpreted it otherwise: the woman only meant to say that a Christian husband may not be any nearer perfect than another Japanese husband, that he may not even be—to put it bluntly—"morally intact" and above having an affair, but that *when* he does something bad, he does it with a bad conscience. Awareness of judgment constitutes something like gauze in a wound that prevents it from healing too quickly and prevents him from succumbing to the illusion that he can emerge with a whole skin, morally. Practically, this means that although even a Christian husband might perhaps occasionally kick over the traces and patronize the geisha houses, the practice could never become an actual "style" of life for him. Being a Christian, he could never elevate it to an institution and take it for granted as a natural part of life. For him it would always remain something contrary to the order of his life, and to this extent would leave a sting behind it. This sting would have something deterrent about it; in other words, it would have the effect of an "inhibition." I must say that seldom have I heard the Reformation doctrine of Law and Gospel expressed in such a compressed, anecdotal, and at the same time veiled way.

We had a small midday snack in a restaurant which, like many of these simple eating places, was like a dollhouse, completely open in the front and enclosed with latticework in the back. We sat on straw mats (*tatami*) spread over planks. All around us was a wild confusion of empty packing cases, boxes of supplies, innumerable bottles in wooden cases, and the stock of a souvenir shop. The same comfortable, magnificent sloppiness prevailed that can also be found in many French stores and pubs. On the whole, many things in Japan remind me of France, especially the charm of Japanese manners (also, obviously, the *ars amandi*).

I spent the evening in the guest house of the state university.

144

I had been invited there by a large number of professors of the state university and the Christian university (Doshisha) for supper and a colloquium.

We sat in a beautiful, noble room, forming a large circle. The various faculties, religions, and sects were represented, and the intellectual tension that was generated by the polarity of these worlds could literally be felt, though it was mitigated by the cheerful atmosphere that prevailed and the good manners of everybody present.

Beside me sat the leading Japanese philosopher Nishitani, whom the others discreetly pointed out to me as one of the most distinguished of all living Japanese. He is a Zen Buddhist, and he has just published a work on the concept of Nothingness in Buddhism and European existentialism. He has a finely chiseled head and an extremely keen, expressive, yet composed face. His social grace and polish present a curious contrast to his intellectual magnetism and the aloofness of his real nature.

On the other side sat the very kindly, fatherly chancellor of Doshisha University and diagonally across from me the only professor of Christianity in a state university in Japan.

I said we were sitting, but of course we were again squatting on the floor with our legs crossed beneath us. I had to keep stretching my legs like a lubberly lout to avoid cramps in my calves and pains in my legs and to keep my feet from going to sleep, and thus I had all kinds of trouble preventing my feet from inadvertently getting into the soup. It required great concentration to combat the fatigue of sitting cross-legged, participate in the ceremonies of the meal, and at the same time keep my end up in the discussion. Besides, I had a headache from the many times I had bumped my head during the day. But these discomforts paled before the kindness of my hosts, the nimble, rapid translation provided by Professor Ito, and the refreshing view into the garden, where a full battalion of frogs was croaking. The typhoon rain, which had spared Nara throughout the day, now began to beat down in earnest, and together with the ventilators gave us a pleasant coolness.

145

So while I continued in a perpetual state of gymnastic exercise, with my body bent and stretched forward as I angled for my victuals with a chopstick, the conversation quickly passed from relaxed conversation into a theological and philosophical discussion. Since Karl Barth has a large group of followers in Japan, and Emil Brunner has just recently been teaching there, they wanted to know where I stood with respect to these two theological thinkers. To my surprise it again turned out that a number were thoroughly familiar with my *Theological Ethics* and that in general they were well abreast of the current discussion in Germany.

Our discussion then circled somewhat longer about the question of religion and science, and we attempted to define together the positions of the thinkers who have concerned themselves with this problem. Towards the end of the conversation we exchanged views on general university questions, and I learned that all efforts to establish a non-specialist department of liberal arts in the universities have taken the same downward course in Japan that they have among us. Our attempt to communicate this parallel experience to each other gave me some fascinating insights into the intellectual situation of Japanese students, who, like our own, have fallen into line with the trend toward specialization and thus are averse to a more general intellectual orientation. The predominance of technical subject matter both here and abroad seems to make calm reflection impossible.

What struck me in this whole discussion was that although I was constantly being asked about the views of European thinkers on this and that problem, the problems themselves were not discussed. Naturally, this may have been attributable to the fact that people are generally more interested in securing information from a guest who comes from distant parts. However, I wonder whether there may not have been still other reasons. It is true that Japan has in its own tradition a great reservoir upon which it can draw, but its encounter with Western ideas would appear to be too recent for Japan to be able to find its own way among them. Perhaps it is still at the stage where it is looking for authorities in order to find a "pro tem" refuge in this or that master (of course, only in fields and areas which have already opened up through encounter with the Western world). Hence the constant questions about Western authors and authorities (in theology about Barth and Brunner, in philosophy about Heidegger and Jaspers, and so on).

In technology the situation is similar. Here the situation is that they must first pass through the stage of imitation (in which, of course, it sometimes turns out that the copy is better than the original). One sees in the streets many imitations of European—particularly German—brands of cars and motorcycles, and in the stores many copies of German cameras. Here Japan is doubtless still at the stage of catching up with the West.

In any case, to me it seems wrong to conclude from all this that the Japanese are fundamentally dependent and perpetually imitative. The quality of the intellectual leaders with whom I sat this evening makes this assumption absurd. In technology this frequently quite unscrupulous imitation of Western models, which we naturally resent because it skips the costly labor of development and thus takes advantage of the intellectual property of others, may also be due to the fact that overpopulated Japan is simply compelled to export on a large scale in order to be able to live. Therefore, in addition to this explanation of imitativeness as a stage of historical development, we must also take into account certain economic factors which may help us to understand many things and judge them more leniently.

In any case, it seems to me, as far as the theory of development is concerned, there is a peculiar synchronization between the intellectual-scientific and the technological encounter with the West: the Japanese are still struggling with set models, with authorities and with patterns. What is scholasticism in the intellectual disciplines is imitative construction in technology. But anybody who is even remotely aware of the intellectual energies in Japan knows that what we are dealing with

147

here are only the earlier stages of the autonomy Japan will one day attain in this respect, just as it has in its own autochthonous culture.

August 27

Kyoto. Typhoon Grace, which has been in all the radio and press news for days, is due to arrive tonight. A phone call to the agency, prompted by my concern about the ship, informed me that, like the other ships, it had received orders to put out to sea and ride out the typhoon outside the harbor of Kobe. It is too dangerous to stay in the harbor because the hawsers break, the ship's side is battered against the pier, and the ship may even be cast up on land. I am concerned about the men on the ship with whom I have had such good comradeship, and I am sorry that I am not with them now.

I whiled away the morning in the hotel lobby. I simply had to stop to digest a bit and catch my breath. And the lively activity in a place like this, enjoyed as a passive spectator from a comfortable chair, transports one into precisely that intermediate state between complete rest and blinking observation which is characteristic of a cat. I was interested to see whether there were any observable nuances of respect in the stereotyped ceremonial courtesy. In fact they are quite considerable, among the hotel staff (but here less, though there is considerable grinning behind guests' backs on the part of the bellboys) as well as among the guests whose courtesy toward the staff varies greatly.

Professor Ito finally arrived, and a short time later Pastor K., a teacher in the universities of Kyoto and Tokyo, with whom I got along famously from the very first moment. Here again— as in the case of J.—is the type of missionary who is the opposite of any kind of clerical functionary. Though he is profoundly dedicated to his task, a high degree of lively self-criticism enables him to recognize both the divine and the "human-all-too-human," both the eternal and the temporal or ephemeral in his position as a missionary, and also to withstand the trial of faith to which this complete submersion in a world of alien values can lead. His sense of mission, which he has allowed to be refined in this crucible of sacrificial understanding, is substantial and convincing. There is nothing of the half-educated know-it-all here and no faith that is made too easy by ignorance of the world. Here is someone—there are such men among the great missionaries—who has gazed into the abyss of relativism, so that, as Nietzsche said, the abyss threatened to gaze into him, but who knows that he has been graciously and repeatedly snatched away from it. I would believe every word this man said.

He has invited me to be his guest, and during the rest of my time in Kyoto I am to stay in his hospitable and comfortable home, which reflects both Western and Eastern culture. Mr. K. is Swiss, and it is a delight to hear the familiar Swiss German spoken here in Japan. So now I have a mentor to replace my friend J., who had to go off on a business trip. Will we feel the typhoon at all in this solidly built house? The radio is following its course with hourly announcements and giving instructions for emergencies. So far five persons have died. All the localities on rivers which it touches on its course have been evacuated.

But before the typhoon passed over Kyoto between eight and nine o'clock in the evening—incidentally, the first to hit Kyoto in five years—I was to experience one of the high points of my stay in Japan.

A great—perhaps the greatest—master and investigator of Zen Buddhism had invited me to his temple for a discussion. In public as an author he calls himself Hosekei, but his real name is S. Hisamatsu. Three Japanese professors and my Swiss host accompanied me. Professor Ito again took over the job of interpreter.

Fortunately, the violent rain abated for a short time as we entered the spacious temple grounds and walked through a number of courtyards, through covered walks, and finally over a carpet of cultivated moss through a garden thickly overgrown

149

with shrubbery to the small, extremely secluded residence of the Zen master. I wondered whether the purpose of the garden was to serve as a kind of botanical ring of fire to screen off and guard the contemplation of the master. The figure of a ring of fire that suggested itself to me may also have been prompted by the fact that the vanguard of the typhoon was already driving into the shrubs, bending them apart and beating them together so that they looked like leaping tongues of flame.

A woman stood waiting on the tiny terrace. Because we were not introduced to her then or later, I took her to be a servant. But one of my companions told me later that she was the wife of the master. As we came closer to the terrace she fell to the ground and bowed low as each of us passed. She then ushered us into a very simple, beautiful room—which again contained not a single piece of furniture—and seated us in a circle on plaited mats. Trees and shrubbery nestled close to the house, so that at first, while the sliding walls were still open, we had the feeling that we were sitting in a tiny clearing.

The storm shook the bamboo blinds that indicated the boundaries of the room. We would surely not have been able to sit there in such a wind had it not been for the protection of the thick shrubbery.

Hardly had we seated ourselves on the floor when the host came in—this was the signal for an exceedingly solemn and complicated welcoming ceremonial. My companions bowed before the master with extraordinary reverence, which is to say, they made more profound and repeated bows.

The master himself, in his great modesty—which in this case was certainly not *mere* form, but an expression of his nature—appeared to dismiss the reverence by bowing even more profoundly and casting himself repeatedly to the ground. Curiously enough, up to this time these mutual reverences had merely interested me; here they touched and stirred me. I felt that here the form was filled to the brim with what it was meant to express.

Finally we sat down again, the master in his simple gray robe

150

taking his place in the center, at the back of the room. During the opening conversation, which was about the weather and my trip, and thus to my relief very generally human and conventional, I was able to observe him. He is a man between sixty and seventy, graceful, with a lively, artless play of expression on his face. He does not have the chiseled, concentrated, restrained look of Professor Nishitani; his features are rather relaxed and open. And his manner of conversing is exactly the same as his appearance. He did not deliver a sage lecture on wisdom but maintained the tone of a straightforward chat even when we came to discuss the profoundest questions. Consequently, in a very short time he relieved his visitors of all self-consciousness.

As a small hospitality gift I handed him the English translation of my book *Between God and Satan,* in which, following Japanese custom, I had placed my calling card. He expressed his thanks warmly and with further genuflections, raising first the book and then the card to his brow. This combination of exceedingly stylized ceremonial with the easy, natural flow of the conversation made a strong impression upon me.

After these overtures Hosekei touched a small bell, giving his wife the signal that the tea ceremony might begin. At first this proceeded in silence. Whenever Mme. Hosekei proffered a cup to one of the guests, both bowed to the floor. This certainly was not a conference dictated by the minute hand of the clock, where one seeks to get down to business as quickly as possible. Here the first concern was the careful preparation of the attitude in which good conversation can take place. Here communication was established first, in order to create receptiveness to the matter to be discussed. The tea ceremony is intended to be an exercise that fosters the "mannering of the soul." As a rule we Westerners feel that we are being objective when we stand off from an object and view it impersonally. Here it is just the opposite; here the object is related to the person. Therefore the person must go through training before he is permitted to meet the object. I suspect that even in Japan this no longer obtains in business conferences. But in the presence of the Zen master the tradition continues.

During the tea ceremony the master showed me the honor of allowing me to receive his own cup, which he takes with him wherever he goes. I was somewhat surprised at this, for it was easily three or four times as heavy as the usual teacup, with thick sides, quite asymmetrical in form, and a bit odd because of its almost grotesque awkwardness.

Hosekei perhaps had noted my faint surprise when he disclosed that this was his own cup. He explained to me that Zen Buddhism loves asymmetry—a feature which is reflected even in the outlines of its temples. It breaks, as it were, the harmony of forms and gives them a touch of imperfection in order to prevent the form from becoming, through its perfection, an end in itself. The form should always be only a path, a bridge to a structure; it must remain transparent and retain the "unauthentic being" of the pure symbol. It can be only a handmaid.

For a moment the somewhat fantastic thought occurred to me whether Bert Brecht (of all persons!) may not have intended something very like this by what he calls the repulsive or "alienating" effect in his theory of the drama. Why did he turn so vehemently against any perfection and virtuosity in the actor? Why did he disdain the trained voices of concert singers and choose—for *The Threepenny Opera* and his songs generally—persons with rough, rusty, uncultivated voices? He was afraid that perfect form would go down too easily with the Philistines in the orchestra seats, that they would get stalled aestheticizing in the limbo of form, and that perfection itself would thus help them to evade real engagement. Therefore the hearer must be shocked by "asymmetry." This precisely is its "alienating effect." And does not Kierkegaard mean something similar with his idea of *skandalon* and offense? He too wanted to prevent the Gospel from being too easily received, from being too harmonious and pleasant. He did not want the hearer to evade its claim and its contradiction, to keep angling for self-vindication, and thus to be able to act aesthetically and not ethically.

Again and again the conversation brought to my mind the remarkable formal parallels to phenomena which can be seen in *our* intellectual life. And as long as we remained on the level of formalities, much of what Hosekei said struck me as being very familiar. I told him so, and he appeared to be delighted by many of the instances.

It would have been a pity, however, if we had remained on the level of merely formal analogies. We had to see to it that there was a meeting between the alien elements in the positions each of us hold. So, pursuing his explanation of the teacup, I put this question to him: "The asymmetrical form is therefore meant to help prevent the form from becoming an end in itself and rather to remain a subservient signpost. But if this is so, then everything depends on how we describe the end to which this signpost points?"

"Yes," he replied, "everything does indeed depend upon the content within the form, and when we define it the difference between our positions will perhaps emerge. I would answer your question this way: The broken, imperfect form points the way to perfection."

I said to him that I knew very well how little regard Zen Buddhism has for definitions, that it regards them as a somewhat vulgar attempt to capture in rational statements that which is inexpressible and can only be experienced in absorption, and thus to force it to become so obvious that it is distorted. I said that I was therefore in a somewhat awkward situation with regard to him, for a discussion operates through the medium of words, and, if I were to carry anything away from my meeting with him, I could do so only by expecting him to attempt to clothe this ultimate thing in words for me. I begged his pardon for expecting of him something that he must necessarily regard as improper and inadequate. It was, I said, like asking somebody to divorce a Beethoven symphony from the idiom of musical tones and describe it in words.

I had the impression that the master was grateful for the understanding I had of his difficulty, since he then proceeded to accommodate himself to me by resorting to a philosophical form of statement. What he said was this: "Perfection consists in recognizing 'the One in everything and everything in the One' "—this is the real Zen principle. Here the distance that separates subject from object, the inward from the outward, is overcome.

I then asked him cautiously—always respectfully conscious of his difficulty with conceptualized thinking—whether he could tell me what significance he would attribute to the human self and whether the position he took did not imply an identity between subject and object, the self and the world outside. "Does the self," I asked him directly, "retain any of its personal independence at all, so that it stands in a genuine encounter with the world it meets, or does this distance, this selfhood, and thus also its ethical quality, remain beyond its reach? Does it not, as it were, evaporate into the world and become one of its anonymous elements?" Friend K. came to my aid and used this brief formulation: Zen Buddhism is manifestly concerned with the identification of the self with reality and not with a confrontation of the self with reality.

I fully appreciated the fact that the master, faced by this Western conceptualized vocabulary of ours—which he knows, but which must appear to him to be a diluted abstraction that has lost its substance—did not lose his patience, but on the contrary made the attempt to meet us on the level of our own terms. He said that the concepts identification and confrontation were not really precise terms for what he meant. It was not a matter of identification of self with reality at all. "It is rather a matter of my discovering myself in my elemental relation to what is around me. I must therefore become aware that I have been thrown upon this reality from the very beginning and that consequently I can come to terms with the reality I encounter—the horse on which I ride, the bow with which I shoot, the tree which I fell or beneath which I rest—only if I have discovered my original 'connection' with it. The Zen principle 'the One in everything and everything in the One' therefore does not mean that all distances between subject and object, inside and outside, thinking and being, disappear and that the self is drowned in a universal primordial plasm. Rather this principle means that I discover myself in my cosmic place as a member of Being and therefore in a relationship of brotherhood to all the structures of reality. It is in this very awareness of the relatedness, the unity of the Whole in which I live and have my being, that I am then enabled to handle it, know it, meet with it, deal with it. I do not first create my world for myself, as perhaps the Western activist and man of action wishes to do—here *I* am, and over there is the *world* in which I must act—rather I discover the world as something related to me, to which I have already been co-ordinated and of which I am already a part. In the kind of abstract identity of inside and outside which you have just suggested, all action, all decision, and thus all responsibility would indeed cease. But, as I have said, I do not mean this kind of identity at all. My concern is rather to discover a human existence which by its very primordial coherence with reality is enabled to be near and related to things and for this reason also to be able to 'handle' them rightly."

It was a fascinating moment of the conversation when we were confronted with this inadequacy of our conceptual language. The man who sat there calmly waving his fan as he talked not only had a different form of thinking but also drew upon different sources of thought. He exists somewhere else. He has gained not only his insights but also his self from springs of meditation that are alien to us. We were still a long way from being able to take up a standpoint over against him or to interject "critical evaluations"; for the present we simply had to stand still and try to understand. (When I say "we," I mean not the Japanese who were present, who were quite familiar with all this, but the two European Christians, my friend K. and myself.)

As though Hosekei had noted our hesitation and our hidden concern, he continued his line of thought and sought to illustrate what he meant with a number of classic symbols of Zen Buddhism, with which I was already somewhat familiar through my philosophy teacher Eugen Herrigel (whose book *Zen in the Art of Archery* is regarded very highly here). The first model to which he referred us—which, coming to us in this situation and from his lips, took on for me a wholly new vitality—was the example of the rider.

The perfect rider constitutes a unity with his horse. This is the only reason he can be perfect at all. Only because this is so can he "handle" the horse. Precisely because he has become one with it, he possesses the relation of authority to this piece of reality which is called "horse." The "one in all," applied to this case, means therefore that "there is no rider above the saddle and no horse beneath the saddle." The point is that the unity in question here can only be expressed by pure negations. The negations, however, arise not because the reference here is to an objective Nothingness, but rather only to a Nothingness in relation to the relationships familiar to us in everyday life.

Hosekei illustrated the same thing with the art of archery. It is well known that the archer who has undergone the Zen exercises is capable of hitting his target exactly in the middle at approximately sixty yards, and that he is then able to shoot a second, third, and fourth arrow into the first. This is not the result of training in the art of bowmanship, but is rather a mystical art, in which the "It" shoots the arrow and takes it to its goal while the archer only serves as an instrument in the process. The fact that he can be this, however, is again grounded in hidden co-ordinations which effect a oneness: the bowman is one with the bow, the arrow is one with the target, the bow is one with the arrow. Out of this mystical insight into the innate contact of all the elements of being, insight which springs from meditative absorption, it becomes possible for the archer, the arrow, and the target to *become* one, because they already *are* one. Consequently, the incredible marksmanship of the mystically trained archer results—contrary to all Western ways of thinking—not from his combatively setting himself "at odds" with the target, but rather from putting himself "at one" with the target, which is nothing more nor less than the recapitulation and realization of a unity of being which is already *given*.

"I must therefore," said the master, "give up myself as an independent factor over against the target; I must become a formless self." This term "formless self" recurs repeatedly in his statements. It is one of his standard terms.

I then reiterated the question whether with this formless self there could ever be any real encounters at all between man and man, man and beast, man and thing; whether this giving up of the self could ever enable us to have any "historical" community which, unlike a mere collective, consisted of personal individualities with their sense of being "for" one another and "against" one another and with their mutual respect; or whether instead we would not be threatened by something like a non-historical existence. Hosekei replied: "Perhaps you are still laboring a bit under the prejudice that the example of the archer is meant to express a hidden, timeless, and non-historical identity, and thus a contourless sameness. Here everything depends upon convincing you that I mean something else. It is not at all a matter of reducing everything to a sameness that would destroy all tension-filled encounters or not even allow them to occur. It is rather a matter of experiencing a communicative relationship in which all the elements of being—including the self and the outside world—are interrelated, and on the basis of which encounter and confrontation, intercourse and manipulation become *possible* in the first place."

At this point there occurred to me a number of thought processes in our own intellectual tradition which may be analogous to what he meant. I made reference to them in order to ask him whether he felt there were any parallels here. Thus I mentioned an idea in Dilthey's hermeneutic to the effect that one can only understand what is "already contained within the living, perceiving being." Hence a previously given relationship exists between a text one wishes to understand and the norms, questions, and criteria of the one who wishes to understand it; likewise, there is a pre-established harmony between the structure of the world and the rational mind that understands the structure of the world. "If the eye were not sunlike, it could never see the sun." This saying of Goethe would appear to point to a previous, original unity of the inward and the outward that conditions our ability to understand from the very beginning.

Hosekei acknowledged that this was indeed a parallel, and appeared to be pleased with the similarities. He was likewise appreciative of certain Platonic ideas that point in the same direction: namely, that the philosophical exercise by which we are to arrive at the contemplation (*theoria*) of the Ideas bases all processes of cognition upon the assumption that there is a pre-existent connection between the knower and the known; therefore all cognition is based upon remembrance (*anamnesis*), and likewise the multiplicity of separated things is grounded in a unity of their prototypes.

Perhaps, however, other associations evoked by the idea of unity in Zen wisdom are even more obvious. So we threw into the debate Hegel's philosophy of identity—his idea that the world is reason and mind and that man the finite is co-ordinated with this conscious reason of the world and so is able to understand it—and also mentioned the concept of being in Heidegger's philosophy—that Being in which I am "contained," without my "standing over against" it as one who exists autonomously, and which I cannot apprehend as a spectator, but which rather "discloses" itself to me of itself (*aletheia*).

The master listened to all this with interest, and repeatedly assented when I asked him whether he felt he was being understood at this point and whether he recognized the similarity of the intentions. Sometimes he expressed and underlined his approval with a touch of enthusiasm. Nevertheless I was not quite sure to what degree his courtesy was playing a part, nor whether here and there he was not secretly thinking: I have seen the sun, and this man (along with his Western authorities and intellectual heroes) sees only the shadows on the wall of the Platonic cave; he knows only the categorical contours of Ideas I have really encountered in person. If this is what he was thinking, he was careful not to let us see it.

In any case, it was clear to us that in the history of oriental thought there are—from a formal, typological point of view—analogous positions and ways of approaching questions. But what do they signify? Are they more than empty, threshed-out hulls? If I have rightly caught the crucial thing in our discussion, it would seem to me that Zen Buddhism is less concerned with the conceptual definition and expression of an insight (and here it appears to be somewhat inept) than with *how* I have gained this knowledge, or better, which organs of perception I have used to assimilate it into myself, and further, into which levels of myself I have received it and to what *extent*. Am I a receiver or a conqueror? Do I merely accept, or do I seize upon this knowledge? Do I allow Being to speak, or do I myself speak?

For anybody who would clarify the structure of a process of cognition merely by applying the rule "two times two equals four" these would, of course, be improper and strange ways of putting the question. For when this rule is employed the only question that arises is: "is this correct or incorrect?" but not the problem of how and to what extent and to what end I receive the truth. The theologian (but by no means only he!) is already more acute at this point; he knows the curse that lies upon mere intellectual knowledge of or assent to the truths of faith, and knows that the precondition for my being able to know a truth of God is the Johannine *being in* the truth. Only "one who is of the truth hears my voice."

Since the rise of Kierkegaard and existentialism, the problem of how knowing relates to our own existence, and thus of what my *relation* is to the truth, has become generally familiar.

159

I have always turned to Plato's doctrine of Ideas in order to clarify for myself and my students the problem which was the central concern of this discussion, namely, to what extent, with which organs, and to what end do I apprehend the truth? Every textbook of philosophy defines the Platonic Ideas, and this definition is almost a routine question in every final examination in theology or philosophy and one for which every candidate must be prepared. But what do these definitions say? In the *Symposium* we can read what kind of exercises in knowing and symbolic seeing the philosopher must pass through before he arrives at the "perception" of the Ideas. In the last analysis, therefore, these Ideas cannot be communicated through teaching at all; they can only be communicated by setting the student down on a road to them that is his own—then he must *himself* travel that road to its end. And here again the proper method of teaching is the Socratic method, which does not force upon another being either a system or a scheme of ideas, but rather puts him through a particular series of exercises that lay claim upon the whole being. No teacher, but only a master of exercises, can bring one to the road leading to the Platonic Idea. And certainly this is also a matter of organs of perception completely different from those of intellectual apprehension — organs which on their part need first to be cultivated.

Furthermore, when we find in Christian doctrine a chapter on the Holy Spirit and Luther saying in the explanation of the third article of the Creed, "I believe that by my own reason and strength I cannot believe in Jesus Christ, my Lord, or come to him; but the Holy Spirit has called me," it likewise points to the fact that mere intellectual understanding is simply not equal to the things that need to be understood here, but rather that this reality can either disclose itself or withhold itself. I communicated to Hosekei all these common elements in our tradition which were going through my mind.

Our conversation then gradually began to move in a direction I had not previously contemplated at all. In other words, I realized that what I had been doing all the time was to point out and think through with the master the epistemological parallels between Zen Buddhism, Christian theology, and Western philosophy. But this made me increasingly uncomfortable. Had I been slipping into the easy berth of relativism? Had I chosen the comfortable and very polite expedient of remaining on the level of formal questions concerning method, on which it is possible to come to some kind of agreement without being exposed to the *status confessionis?* Was there no point here at which I as a Christian theologian must say nay, was there no obligation to proclaim? I began to distrust myself. The passion of thought is a strong emotion that must be controlled by faith and not enjoyed for its own sake.

Our conversation had indeed arrived at a curious point. When I looked back at its previous stages it struck me that the theological problem of "heathenism" had not yet become acute at all. For up to this point we had been concerned only with the question of how I "appropriate" reality and how I am "coordinated" with it. In other words, it dealt with a part of the theory of knowledge, of epistemology, or more correctly, with a part of exercise in knowing and thus with a neutral problem of form or, as the theologians say, an adiaphoron.

The real theological problem, it seemed to me, lay altogether elsewhere, specifically, in the question which I then put to the Zen master: "How is this Being which is perceived and appropriated—the Being which is referred to in the phrase 'Everything in One, One in everything' — how is this Being understood among you as a whole, that is, with regard to its ground, purpose, and goal? Where does it come from, where is it going? Does it have a Lord? Or, instead of starting from the outside, I might put the question this way, starting with the *subject*. What do you mean by the formless self? Is it autonomous? Is it guilty? Is it redeemed? I am not asking for answers to these details, but simply trying to indicate to you the direction of my question."

Hosekei replied, "I believe it is best to put the question as you have in your second variant. So if you ask me about the

161

formless self, this must not be thought of as a problem of subtraction in which the answer is zero. The formless self is not a nothing. Rather, formlessness means only that the self is no longer *fixed* by what is external and therefore alien, but has gotten away from everything and thus is free."

Though for the first time this brought into sharp focus a problem of content, namely, the problem of freedom, and therefore the moment might finally have come when the latent tension between our differing convictions would clearly emerge, nevertheless this answer too had in it something that at first was confusing to me. For it too set me to thinking of some familiar analogies. The term "fixed" which Hosekei used immediately recalled Sartre's use of the term "fixation." After all, Sartre's doctrine of freedom is also constructed in such a way that a person can achieve his own free existence only by refusing to be bound by the standards of value held by his environment, by the demand of "one does thus and so," and not allowing himself to be fixed by all this. Had not Nishitani worked on the concept of Nothingness in Buddhism and in existentialism? So here again I was aware of certain similarities in the way the question is approached.

When I called this to Hosekei's attention he agreed that the similarities and differences pointed out by Nishitani might be possible; yet existentialism seemed to be something unfamiliar to him. For me the charm of this conversation lay not least in the fact that we were listening to a genuine, self-contained Buddhist who was fundamentally isolated from Western thinking.

It suddenly occurred to me that the concept of the formless self and of freedom presented a totally different and better chance of bringing Christianity and Buddhism into encounter and allowing their messages to clash on a level beyond all formal analogies. I mentioned Luther's statement on the freedom of the Christian man and asked Hosekei whether he was familiar with this doctrine of freedom or whether I might sum it up briefly, and ask him to comment from his standpoint.

When he indicated that he was interested, I briefly outlined the main points as follows. This freedom means that the believer is no longer subject to any man or any thing and that despite his standing in full engagement with the world (as a sufferer, a lover, a worker, as one who dies, and so on), he can "have" the world "as if he had it not" (See I Cor. 7:29 f.). Consequently, he is no longer "fixed," either by Mammon and a false need for security, or by his finitude which delivers him over to anxiety, or by the spell of his passions or even the spell of his mind which prompts him to fabricate images of the world that no longer call him in question but rather buttress him.

The Pauline reference to "having as if one had not" seemed to make an unusual impression upon the master. He actually underscored it and wished to appropriate it as an expression of *his* fundamental attitude. I suspected why he would think of this phrase as being spirit of his spirit, for though Buddha did indeed advocate detachment from external things, he did not mean that one must then proceed also to withdraw *de facto* from things and from active manipulation of them. On the contrary, the inwardly detached person by his very detachment acquires the freedom to deal with the world without falling victim to it. Characteristically, this knowledge of a new possibility of being-in-the-world did not come to Buddha during the time when he was subjecting himself to the severest of self-mortifications and eating the dung of calves in order to force his way to illumination and detachment. Rather, this insight came to him when he discovered the *hopelessness* of the way of asceticism, when he began to eat again and even accepted invitations to prepared meals. "Having as if one had not"—this expresses being in the world and yet being aloof from it.

When the master began to play with these associations of ideas, as if he were turning this Pauline saying in his hands like a precious stone in order to make it sparkle in the light of various thoughts of the Buddha, I was, of course, obliged to confront him with an objection. "I am afraid," I said to him, "that now we could also use the idea of freedom to salute kindred ideas on both sides and, so to speak, meet our own doubles. This does not mean, of course, that we should not welcome with due gratitude such manifestations of the *logos spermaticos* (the generative reason scattered like seed in the world). But these meetings with doubles frequently turn out to be illusions brought about by the effect of shadows and the refraction of light in the fog. Here one may be subject to optical illusions. And I do believe that we are now very close to such an illusion."

Then Hosekei made the point that the nature of freedom is interpreted differently on the two sides, and I could only concur with his conjecture. He added that the nature of freedom can only be defined if it is clearly understood what freedom exists for and where it leads. I conceded the point with qualifications, but refrained from asking how he would define this goal; for I think I knew that this question would be improper. After all, he could not define the goal of freedom as an intra-worldly mode of conduct on the part of the self or as the self's becoming free for God. Hence the master would again have been obliged to resort to negations. And if Nirvana—the final coming to rest of the individual soul—were to appear in his reply, it too could only be expressed in negative terms. In this conversation I did not wish to get myself into a situation where Hosekei could point out that, certain things I was inquiring about being beyond expression in conceptual terms, my question was improper. Therefore, I contented myself with the reply that the nature of freedom can be seen only from the vantage point of its goal. I did tell him, however, that as a Christian I was not only concerned about the *goal* of freedom but far more about the antecedent question of *whence* I gained this freedom and how I was empowered to exercise it at all. I added that I could speak of this source of freedom only in the form of proclamation.

What I said here—as the conversation continued back and forth—can be summed up as follows. "The opposite of freedom, that is, what we have just called 'fixation,' appears in Christian terminology under the label 'bondage': I am under the dictatorship of fear, anxiety, guilt, and false hope. The opposite of this bondage is not, however, to be described simply negatively, as mere emancipation from bondage, but positively, as sonship, as acceptance by the Father. And it is Jesus Christ who establishes this peace between the Father and me. Freedom is therefore not the opposite of bondage but rather a new form of bondage."

I then told very simply the parable of the lost son, who went out into the far country in order to be free from his father, thinking that he would find himself in the broad hunting grounds of a strange country. Because he understood freedom only negatively, he did not find it, but instead fell into the grip of new powers of dominion, under the dictatorship of his passions, his need for recognition, and finally his loneliness and homesickness among the swine. Not until he turned homeward did he discover that he could find himself only when he had found the father. For the fact is that it was his nature to be a child, a son. The secret of our life is not that first we are children who are under the authority of a father and then we become autonomous adults; the way of existence, as Christians understand it, is that we begin as children and become responsible sons, but real *sons*.

I apologized for having to speak so long without interruption, but Hosekei begged me to go on. I was grateful for this. Our discussion had long since passed the boundaries of debate. Now we were able really to "address" each other.

I went on to make a further comment (the subject could, of course, only be touched upon in this conversation). In my opinion, this is the problem: If I have freedom only as I pass through Nothingness (but is this not too superficially expressed, have I not trivialized it by saying this?), then immediately the question arises whether I do not then gain that freedom by my own mastery through an act of obliteration of the self, through training in extinguishing all feelings, and through

165

trained exercise in the art of dying to oneself. Christians too know something about freedom being gained only through dying, through *mortificatio sui* (Luther). But there—despite all the seeming parallelism of processes and concepts!—it is specifically a matter of dying with Christ, of being graciously incorporated into his death and resurrection. "Therefore," I said to the master, "even though among you it is a matter of acts directed against the 'natural' self, it seems to me, since it is not a matter of grace and pardon, to be a matter of a kind of self-creation on the part of man and therefore a subtle form of self-assertion by which he achieves his higher self. And the term formless self would then, by its very negative structure, only disguise the fact that what we have here is a shocking upsurge of the self, an upsurge which, for someone who reckons with God, could perhaps take on the meaning of desiring to 'be like God' and thus signify a usurpation of divine prerogatives. If I rightly see the decisive question that lies between us, I should formulate it in this way: What everything depends upon is by what authority or power the human 'I' becomes a self, becomes an 'existence.' Does this becoming a self occur by way of a man's extricating himself from the domination of that which 'fixes' him, or even from the clutches of Nothingness, through some form of self-assertion, even if that self-assertion be a training in self-obliteration in order to achieve freedom? Or does this becoming a self occur by way of my learning from someone that he recognizes me, loves me, judges me, and lifts me up, and my learning that this someone is the Almighty God and that in Christ this Almighty God is my Father? The relationship upon which everything depends could also be stated in this way: Do I determine myself on the basis of my fundamental relationship to the world that I want to overcome, or do I determine myself on the basis of my relationship to him who overcame it for me and who now accepts me and includes me in his overcoming of the world?"

It was amazing how the master was able to listen, and I did not gain the impression that this was merely polite patience.

166

Although, when we arrived at the kernel of the conversation, I occasionally fell into a monologue, whereas at this very point I should have preferred to listen and learn rather than speak myself, I console myself with the fact that Hosekei repeatedly asked questions and encouraged me, indeed, insisted that I state my objections and my position. However, it may be that there is a deeper reason why the conversation took this course, which is that the Gospel lives by words and seeks words, whereas Zen Buddhism flees from words and dwells in totally different regions. So in the course of conversation, which must necessarily employ the idiom of speech, both of us remained in our different places.

The conversation had already lasted a long time. The rain and wind had become stronger, and the paper walls were drawn shut. The feeling of being enclosed in the small room grew even more intense. Only for a few moments was I conscious of what was happening outside, otherwise we were all absorbed in our theme. I was hardly aware even of the pain in my legs caused by sitting cross-legged so long.

I resolved to present to the master a question Romano Guardini once raised in a lecture. Guardini set forth the thesis that the Eastern peoples, especially those who live by Buddhism, are probably better able to contend with the world of technology than the secularized Westerners. For Western men, he said, have been largely robbed of their inner substance and thus are helplessly exposed to outer-direction; therefore—repeating the fate of Goethe's sorcerer's apprentice—they have been misled by technology. The Eastern peoples, however, are still more inclined to live by inner-direction and to this extent can meet the phenomenon of technical knowledge with more poise and aloofness. And though I knew, I said, adding my own little report, that the wisdom and inner-directedness represented by him, Hosekei, was exceptional and that "secularization" was rife in Japan too, Guardini's thesis nevertheless appeared to me to be plausible. The continuing effects of ancient traditions were still clearly apparent to the visitor, in the form of greater tranquillity and in many ceremonial forms of composure.

The master was delighted at my mention of Guardini, and we talked for a moment about our gratification at having a mutual acquaintance in him. He then very unassumingly and circumspectly affirmed Guardini's conjecture. It could be clearly sensed from his words, which were obviously intended not to offend his Western guest, where he saw the chief dangers of our inner situation.

In this connection, however, I felt obliged to pass over to a minor offensive and ask him something which I myself as a Christian theologian have by no means solved. I said to him: "In our Christian ethics too the question of what inner counterbalances to the external pressure of the technical world are made available to us through faith naturally plays a large role. The subject of 'meditation' and 'spiritual exercises' has therefore gained increased interest among us. And not a few are asking what a master like yourself might have to say to us about this. I must admit, however, that this question no longer suffices, though I take it very seriously. Rather, I believe that the problems lie not only in our inner attitude toward technical knowledge but also in the objective realm of technology and in the whole structure of our society itself. We have detected a certain autonomy of processes that permit themselves to be only conditionally influenced by ethical decisions. Thus a research scientist, for example—an atomic physicist, let us say—is not at all confronted with the decision whether he should choose a particular problem. Rather, the problem simply "arises." Nor is the *application* of knowledge something that depends upon the decision to put it into practice and realization; rather, the trend toward putting knowledge into effect technologically is already inherent in the theoretical thinking. For me the exciting problem that results is this: What, if any, possibilities are there for guiding autonomous processes? In other words, how can I influence, not merely my *inner* relation to the technological process, but the techno-logical process *itself?* And how do we as theologians and ethicists interpret autonomy itself? Is it an irresistible process like that of natural law? Do we have here the irruption of a natural process which is completely neutral so far as values are concerned, and is humanity consequently confined to an ethical minimum? Has Zen Buddhism—this would interest me very much—also grappled with this problem of autonomy?"

I hardly need explain why I was anxious to hear the master's answer to this question; for though it is true that Zen Buddhism locates the dominant factor of the existential process in areas that lie deep below the level of action, it then radiates out from these areas into the realm of action, in a certain sense makes action possible, and thus it has very definitely influenced a culture as active as that of the Japanese. What interested me in the extreme was whether Zen Buddhism concerns itself only with the *inner* capital on which the "actor" lives or whether it also concerns itself with the structure—let us say, the autono-mous structure—of that *reality* upon which the "actor" acts. Did Zen Buddhism have an answer for both forms of the threat? By his nodding and otherwise showing his participation I saw that Hosekei was much interested in these reflections. But his reply yielded nothing. He said only that he had pon-dered this question repeatedly with his students, because he was thoroughly aware of its fateful significance, but that he was still unable to say anything about it since he was not sure of the solution and would have to do a great deal of thinking about it. When he asked me what we Christians thought about this question, I briefly indicated the thoughts I have had on this subject, but frankly admitted that I was still wrestling with it and that here all of us were only travelers on the way.

This ponderous discussion gradually came to an end. Though it had lasted for several hours, we were able only to touch upon things, and had to leave many of our tensions and differ-ences unexplained. Throughout, we felt the strong radiation emanating from this man who does not subsist purely by the intellect and whose life discipline includes totally different dimensions of his self. Despite all the concentration the discussion demanded, his attitude remained one of relaxed kindliness, which was in charming contrast with the involuted Japanese ceremonial of his home. Thus he knew how to impart a human climate to our meeting. In his appearance he impressed me as strangely asexual. He could just as well have been a wise old woman.

In the presence of this man and his eminence—I sense this eminence even more intensely in the reverence shown him, particularly by my Japanese companions—I see very clearly what Albert Schweitzer means when he dismisses any kind of half-education for missionaries and considers only men of theological and cultural rank fit to practice the calling of a missionary. In the face of this crowning pinnacle of an ancient culture it would be preposterous and absurd if the only diagnosis that occurred to a person were that of "benighted heathenism" and if he then proceeded to launch a conversion attack on the culture without any sense of its greatness and without even evaluating what he is confronting. It would be like a mouse gnawing at Mont Blanc. (The question, however, is whether this inferior type of missionary actually exists. May it not be that he exists only in the imagination of the opponent?)

Not that I wish to eliminate or even merely relativize the concept of heathenism or even of conversion. (On the contrary, I believe that here we have the unredeemed condition in its ultimate sublimation.) The only thing is that the term "heathenism" cannot be had so cheaply and cannot be applied so cocksurely as it was perhaps in many missionary circles (of, it is to be hoped, a bygone style). The word "heathenism" can never be given as a wholesale judgment; at most it can only signify the final result of a diagnosis. I am glad that my particular European missionary friends in Japan are men of high quality, whose self-criticism and whose skepticism, constantly conquered by faith, command my admiration and trust.

Before we departed, the master took us through his temple.
We stopped for a while before a bell that once hung in a
Christian church, dating from the activity of the Jesuit missionary Francis Xavier in the sixteenth century. The Church of
Jesus Christ will endure till the day of judgment, but the
churches may pass away. The passing shower of the Gospel,
of which Luther spoke, may go its way elsewhere. I grasped
the mallet hanging beside the bell, looked at the master inquir-
ingly, and when he nodded his permission, touched the bell with
several light blows. Its clear tone resounded through the Buddhist temple. Centuries ago it called together a Christian
congregation.

At the formal farewell ceremony Hosekei handed me a fan
on which he had painted the word "Nothingness" in ornamental
Japanese characters, thus recalling many stages of our discussion. In addition he gave me a scroll of Japanese paper, likewise inscribed by his own hand. Professor Ito interpreted the
characters as follows: "Through great doubt—and thus again
through confrontation with Nothingness — to great questions
and knowledge."

By the time we had gone the few steps back to the car we
were completely drenched. The trees were swaying beneath
the impact of violent gusts of wind and pouring rain. The
empty streets were already flooded.

At the home of my kindly host K. everything was prepared
for a pleasant evening. In the face of a menacing event of
nature, from which one feels fairly secure, the primary meaning
of what we call culture can manifest itself more demonstratively, as it were, than at other times. We realize that, as I
had already learned on shipboard, culture establishes a sphere
of security by which man declares that he is more than a mere
product of nature, that he does not merely accept and endure
it, but resists it in freedom.

So I observed that during the preparations for the evening—
the adjusting of the chairs, the provision of drinks and smokes

171

—something like euphoria settled down upon us: we were close to the elements and yet sheltered in the midst of them. At increasingly briefer intervals the radio announced the position of the typhoon and continued giving directions for safety measures. The typhoon, which had been moving toward the north at about eighteen miles per hour, had just swerved slightly toward the east. Its rotary speed was eighty miles per hour.

Meanwhile all offices, stores, schools, and factories had closed in order that everybody might get home in time to take the necessary safety measures. We too fastened the doors and windows and secured everything that might be flung about. From the radio came "serious music," the familiar sounds of classical European symphonies. All this reminded me of the hours of catastrophe in the last war, the days of Stalingrad or the air war, when the radio broadcasts did the same thing for us. Outside, the storm roared and sent the rain drops smacking against the windows.

Just as we finished our supper the typhoon itself arrived, and with its savage and awful splendor outdid all its harbingers. It is indeed the lord among the elements. The house shook and trembled. We heard the trees groaning and cracking, and there were moments when we involuntarily ducked our heads. After a little less than two hours it was over and we took a walk about the city. It still looked deserted, as if life had been arrested at its moment of terror. The streets glistened in black emptiness, strewn everywhere with leaves, with shattered branches, and among them roof tiles.

August 28

Kyoto. In the wake of the cloudy and humid days of rain, today the brilliant sun shone, sparkling in the multitudinous raindrops. The typhoon was a drastic cleansing storm that swept everything clean. And now that it is past, a burden seems also to have gone from people's spirits; they appear to me to be several degrees more cheerful and relaxed. And finally I can also take pictures again.

172

Passing by a great Buddhist temple, we heard the muffled sound of a gong, announcing the beginning of a service of worship. We took off our shoes, ascended the broad flight of steps, and found ourselves enveloped in the dusky light of the temple, in which only the feeble glow of colored tapestries and metalware could be seen. Six monks were assembled for a funeral service in which several peasant families reverently participated. Their rough, honest faces were immobile as they squatted on the floor. The service was conducted by the abbot, who was seated upon a throne and dressed in splendid vestments.

The liturgy the monks were celebrating produced upon our ears the effect of a weird, atonal bleating, full of whining and long drawn-out lamentations, crisscrossed in jungly confusion, interspersed with syncopated strokes of a gong, and in a rhythm accelerated at intervals of about a minute and accentuated by the crashing of gongs and cymbals. The more one listens, the more this furious acceleration of tempo creates something ecstatically exciting. One feels gripped and sucked into something strange that will not brook his desire to remain a spectator on the sidelines. "Japanese life can only be understood through the dance," said K. He explained to me that these same rhythms recur in the ancient Japanese theater.

Beyond the bounds of the altar, the public traffic in the temple went on unconstrained. Here as in all the temples the stream of museum visitors milled past, people for whom the service of worship was something like a historical exhibition. Throughout the service people "shamelessly" took pictures, even flash pictures. Secularization is a global phenomenon. To be sure, I knew this before, but this demonstration leads to a different kind of knowledge. Its evidence is more frighteningly direct. Suddenly I knew it, not only with my mind, but with all my senses.

Observing these things led to a discussion of missions. It would appear that it is no longer a question (at least not primarily) of establishing a point of contact with the thought content of the non-Christian religions, as it was in the past, but rather of the Christian message's addressing itself to the predicament of being caught in the grip of the meaninglessness and nothingness inherent in secularism. Missionaries encounter another form of Nothingness apart from that peculiar to Buddhism. The variations of Nothingness—this could be a new theme for theology.

This whole problem of "point of contact," the problem of positive and negative contact! — every conversation of these days had this as its hidden central theme. And in this connection we were also troubled by the problem that the Japanese find it hard to understand the Christian sacraments, since in Japanese life the elements of bread and wine have no elemental significance and thus they are obviously prevented from producing an elemental effect, that is, a dynamic symbolic and community-creating effect. Ernst Benz, who was in Kyoto shortly before I was and who commanded universal admiration because of his penetrating observations, has said: "The sacrament is as alien to them as it would be if we were obliged by some exotic mission in Germany to celebrate a sacrament in which lotus roots and bamboo sprouts were eaten."

Does this not indicate in a downright shocking way how little we trust that the Word is constantly seeking to become flesh and *other* flesh?—that Christ desires to sacrifice himself in *alien* cultures, and traditions besides our own, but we hinder him from doing so and are constantly doing nothing but hinder him? For we bring Christianity to the peoples of Asia in our Western form, that is, mixed with foreign matter (which, of course, is for us not foreign matter—only our own form of appropriating it.) However, this matter cannot be absorbed by the alien organism. Often we do not missionize at all, but simply export a foreign religion.

This is very harshly stated. But where there is unbelief the rebuke must be harsh. Or is it not unbelief that we should insist upon our forms of confession, our symbols, instead of proclaiming Christ "alone"—really, in the full sense of the word, "alone"—and thus daring to trust that he will construct for himself new structures of symbol and doctrine and that he does not need our defensive dogmatic fortresses? Is it not presumptuous to wish to secure and safeguard God by delivering him in protected packages for tropical consumption?

I ask myself seriously whether it is not a judgment upon *us* that ever since the beginning Japanese Christianity has remained constant numerically and has not grown. Can it grow if instead of the living Christ, the living Word, and the living sacraments, we supply the Japanese with these protective straw wrappings, all our confessional hedges (however honorable their origin!), and the whole welter of our communion doctrines?

Perhaps these scars and battle flags of the human struggle for faith are indispensable. If so, the Japanese should set up their own hedges and let their own doctrines develop; we should not sow the mission field with the debris of our own traditions, nor burden hungry souls with our mortgages. They will find it hard enough to carry their own.

The way we have carried on mission work up into this century makes it altogether too hard for the Japanese theologians to arrive at their own elemental encounter with Christ. In the main, they seem to be threshing about with the nuances of Brunner's and Barth's theology, while among the lay Christians—like the miracle of stones turning into bread—again and again we find people making contact with the bedrock of Christianity. How foolish it is to ask whether Christianity is suited to the Japanese! We *ourselves* have not conformed to Christianity, or more correctly, we have not conformed ourselves to the Gospel; instead, we have produced a Christianity which all too often is only a sum of the misunderstandings which have gathered about Jesus Christ. Are we really preaching the Good News, or merely exporting our misunderstandings? What actually are missions? It has been said that in times past there were missionary societies in which pious ladies sewed bathing drawers for the poor natives who went about so

175

shamelessly naked. This—if it is true!—is a trivial variant of what has often occurred on higher levels.

When I talk with present-day missionaries I become convinced that God's promises are coming true, that they are still operative. These men have the earnestness of men under judgment, of men who have been awakened by judgment. Probably all the hard weather that has gone over our planet was necessary to teach us to see the critical point. Therefore we cannot indulge in any supercilious contempt for the failures of previous generations. Our generation has been blessed with new insights. But blessings are never criteria given to us in order to judge the past, but rather incentives for our own repentance. The field is ripe for harvest. No longer dare we trample about in the sown fields.

No matter where we went on this fresh morning, though the sun was already blazing hot, at all the historical sites and beautiful vistas in the parks we saw group after group of children painting. Indeed, we saw them painting at other times, whenever the weather was at all tolerable, and even in the intervals between rainstorms. Adults walked up and down among them, criticizing, stimulating, and encouraging. I jokingly asked whether the children were given nothing but painting instruction in the schools; K. called my attention to the fact this was vacation time. So we stopped at several groups and asked where they came from. In every case it turned out that they were groups of neighborhood children who were being taken on these painting expeditions by various mothers and fathers. What a people! Almost involuntarily K. asked: What can we really bring to them? Haven't we ourselves got plenty to learn from them? They have so many perfect and lovable ways of living. Where else in the world would one find this simple, everyday, taken-for-granted pedagogy? Where else would one find this vital kind of play that gives character to life itself?

Again we were plunged into reflection and self-critical questioning of our way of proclaiming the Gospel. Is it sufficient to preach only faith? Must we not also preach the faith that is *lived,* the faith that stamps and molds our life with one another? We spoke of our danger of falling into a merely dogmatically correct faith, the kind Luther disparagingly called mere "holding something to be true." This kind of "faith" which has been delivered over to the esoteric prevents the Word from becoming flesh in the life of society and community. We spoke again of how the Japanese loves Hilty, who provides him with the wisdom to shape his life in a Christian way, shows him how faith produces a style and atmosphere, and tells him, as he goes into the sanctuary and back into life, how to order his thoughts, how to prepare for sleep, how to eat, drink, and read sensibly, and how to relate himself to the inner-direction and outer-direction of life.

Dietrich Bonhoeffer, too, expressed a demand for this kind of Christian wisdom literature. We have many expositors and preachers but no Solomon. A pitiful remnant of the longing for practical Christian wisdom manifests itself in the way we seek out Christian biographies. In them we have not only the faith that is preached, but faith that has "arrived" in a person's life; there the power of the operative, life-changing (and by no means merely instructive!) Word becomes clear in the way it makes its impact upon a life. But is this enough? Japan is a country which is constantly confronting me with questions.

The fact that this is so is owing not least to the circumstance that I met my friend K. Seldom have I encountered such agreement in interests, questions, and opinions. K. lives in constant concern lest he indirectly communicate Western ideas along with his Message, for in his view everything depends on the Japanese finding their own way to Christ. He and other friends actually grieve over the fact that the Japanese Christians have not yet discovered their own voice, that they still copy Western styles in church buildings, that they sing Western hymns. When a people so gifted in plastic creation remains addicted to imitation in its Christian art, it indicates an alarming failure.

177

Starting with this point of view, these men subject their own activity to relentless criticism—not in the name of any kind of nihilistic pessimism, but rather in the name of Him whom they want to follow. Are we not merely erecting Christian facades? Are we not importing our own "Christian" ideas, are we not giving stones instead of bread?

Again and again the subject of a new incarnation of the Word that must take place in Japan crops up in our conversation. But it is only the unprotected Word that can take on flesh, not the Word shut up in our armor, with which we foolishly and faithlessly try to protect it. The chief danger of missions in its present acute stage lies in the fact that the post-Constantinian church of the West is bringing Christianity to a world which is still definitely living in a pre-Constantinian age, which is therefore living in a stage *before* there is a Christian public, *before* there is a Christian state—or better, a state determined by Christian ideas.

The only way that is indicated for us is obviously the one by which Western missionaries allow the younger churches to take their own initiative, because only they themselves can discover the style and form of life proper for them. The West must help to train native theologians in the West—but really only "help" to do this; the chief task must be done by training centers on the spot.

Perhaps the time of *direct* missionary activity in these countries is past. Perhaps the expulsion of Western missionaries from Red China is an unmistakable handwriting written on the wall of our world by a higher hand.

We may have *been* the teachers of the Good News—but the pupil who always *remains* a pupil gives ill thanks to his teacher. Everything depends upon us Christians helping and allowing one another to "come of age," by exposing others to the hazards of adulthood, and not always practicing a solicitous, monkey-like mother love that allows them to remain children forever. (Actually, the term "monkey-like" does not fit, for in this respect monkeys are far more rational than many specimens of *homo sapiens* and *homo christianus*.) We are Eastern and Western members of the same Body of Christ.

The truth is that the missionary of today no longer has anything to do with the bourgeois prosiness and narrow horizons of the "missionary circle." And yet it would be ungrateful and also unrealistic to overlook the sacrifices and the contributions made by that past epoch in the history of missions. It is true that the term "heathenism," which was then quite generally used, should not have been applied so indiscriminately, and it would be lacking in respect, and in a deeper sense even untrue, rashly to subsume a figure like Hosekei under such a term. And yet this initial, and often naive, stage of mission work included people who possessed what we call a loving heart. And this love—like all love—teaches us to understand. Thus these people knew the anxiety and meaninglessness of the unredeemed life, and with great sacrifice and a devotion that only a few can estimate they sought to be bringers of peace and to dig wells in the wilderness. In any case, the more refined and self-critical knowledge our generation has perhaps arrived at, by way of completely different sufferings, can prosper only upon the soil which they prepared, and none of us are permitted to despise the first sowers.

August 29

After my taking leave of K. and his lovely family, which was not easy for me, the train, traveling at terrific speed, took me to Kobe and my ship. On the way I talked with students from various Asiatic countries who were returning from a university course and who filled the entire car. Sympathetically they sought to help with all the difficulties with my baggage and schedules, and they never grew weary of quizzing me.

Coming home to the ship was a real joy. I was greeted like a lost son. I could hardly get to my cabin, because somebody was always stopping me to tell me about his experience on the ship during the typhoon or asking me about my own experiences. On the coming evenings when we sit around on deck there will be no lack of topics of conversation.

Kobe is hemmed in on one side by a chain of high mountains and on the other by the harbor and ocean. In the afternoon a taxi took me on a steep ride up the Rokko, where I met my friend J. again in his home. He lives on a precipice high above the city. From the terrace where we enjoyed the soothing coolness of the heights the eye ranges far out over the ocean and sees distant ships passing by. I subjected my impressions to comment and correction from this penetrating and critical analyst, and in retrospect I was glad that during these days I had been in such close contact both with Japanese friends and with Western friends who have been in the country for a long time. When the two different ways of seeing things that these two sets of friends provide (and share with me so far as this is possible) are synthesized, they give a more rounded view, and furnish a kind of sharpness in depth to the world through which I have traveled. Even though as a hasty traveler I must remain in the realm of inference, I have been given two geometrical points which at least permit me to surmise the point of intersection.

Today I feel as if I had been here a long time and Japan were greeting and beckoning to me all over again.

From a nearby school came the noise of children playing, the typical international signal that it is recess and time for frolicking in the schoolyard. Subconscious memories made me wait for the shrill bell that would recall the skipping lambs to serious business. But again Japan revealed its charm; instead of the expected bell, there came the sound of a fluted signal— a few bars of a melodic folk song. Instead of alarm whistles and furious bell ringing, just a few notes on the oboe—a poetic caesura in the midst of work, which is not made any the less serious thereby. That is Japan. It is the same on the ships. The various watches are not whistled on and off duty; rather, the foreman blows his oboe, and each group has its special melody. They do not "know their master's voice," but each knows the melody of his group. These sounds are like the smiles of the Japanese that pass over their features even when pain or discomfort or weariness of spirit overtakes them. But the form, which parabolically represents the intrinsic values in life, is maintained under all circumstances. The banner with its message from the deeper levels of existence is kept flying. One must not become the slave of the moment and let himself go.

It would certainly be important, and also rewarding, to reflect upon the secret of form in Japanese life. What do we mean when we say that all this is nothing but politeness? What, then, is politeness? If it were only a superficial convention observed in order to ease interhuman contacts, then it would be as unstable as it is among us and would be disregarded whenever it ceased to "pay." When we find it being maintained in Japan as an almost sacred constant, it is probably because form constitutes—as is actually the case in Greek, Aristotelian usage—the representation of the being itself. By keeping himself in form one preserves his being—and therefore not merely the outward facade!—and holds on to it through everything that is commonplace, trivial, and monotonous, and even through pain. Then none of these can overmaster him. His form is his victory and his self-assertion.

I do not know whether I am right about all this. But instinct suggests it very strongly. My opinion is that all this is not merely a matter of frills on the periphery of everyday life, a bit of ornament to cover up the harshness of life, but rather a matter of the presence of what the Japanese perceives to be the meaning and essence of life.

August 30

We are now at sea again. Never before when we put out to sea did I stand so long on the bridge, looking back until my eyes were quite sore and the last faint glimmer of a beloved country disappeared from view.

Last evening I strolled through the city of Kobe for several hours. In the harbor area and around the nearby railroad station prostitution is unmistakably evident, though it is not so importunate and aggressive as it is in similar European quarters. Here too one perceives the last decaying remnants of a phosphorescing charm. But neither my own observation nor inquiries of others have shown that the prohibition of prostitution and the closing of many establishments a year ago has brought about any essential change.

Inevitably I thought of the similar problems which arose at the time of the American Prohibition. In the place of the demon Alcohol, which had seemingly been driven out, Prohibition let in seven much worse spirits, above all smuggling, corruption, and the whole black crew of underworld organizations. The attempt merely to remove the dark façades, without being able to exterminate the evil at its root, leads to social hypocrisy which must be paid for with heavy penalties. If appearances are not deceiving and the comments of my friends are not completely mistaken, the amount of prostitution has diminished very little, but hygienic control has ceased, and this produces worse problems than before.

I walked through the amusement section of Kobe. Such places seem to have their own peculiar autonomy, so that here as elsewhere one finds certain standard types of game rooms, music boxes, and amusement places. Except that here there is a trace more of gay colorfulness and poetry than in the drizzling rain of Hamburg. But this too may be an illusion evoked not only by the summery warmth and the gleaming white shirts, but also again by the ornamental characters on the signs. The strange script reveals nothing, but rather conceals. The illusion of strangeness which results has the effect of toning down the harshness of the picture.

Up to the last minute today the hucksters' stalls remained on the pier beside our ship. Fabulously cheap optical instruments and luggage offered for sale by courteous and remarkably un-blatant vendors tempted one to look about and take something along. But finally even this charm of farewell came to an end. The siren tooted. The oboe sounded for the last time, calling the harbor workers from the ship, the gangway was drawn in, and the hucksters loaded their treasures on improbably tiny carts.

But how could a departure from Japan be complete with only these prosaic transactions and the business of papers and tickets with the port authorities? Why shouldn't there be a bit of the comforting presence of symbolism here too? And sure enough, there it was, and it touched our hearts. Our friends stood on the pier, holding long colored paper streamers by one end as we held them by the other. We could not rope ourselves together with them and bind ourselves together for a permanent stay, but we maintained the contact as long as possible. As the ship slowly moved out and reached the end of the pier, our friends walked along with it to the extreme end as we continued to hold on to the colored streamers. And finally—it could not be otherwise—one after another the streamers parted and fell into the water. With the broken ends in our hands we continued to wave until we became only far-off points to one another and the ship glided quietly into the broad expanse of the sea.

August 31

Last evening when I entered the dining room for supper, a young man, obviously a passenger who had just got on, came in and started with surprise when he saw me. "Is it really you?" he asked, completely flabbergasted. He was a young physician, Dr. G., from Kirchheim in Swabia. He had attended my lectures when he was at the university and was now utterly perplexed to meet me here, of all places. Never before was the real Swabian dialect, which he fondly cultivates and quite consciously lays on rather thick, so welcome to my ears—for he was a real dyed-in-the-wool Swabian.

The whole evening we warmed up mutual reminiscences of Tübingen, and thus the name of "Aunt Emily," the hostess at the Tübingen students' inn and a real character if there ever was one, cropped up even in these latitudes of the globe.

Dr. G. had a two-year cruise around the world behind him. "How did you get the idea?" I asked him. Again the answer was typically Swabian. "My colleagues, the blockheads, kept yapping that I would never get away from Tübingen because I was only a Swabian. So I thought to myself, now's the time, and in no time at all I was off with my fiddle and bicycle." *

"What, with fiddle and bicycle?" I burst out.

And so he had. With fiddle and bicycle he walked and pedaled all over America, visiting hospitals and acting as an assistant for months at a time, climbing innumerable mountains, traveling all by himself, and being marveled at by the American motorists who stopped to pick up the tramp. Then for a long time he was in Honolulu—the Swabian spirit twinkled in his brown eyes, and one surmised who it was that brought the soft glimmer into them and what it was he left unsaid. Then finally all through Japan. In the evenings he sat on the temple steps in the villages and played Japanese folk songs on his fiddle until the young people gathered about and sang to his accompaniment.

When we expressed some doubt about the whole thing— meanwhile he had attracted a group of attentive listeners around him—he fetched his violin and enchanted us with his playing. He also promised us some Mozart: "I have a whole stack of scores in my bag." This may turn out to be wonderful for us!

He is a nice fellow, with a certain amount of resentment toward things "back home," and he has a bit of the unsteadiness of the Swabian who has broken out of the narrow bounds of his native horizon and had a taste of the world outside. He also has the philosophic vein of the Swabian, and by his seemingly foolish questions — much in him reminds one of the Munich comedian, Valentin—he immediately set off all kinds of furious debates. On the very first evening he demanded that

* These lines hardly catch the flavor of the dialect in the original. (Trans.)

the officers give him instruction in the use of the life-jacket. "You never know, and believe me, I'm going to hang on to my life." This fellow will keep us on our toes, no doubt of that. And this is something we can make good use of on shipboard.

Sitting with him at our table was a young Englishman, a leading Jehovah's Witness, who is on his way to visit his friends in Shanghai. He was visibly a bit suspicious of me because I was a theologian and therefore a subject of the whore of Babylon. Fortunately, however, he has the easy ways of the Anglo-Saxon and is very cheerful and on the whole a nice chap. In any case, he does not have the sectarian gleam in his eye which is characteristic of many of his coreligionists in Germany. Late in the evening we sat beside each other in our deck chairs with our Bibles, but did not speak to each other. Yet it was the same Book in which both of us were absorbed. And somewhere in the infinite—only the Good Lord knows just where!—even these parallels will intersect.

At the other table sat a young married couple. They are both animal trainers in the Hagenbeck Circus, who several months ago had brought a group of trained bears to Japan, exhibiting them at circus performances throughout the country. In Germany they live in a trailer.

Suddenly we were all young boys caught by the romance of the circus, and we pelted them both with questions. What is it like to live in a trailer? What kind of people are performers? How does the organization of a circus work? How are lions, bears, tigers, and horses trained? Material for weeks of talk! And here we have the time for it. And where in the world would anybody like us ever live with lion tamers except on shipboard?

This time the evening refused to come to an end. And even as I slipped into sleep I kept seeing "Doc" sitting on the temple stairs playing the fiddle while Japanese maidens in bright kimonos sang, and heard the music of the circus and smelled its ineffable odors. The nose—I mentioned this before, didn't I? —is the most intimate organ of memory. It preserves the irrational elements of life in the memory. Yes, the nose has a memory. Perhaps it is memory itself, its subtlest level.

September 1

The last of the Japanese islands now lie far behind us. Through the telescope we were able to see their rugged terrain clearly. Mount Asso, the volcano which erupted several months ago, towered up majestically. Our animal trainers had lived there for some time. The people who live there, they said, are a tough and surly breed; most of the Japanese suicide-fliers came from there—trained only to take off, not to land.

The captain again had the floodlights put on the German colors painted on the top deck, for repeatedly American observation planes came over to inspect us. Anybody who is going to Red China, as we are, is a somewhat questionable character and must be kept under scrutiny.

As I lay dozing on a deck chair my mind was immediately filled with memories of Japan. It is remarkable that one problem above all has pursued me ever since our departure: the "galloping" secularization, which quite obviously appears to be pressing toward an acute stage in all religions, in Asia as well as in Europe and the New World. There came into my mind the symptoms of complete indifference among the temple visitors, in both the Buddhist sanctuaries and the Shinto shrines. The shrewd look of business cunning on the faces of the priests lingers in my memory.

(*Later entry:* All this was far surpassed by the commercialism of the priests in Ceylon, especially in Kandy, though there, particularly, there were still monastic hermits who exhibited great power. I actually saw priests with the faces of gangsters, in whom not a trace of any kind of vocation could be seen and whose crafty money-madness was given a touch of the sinister by their smooth-shaven skulls and lack of eyebrows. Such a secularized "priest-look" has something oddly penetrating about it. Here religion appeared not only to be dead but to have passed over into demonic forms of decay.)

Is the era of the "religions" really coming to an end? Is the Bolshevistic doctrine in Russia and China perhaps right in calling this tradition outworn and ripe for extinction?

These Communist ideologies possess a highly developed instinct for spotting any kind of fissure in any kind of structure. They usually do not make frontal attacks upon sound and inconspicuous organisms; rather, they provide fertile soil for germs already present—they are like vultures who prey on the cadavers of the past. So in the area of religion, quite apart from the Communist *theory* of religion, they would say that they have discovered the germs of self-disintegration and would base their prognosis that "the era of religion is ended" not only upon their ideology, but also upon empirical observations.

It is such reflections as these that make me realize how important has been the thought we have given in the last decades to the fact that the Gospel is not intended to be simply "religion" and how important is our unwillingness to apply the term "religious instruction" to Christian instruction. The fact is, of course, that the Gospel seeks out man at every level and stage of his historical possibilities; it seeks him out in the structure of his religion and on the icy flats of his nihilisms; it seeks him out in his belief, his superstition, and his unbelief.

And yet I am afraid of the false security that may be inherent in this thought. I believe that for not a few of us Christian theologians it can be misused as a dialectical trick. We see the downfall of the world of religion and then quickly seek to produce an alibi by saying it was not our world anyhow, in the delusive hope of thereby getting hold of a shibboleth to prevent our own end. What is required here is the most alert kind of self-criticism. An ark which will float upon the floods of a passing world cannot be carpentered together with the faulty beams of a few trick ideas. The Noah who survives the Flood must be able to believe. He cannot invent and construct the instrument of deliverance, but must allow it to be bestowed upon him. Only a miracle, which he himself is powerless to perform, can avert the disaster.

187

And are we not proceeding at full speed—this is the depressing thought that comes out of the honest self-criticism I have referred to—in this very attempt to make a religion out of the Gospel? Are we not doing this despite everything we assert theoretically and theologically? Are we not taking flight—this figure of speech simply urges itself upon me—from the actualizing Message into the liturgical operatics of worship?—and therefore into a formalistic antiquarianism which does not lead to direct encounters with the reality of God, to an acceptance of the Word in our actual life, but at best produces merely secondhand sentiments adopted from others and experiences that go no deeper than the mind?

Under the compulsion to pursue these reflections further, in these last days some instinct impelled me to read the hymns which have been produced in our own time, some of which have also found their way into the hymnbook of the church. I must admit that many of them contain the substance of faith and that not infrequently the comforting biblical thoughts concerning sin and forgiveness, suffering and eternal redemption have found an expression that deserves to be called credible and convincing. They endeavor throughout to achieve a chorale style of statement which by its objectivity is something other and more than a mere lyrically devout statement.

For the first time, however, it struck me—doubtless against the background of my recent experiences—that only the classic themes of Reformation hymnology are dealt with and that even this is done in forms of rhyme and meter which not infrequently appear to be consciously archaic. They have a patina which perhaps comes not from a natural, but rather from an artificial, process of oxidation, a labored process of poetic chemistry.

Perhaps I am doing these hymns an injustice, but I find it difficult to resist this suspicion, for I miss in them certain themes of our own time. But should these not appear, if these hymns are to be genuine poetic "objectifications" of contemporary Christian existence?

Where in these hymns do we find the themes that have been

dealt with by existential philosophy, which because it dealt with them made itself the spokesman of certain fundamental attitudes of our age? Where, for example, do we find these hymns dealing with the anxiety, the fear of being swallowed up in unauthentic, impersonal being, in the anonymous collective? Where does the theme of the anxiety of life (as distinguished from the mere anxiety of guilt) appear at all? Where is the experience of nature, in the way *we* experience it today? (We shall always cherish Paul Gerhardt's hymn *"Geh' aus mein Herz und suche Freud' "* * with delight and gratitude, just as we shall always admire Mozart, but must we not also catch something of the tone of our *own* times? Is it not possible that the depths from which we cry have grown deeper? May it not be that we have a longer road to travel to get out of our own peculiar deserts and delights? Where is the poet who takes us by the hand as we go through *these* particular deserts?) Where in our hymns is there any mention of our mechanized life and today's workaday world? Where is there any consideration at all of our broken relationship to work, an attitude which in so many areas delivers us over to meaninglessness, because work, instead of being a calling *and* a curse, has in many areas of life become a soulless, indifferent performance?

All honor to Johann Hermann's *"Gib, dass ich tu' mit Fleiss, was mir zu tun gebühret"!* † How much poorer we should be if we could not sing and pray what that hymn says, and says in those words! But again the question troubles me: when *our* generation sings songs about labor, are they not written in a different key? In any case, the Bolsheviks have tried to find their own key; they have songs about "Tractor Betty" and similar horrors. But, after all, they are their *own* horrors. Are not our songs, whether in the province of the sacred or the profane, in danger of losing relevance to our inner situation?

* A hymn that exults in the glory and beauty of nature (to my knowledge, never translated into English). (Trans.)

† George Herbert's hymn, "Teach me, my God and King, In all things thee to see, And what I do in anything, To do it as for thee" would be an equivalent. (Trans.)

Where is there any mention of the theme of freedom, the misinterpretation of freedom as mere freedom from restraint, and the purification of freedom in mature acceptance of responsibility as children of God? The poem "Freedom, which I love" * is no longer adequate even in the secular area. Many people would much rather sing, "My joy is to be a functionary, merely to carry out orders." Where is anything said about the curse of dehumanized organization, the sterility of welfare which is loveless because it is impersonal, the terrors of meaninglessness?

Whole hosts of questions rise up around me with couched lances, ready to spring upon me in the quietness of these hours on shipboard. During the rush of everyday life they lie hidden in their dark caves, but here they suddenly emerge. However true it may be that all of these themes of possible hymns are related to original sin and therefore can be theologically subsumed under the general theme of forgiveness, must we not *show* people how we arrive at this theme and then also, if it is a spiritual artery vital to life itself, *sing* about it? Must our message not be particularized, since God is always a God of "minute details"? Of what use are the pious conventional ways of expression if a person can go only three-quarters of the way toward comprehending that you are actually dealing with *his* particular, private predicament and his antennae do not even reach far enough to understand this three-quarters? Should the poet not really represent the church today, and therefore should he not do *more* than merely reproduce the venerable texts of early generations? Is he to remain on the level of antiquarian imitation and repetition? Must the poet not do what the preacher and also the "pray-er" must, namely, preach in *our* situations and cry out of *our* depths? In our hymns we act as if there were no prayers except liturgical prayers, as if there were no free prayers, prayers which are improvised groan-

* *"Freiheit, die ich meine,"* first line of poem on liberty by Max von Schenkendorf (1783-1817). (Trans.)

190

ings, yearnings, entreaties, and thanksgivings that come immediately out of our momentary fears or joys.

As I turned these melancholy questions over in my mind, the force of them began to increase. Again I thought of the "topical" songs of the Bolsheviks. Are we not making it much too easy for ourselves when we simply pour contempt on the barbaric lack of taste in this Communist doggerel and reassure ourselves by maliciously pointing out that this is what always comes out when poetry is opportunistically written to order and that poetry simply cannot be produced by Stakhanovite compulsion? May it not be that here we are confronted with something *genuine* in a distorted form and that Bolshevism is in a very hidden way passing a judgment upon us? But if this is true, then we must admit that we have failed tremendously and face up to an alarming contradiction between what we have recognized to be right and tried to practice in our preaching (namely, the obligation to make our expression of the Message actual, topical, and relevant to the situation) and, on the other hand, what the modern additions to our hymnal very largely do *not* do.

I feel that this analysis is confirmed by what I read in the Christian poems written during the war and the bombings. Here we find the apocalyptic terrors of the situation and also the very special consolations of God. Here everything is instinct with the sense of contemporary existence; here one begins to sense the direction which the modern hymn must take.

So I am troubled by the question—without really knowing how to answer it—of whether our church hymns and poetry are not pretty much like the neo-gothic churches of the turn of the century, employing venerable styles—forms which at one time were true, but which now provide us only with crumbs of what is left of that truth. We would thus appear to be taking refuge in a religious structure of the past, and it may be, as Bonhoeffer said, that without our knowing it our faith may be turning into a "religion," a bomb-shelter of the past, in which we take refuge because we are no longer meeting our own time in faith.

Hence my fear that we may be taking too easy a way out when we say that the Gospel is not a religion and therefore will not, like religions, be sucked into the vortex of global secularization. It is quite possible that we shall be involved in a first act during which our faith disintegrates into a religion (which is the illegitimate successor of faith), and that this will be followed by a second act in which this religion is undermined by secularism. Then the "profane" would go on growing, while the "sacred" would revive for one more flash of illumination only to fall back into embers and ashes.

I know, of course, that it is not sufficient merely to see and to state these ideas. To do this could mean that we would never get beyond analysis and thus would become sterile. And, necessary as analyses of our culture and situation may be, they have never yet been of any help, and in Germany the very excess of them has even harmed us. Perhaps we still have not discovered the way to preach and write for our time. Our lips may still be sealed. But we ought at least to pray that they may be opened. Love for those who are as sheep without a shepherd and who do not understand our code language should make our hearts burn.

If we had this love, we would at least find a few poor, stammering words. Perhaps they might not even be our own words, but actually borrowed from our fathers. But then at least we would realize how poverty-stricken we are and learn to rely upon the blessing that is promised to those who come with empty hands. Then we would know that we should have to go on speaking with borrowed words until our own were bestowed upon us.

But I perceive very little of this godly resignation (which corresponds to what Paul calls "godly grief") in the liturgies and religious poetry of our time. I cannot discover in them anything but plunderings from the past and, not infrequently, adornment with borrowed plumes. We are driven by the fateful urge to be rich, and thus turn out to be snobs who are proud of their tradition. We repress the very thing in which the blessing might lie hidden: our poverty. Like the prodigal son, we go spending and squandering the inheritance from the fathers, with this difference, that we do so, not in the far country, but in our own church home. We must first learn to be poor, in order that God may be able again to say to us, "Blessed are the poor in spirit."

Mainland China

September 2

Early morning. I am still thinking of yesterday, Sunday, when all these thorny questions descended upon me and I was obliged to write them down. It was certainly not the weather that provoked them. Yesterday's sunshine is still burning in my skin today. It was much cooler than before, the air light and invigorating, as on an autumn Mediterranean cruise. For the first time in a long time we did not avoid the hostile rays of the tropic sun but again basked in the sunshine. And despite all the melancholy reflections that troubled me, I was still conscious of the glory and the joy of light.

On Sundays I greatly miss the service of worship. Dr. G., however, was good enough to consent to my suggestion that we give at least a little Sunday spirit to the morning by playing some chorales on his violin. The others listened too and seemed to be grateful for it.

Five in the afternoon. A good two hours ago the anchor was dropped. We are lying off Taku. The pilot, Red Chinese commissars with red armbands, and other officials have come on board in order to begin the expected but unpredictable process of checking passports, etc.

We passengers have been required to remain in our cabins. The crew is penned up on the boat deck. The ship has become as quiet as a churchyard.

The stranger is in our midst, and the unaccustomed lack of all activity is oppressive. Only the sunny brightness of the day somewhat alleviates the pressure that lies upon everyone. Even from the boat deck hardly a sound can be heard except the quiet hum of voices. This is completely different from what usually happens when young men of the crew's sort are together in such numbers.

All cameras and telescopes must be kept in our cabins for the whole time we are here. We received elaborate forms on which we were required to enter all our optical instruments in the utmost detail: brand names, factory numbers, and separate entries for exposed and unexposed films. We are therefore limited to our natural eyes and will have to entrust to our memory what we would otherwise record in pictures.

The agency office brought some good news for me: some basic preparations have been made in various quarters to make it possible for me to get to Peiping. The captain, who is always so kindly concerned about my wishes, has received the same information.

Six-thirty in the evening. We have just put in at the port of Tientsin. Standing on the pier, strangely reserved and motionless, are several families who are obviously awaiting our Chinese passenger. I have written nothing about him because ever since we left Kobe, where he came on board, he has scarcely left his cabin at all. He has avoided all contact—to be sure, he may have been hindered by the fact that he speaks only Chinese.

Hardly had the ship been made fast when the waiting Chinese were driven from the pier, leaving behind only commissar types in characteristic Communist uniforms. Every once in a while they smile at each other. How gratifying it is to see even this paltry sign of human feeling!

In remarkable contrast to the silence and desolation of the pier—how different is this reception from the one that would occur anywhere else!—is the bellowing of the loudspeakers, broadcasting a succession of whining, yowling Chinese records and propaganda slogans lashing the people forward. It is true that I do not know Chinese, but I know this sound. It is the same in all totalitarian states.

Likewise I can read the mammoth red sign with its strange characters just opposite the ship—though I do not know the language, by a perverse Pentecostal miracle, I know what the sign says: "We fight for socialism, for peace and freedom," or "The wheels must roll for victory." We are quite familiar with these placards with their uniform slogans, having seen them beyond the Brandenburg Gate. My interpretation hardly requires the confirmation it has received through the Chinese agent, who has just translated the message for me at my request. He complied with my request, incidentally, with the air of a friendly, neutral service department employee, without any sign of aloofness or undertone of irony. As we already know from reading the literature, Chinese communism controls men's words and actions; it appears also to control their gestures and their unconscious minds. Even this young man betrayed no attitude, though his face did not have the rigidity of the commissars' but was rather quite cheerful and relaxed.

We have now been required to come back to our cabins for further examination. I brought back with me the rather somber rumor which is going about among the crew, namely, that the tension over Quemoy, which is now being bombarded daily, is coming to a head. "We'll be lucky if we ever get out of here," said one of them. During the waiting period I have read books twenty-two and twenty-three of the *Odyssey*. The story of Odysseus' revenge upon the wooers of Penelope, their torture and death, is told there with gruesome convincingness of style. Involuntarily one gets the pleasant feeling of having been shot in the neck.

Seven-thirty P.M. The commissar, a very young fellow, just arrived, with a companion who was quite obviously an interpreter, for examination of passports. He looked grim and hard-bitten. An Asiatic face the like of which I had not seen before —the chemistry of communism had bleached every bit of laughter and charm from his face. The impression his death-mask face made was accentuated by the fact that the man did not utter a word or even touch his hand to his cap or make any gesture whatsoever. The interpreter merely demanded the passport. I handed it over to him, and the commissar proceeded to compare the entries with his list, which was written in Chinese. He then handed back the passport without a word and slowly walked out. His face was so impenetrable that I did not know whether I was dealing with hatred, indifference, or suspicion.

Eight-thirty P.M. We are still in our cabins. Nor have we as yet had anything to eat. The ship remains quiet; no stevedores can be seen. No sound indicates that the hatches have been opened, but the passing of inspection groups and alien voices can still be heard. At the beginning of this voyage I wrote in my diary that all of life is in a sense a voyage. But here one could say that life is nothing but one unending inspection and submission to inspection.

Ten P.M. At supper, which was not served until an hour ago, we heard the details of what has happened in the last several hours. In the cabin of the second engineer, a grand old seadog, hung a pre-war map of the world on which he had marked all the voyages he had made. The police were snooping about in the crew's quarters, even inspecting their private property—this had never happened before—and they discovered the map. Furious with rage, a functionary pointed to a place that still indicated the boundaries of the Japanese occupation zones. The map had to be torn into pieces at once. The commissar insisted that the ship's large flag chart also be removed immediately. The lynx-eyed fellow had discovered that a small space on the chart included the flag of Formosa.

September 3

Noon. The night was abominable. Since we are lying starboard at the pier, the two windows of my cabin are exposed to the glaring lights of the warehouses and, worse yet, to the howling sounds of the gigantic loudspeakers distributed about the whole harbor area. The same thing obtains in the city, we are told by the first ones to return from procuring supplies. The propaganda whip constantly keeps whistling down upon the plodding coolies. "Big Brother" is always standing behind them. We hardly trusted our ears when, among the urging, appealing, and whipping slogans, suddenly "Annie from Tharau" * came roaring over the air, though it was robbed of all its tenderness and reminded us more of a bawling fishwife. The stepped-up tempo along with the volume gave the impression that they were furiously providing poetry "beyond the required norm." The loudspeaker began its howling today at seven o'clock in the morning. First on the program was something like morning setting-up exercises. A Chinese businessman told us after breakfast that each morning he had to stop his business as soon as the radio gymnastics began and go out into the street with all his employees to take part in the exercises.

For the moment I have partially escaped this onslaught upon the ears. I have found a place on the ship where an obviously defective ventilator, badly in need of grease, makes a clanking noise. I am sitting as close to it as possible, and it is really wonderful to be released from the premeditated roaring of the loudspeaker by an unpremeditated mechanical racket.

At breakfast we heard that the poor man whose map was torn up last evening had been subjected to another trial. After midnight, just as he was about to fall asleep, he was roused by the stealthy opening of his cabin door and the light this let in. The Chinese commissar slipped in without knocking, felt about with his hand on the empty wall where the map had been hanging, and then left the room as quietly as he had come in. Obviously he thought it possible that the German seadog had pasted the pieces together again and put them back on the wall.

Shortly before noon a kind of Intourist agent, an alert young Chinese, came on board to secure our passports and inquire about our plans for sight-seeing. He said he would secure the necessary stamps from the authorities. "Of course you can go to Peiping," he replied when I asked him, "but it may take

* "Ännchen von Tharau," popular German folk song. (Trans.)

some time." Mr. H., who is familiar with the whole business, said, "These are the usual delaying tactics. They never say no, but the permission will come about an hour before the train leaves."

Well, we shall see. I am somewhat skeptical, for in the spring, when my plans for the trip became known, the Young Men's Christian Association in Germany had suggested to its branch organization in Peiping that they invite me to give a lecture. At first they had replied with delight, and they had immediately made the necessary applications to the authorities. At their request, I had even furnished them with a detailed list of my dates. But after that they were silent; only later, and only after repeated requests for clarification, did they indicate very indirectly that, unfortunately, the arrangement was impossible. Though they gave no reasons, the difficulty was clear to anyone who could read between the lines: the authorities had vetoed it. Since I am often attacked by the East German press, it is obvious that the authorities had made inquiries in Pankow [East Berlin] and received a negative report. In any case, they know precisely who I am and by which ship and at what time I shall appear in such and such a port. Hence, the matter of permission to land looks fishy. If they have a quarrel to pick with me, I hope my fellow passengers will not suffer because of it.

Five in the afternoon. The agent has come back. The authorities have refused to stamp any of the passports; no passenger is permitted to land, and thus only the crew is "free." The captain took it harder than we did. He was kind enough to say, "Then I'll stay here too." If only the loudspeaker would be quiet for a moment.

September 4

Morning. Last evening as we were strolling on deck we noticed a tremendous string of lights in the distance, consisting of thousands of electric light bulbs. It could not very well be a city, but what was it? None of us had ever seen such a display before.

As luck would have it we were able to ask the agent who happened aboard. What he reported is amazing: a gigantic dam is being built over yonder to separate the salt water from the fresh.

"So that's where the people are who should be here loading the ship," said one of us. The cargo officer is very unhappy that so few work gangs are available and that despite the industry of the few that are working we are making such slow progress.

"By no means," said the Chinese. "On the contrary, there are hundreds of thousands of voluntary laborers who have offered their services." This was the case, he said, all over the country, and the reason construction was going forward so rapidly.

Naturally, we questioned him further: "How do they recruit the laborers, then, and what kind of people are they?"

They are, he told us, professors (he smiled at me knowingly), students, business people, clerks, factory workers, and functionaries. Lists are handed around in factories, places of business, and universities, and anyone who wishes to volunteer for such work can sign up.

"During regular working periods?" we asked.

"Oh, no," he replied, "during vacations, naturally. Everybody signs up. The only exceptions are special cases where there is justification."

"Aha, voluntary compulsion . . . we know," interjected one of the group.

The good man refused to be ruffled, however, except that he let us know where he himself stood, which is to say he was all in favor of it. (Yet one never knows whether this is his real opinion.) He said very simply that it was really voluntary. "These people receive no wages, they must even bring their own food with them. And besides, you would be amazed at the spirit they show. Good comradeship prevails. They sing and laugh while they are working."

An amazing conversation. I hope very much that I run into some others whom I can ask about this matter of control and supervision.

Three in the afternoon. I find myself in a curious state. Here I am under house arrest, experiencing China as seen through cabin windows and through the medium of those who come in from the outside, the officials who come snooping about the ship—those who will talk to us.

A strange, Homeric experience, to sit here watching the walls of Troy! But the various little stones in a mosaic form a picture nevertheless, and a lot can be seen through a hole in the hedge. The general atmosphere and temper of things adds its contribution to the picture. No newspaper article at home, no matter how well informed, can provide this commentary.

To be sure, I must remain self-critical enough to be aware of the possibilities of error in this view: the "psychology of the interned prisoner" and the constant threat of "barbed-wire blues" may cause me to lapse into a very one-sided perspective, especially since the sailors too are dull and depressed. They have no diversion at all of the kind that is usually sought and found in the ports, and they are ill-humored and inclined to be sulky. I must guard myself against transferring this unusually gray atmosphere to our picture of China. If just *once* I could meet a decent sort of official so that I could prove to myself that I was willing to be self-critical!

September 5

Eleven P.M. How unexpectedly rich the rest of the day turned out to be! I had hardly finished making yesterday afternoon's entry when the captain sent word inviting me to come to his room. Three German businessmen and the director of a Goethe Institute had fought their way through to see me. They had come from Hong Kong and were staying for several days in Peiping and Tientsin in order to visit an exhibition. Two of them have lived in China for decades and speak Chinese perfectly; they are thoroughly cultured and open-minded men who know the country and the people, good observers, and obviously men who have a sense of the deeper intellectual things. I shall not set down in detail the adventures they went through before they finally obtained permission to meet me on the ship, or rather "to visit the captain." Unfortunately, they had to leave everything behind that they wanted to bring along to show me. It was too dangerous even to bring along a program of the exhibition to the ship.

Naturally, I immediately asked them whether the story about the string of lights was true. It is. Within the last few days they had driven for miles along new railway embankments where people were working in similar fashion.

I asked especially about the communes, which are a kind of institutional symptom of the accelerated transition into communism. What interests me in this is less the economic than the human side.

On this point I get the impression that the primary struggle is over the family, because it is the intimate sphere within which uncontrollable resistance to the new regime could occur most easily and the older generation could influence the younger. Naturally, the reason is never directly stated, but rather in the way the *Red Banner* recently put it: the family is "a wretched prison cell for the workers." Above all, women must be freed from the serfdom of housework and incorporated in the production process.

Characteristically, in genuine Marxist fashion, tools of family living are being taken away from the home: collectivized sewing rooms and laundries force families to do their chores outside the home. In many areas cooking pots by the thousands have been taken away from the people in order to force them to use the communal kitchens. Furthermore, the children, the determinative vital cells of the family, are being claimed by the state, taken away from the parents, and lodged in educational collectives (something like kindergartens and boarding schools). The radical abolition of private property must inevitably dissolve all family ties. The transition from socialism to communism, which the Chinese regime, unlike the Soviet Union, is already undertaking, leads not only to the step-by-step liquidation of ownership of the means of production but also to the gradual liquidation of hitherto existing corporate and private holdings. Bedding and clothing, a few fruit trees and chickens, and perhaps a clock are the only relics of private property still permitted.

Our conversation increasingly took on a minor key. Once criticism begins, it very quickly tends to become a riot of criticism, the way the negative always seems to be subject to the law of accumulation. In situations like this we need to be careful not to lose our clear-sightedness. So it was almost a relief to me when the man from the Goethe Institute blew the whistle on this trend of criticism and said:

"It would be unfair simply to let this thesis concerning the regime's hostility to the family stand, without any qualification. Every thesis gains meaning only as one sees the significance of its antithesis. And here we must say quite simply that Mao is not against the family as such, but primarily against the family clique. By that I mean the dictatorship of the head of the family. One can hardly realize the extent of his authority when one judges by Western standards. Naturally, Mao knows very well that he can no longer fully win over the older generation. But then Mao must break their authority in order to prevent them from removing the young people from his influence. Consequently, his opposition to the family has no primary connection with communism at all, but is based upon a simple political consideration. In the second place, what I have called the 'family clique' has actually played a devastating role in Chinese society: every process of life became a play of 'relationships.' One can see that when such significance is attached to the family and the family group that a state administration cannot function, it is a source of prejudice and corruption." This sounded reasonable to me, and the other two gentlemen agreed.

Naturally, here again I threw into the discussion my old

question of how it can be explained that the Chinese, who are stamped by a millenniums-old tradition, should have subjected themselves so compliantly and unresistingly to such a revolution of society and mind.

This time I received from Mr. N. a thoroughly reasoned answer based upon incisive knowledge and profound emotional penetration. I therefore immediately recorded an extract of his account, which was given added weight by the concurring testimony of the others.

In the first place, said Mr. N., there are certain definite *historical* facts that help to explain the reaction of the Chinese people: the end of the unimaginable corruption of the former system of government, the improvement of the living standards of certain classes of people, the establishment of China's international position as a great power, which gave them a sense of national pride, the attack upon and fairly successful elimination of catastrophic floods and famine, and other similar things. All these things, said Mr. N., certainly produced a certain popularity for the new regime, although they do not provide a complete answer to the question of how a voluntarily accepted revolution of the Chinese *mind* or *soul* could be accomplished.

To explain the latter event, Mr. N. put forward this thesis. There is one thing the Chinese—for all his eminent intellectual ability—does not possess or possesses only in small degree: perhaps our word "character" comes closest to describing the deficiency. An ethical act, like those of neighborly love, for example, is something generally alien to him, especially if it involves personal disadvantages. He is, so to speak, a constitutional opportunist.

In reply to our questions, which were critical of this opinion, Mr. N. himself felt the need to qualify this wholesale judgment more precisely and admitted that of course it would be wrong to characterize the Chinese as utterly "unethical." However, with them—and even in Confucius!—ethics does not even begin until its expediency becomes evident. The principles and maxims for an ethical order are not laid down for their own sake on the basis of an ethical imperative, but are rather intended primarily as a means to a smoothly running social life. It must be admitted, he said, that in this sense they have been wisely devised and that they have proved successful in practice. But, after all, the intention is still determinative in ethical problems. And as far as intention is concerned, it may be quite clearly stated that for the Chinese the ethical question "Is it right?" is subordinate to the pragmatic question "What will come of it?"

Pursuing this further, Mr. N. stated emphatically that he had hardly ever seen a genuine friendship in our sense between a Chinese and a European or between two Chinese, even though some Europeans believe they have had such friendships or observed them among others (Pearl S. Buck!). By genuine friendship Mr. N. means a relationship in which one person will stand up for another unconditionally, regardless of the consequences. "I know many 'old China hands,'" he said, "who swore by the loyalty of their old servants, who frequently had been with them for decades. I do not know a single one of them who was not disillusioned in this matter after the Reds took over the power, when it really became a matter of life and death. How often it happened that cooks and houseboys regarded as pillars of loyalty after serving for forty years turned out, when the test came, to be foul denouncers. I have never been able to understand the violent condemnatory reaction of those who were thus disappointed; it doubtless shows that they never understand the Chinese mind at all."

Mr. N. saw further confirmation of his theory in the complete absence of any love for animals in China. Any deeper sense of communication with the creaturely world is also lacking. In marked contrast to the Japanese, from childhood on the Chinese are allowed to torment animals in every possible way, whether for pure pleasure or for the purpose of producing subtle changes in the taste of animals when they are eaten. What is lacking is the ability to sympathize, the capacity for entering into the feelings of another creature or another human being. Everybody who has lived in China is familiar with the sight of the pedestrian or bicycle-rider who has been run over, writhing in pain in the street while an interested, gaping, but otherwise completely passive circle of curious people gathers about him. Nobody pitches in and lends a hand—this is the "affair of the authorities." Besides, the person who gives help runs the risk of being held liable by the relatives or survivors of the injured person.

This far-reaching lack of any "reverence for life" provides, according to Mr. N., the key to the question asked at the beginning—the question how this "total reversal of mind" among the Chinese could have been possible. "Actually, it was not even necessary to reverse these minds, at all, for there was no basic anticommunistic or antidictatorial attitude to begin with, in any case not in a degree that could have fostered any considerable resistance to realistic and opportunistic thinking. One might go further and say that there was no basic mental attitude at all, but only what to our minds would be an incredibly soft mass which, under certain conditions, could be rather quickly and easily pressed into desired forms; possessors of those minds were always ready to sell small bits of them at suitable prices."

The Chinese therefore remained an individualist who behaved in a passive, meditative fashion as long as it was impressed upon him that this was worth aspiring after and as long as it appeared expedient to him. But he became a demonstrative and marching activist as soon as he recognized that his life would become intolerable if he rebelled and refused to cooperate.

Mr. N. took the position that in China co-operation is "indivisible." The idea of a "seeming fellow-traveler" who has his inner reservations is non-existent here. Such an attitude would be very quickly detected, since every Chinese is a skillful psychologist and almost instinctively divines the thoughts of his fellow men. Nor is there really any room here for the "oppositionist" type. True, there have been many revolutions

206

and revolutionaries in China, but only when there was a calculated chance of success. A true martyr as well as a pure idealist would be essentially un-Chinese; if there were one, he would be regarded by his fellow men as a blockhead or as just unlucky.

In the course of the conversation Mr. N. moved toward increasingly recondite interpretations, which inevitably became more conjectural. And I record this conversation, not because I am convinced of every statement—it would be pretentious of me to presume to make a judgment upon it—but rather because there is something plausible in the argument, because I sensed the thoroughness of Mr. N.'s analyses, and because, while the other participants in the conversation made supplementary and affirmative comments, they never really took any critical position.

Mr. N. believes that the ultimate, and not the least important stone in the mosaic of Chinese re-education is furnished by that peculiar feature of the Chinese character, the talent and the love for play-acting. The Chinese are "the most magnificent play-actors in the world," who are "constantly playing themselves. Yesterday they played the traditional Confucian oriental; today they are playing the co-ordinated Marxist. In both cases they are playing themselves. In both cases, paradoxically, they are at the same time true and untrue."

One of the other gentlemen threw in an anecdote that illustrated what was just said. Recently a Lloyd captain asked a curio dealer in Shanghai, whom he had known for decades, how the Chinese could stand the continuing indoctrination meetings, demonstrations, government interference in private affairs, etc. The Chinese answered very briefly: "We are in ecstasy!" This reply, the narrator believed, is symbolic; today all China is "in ecstasy"; they are overacting, and outdoing themselves in going along with the parade. The will to be individual human beings, to be themselves, does not exist; they are playing a magnificent performance, even though, as Mr. N. quite rightly said, they "are playing themselves."

207

"For me," summed up Mr. N., "that is also the answer to your question whether Chinese communism is a permanent institution or whether one day it will disappear. It will disappear if ever the 'stage-management' should fail, if another play should turn up in the repertory that seems to the actors to promise more success and offers a higher price for the soul, or if the new stage-manager removes their fear of the old stage-manager, or if he himself is able to inspire them with a still greater fear."

Before my visitors took leave, the director of the Goethe Institute posed a final thoughtful question: whether the present system might not—perhaps for the first time in Chinese history —release something like a character-building impulse, and whether, through the importation of an originally European set of ideas like Marxism and Leninism, certain remnants of European humanism might not infiltrate the Chinese mind. True, these remnants are distorted, but nevertheless in the education of the youth and the building up of the army there has been an appeal to certain elements of comradeship which move in the direction of a kind of helpfulness and neighborly love. ("Do they really mean 'neighbor' here?" I interjected briefly at this point. But it was too late to go into this question.) It is true that the accident victim is still idly stared at by the passers-by, but he is transported to the hospital much more quickly than before. "These 'un-Chinese' by-products of Marxist practice could cause (of course only among the youth and the coming generations) certain mutations of the Chinese soul, which in turn—and this would be even more paradoxical —could one day be dangerous to the system itself."

It was an exceedingly rich conversation this afternoon brought me. Never before have I been so much impressed by the enormous ramifications and intricate complexity of this problem as I was this afternoon. House arrest on board ship has brought me to several facts and questions it certainly would have taken me months to arrive at by my own experience.

To be sure, there may well be differences of opinion about

one point or another. When one is dealing with such a far-reaching and complicated subject as this, there can never be complete clarity. For me, much more important than the question of individual analyses is the fact that I have been introduced to the crucial approaches to the question by intelligent and self-critical men. After all, the dignity of good conversation lies in its teaching us to ask the right questions.

Perhaps I shall have no experiences at all to record during our stay in China—only conversations. Nor would that be the worst thing that could happen. Let us hope, too, that the right partners will continue to show up!

September 6

As I read and write I keep looking out of the cabin windows. The noise of the loudspeakers no longer disturbs me so much as it did before. The funniest thing I see is the donkey carts loaded with sacks for our cargo. Behind each donkey a sack is fastened to catch the droppings. This saves street cleaning. And besides, not a drop of manure must be lost. A remarkable combination of primitive times and rationality!

Nine-thirty in the evening. The cargo we anticipated early this morning, expecting then to forsake this dismal port in the afternoon, still has not arrived. Whether the cargo comes in the next few hours or not, it has begun to rain, the weather forecast for the next several days sounds rather bad, and loading is out of the question. Our hatches have already been closed down—also those on the feeder ship lying alongside of us. The coolies have disappeared. My fellow passengers and the crew have fled from the gloom to their bunks. Only the Red commissar stands unmoved in the rain, keeping watch over the ship. I am reading once more Adalbert Stifter's *Nach-sommer*. What a tremendous gap between these two worlds!

September 7

Seven-thirty in the morning. Contrary to all expectation, we are now making progress. The cargo arrived around midnight.

209

The weather has improved; the sun is shining but it is not too hot. And now we are off! The captain has just brought us this good news. In the adjoining cabin I hear Dr. G. playing the violin. For our departure from this inhospitable harbor he is playing "Now thank we all our God."

Six o'clock in the evening. When the captain dropped in to see us at afternoon coffee, Peter, the nice little steward, handed him a telegram. The captain rose quickly and went up to the bridge. We had some misgivings, and a short time later we learned that typhoon "Helen," which had been lingering in the distance for some time, was expected to be in precisely the area toward which we were heading by morning. It had changed its previous direction; therefore the surprise.

The captain wants by all means to avoid this rendezvous with the wind, and therefore he has ordered the ship turned in an opposite course. We shall attempt to run away from the typhoon. So again we are cruising, though at half-speed, in the direction of our "beloved" Tientsin. The barometer recording morale on board took a nose-dive. I find that even Adalbert Stifter cannot entirely engage my attention.

Despite our flight from "Helen," she has nevertheless hit us with her outrunners. The ship is rolling very considerably in the swell. Everything movable on board is again securely lashed down, seats and tables are screwed fast and the table-cloths have been sprinkled with water to keep the chinaware from sliding off when we eat.

We cherish the godless wish that the typhoon, in order that it may accomplish *some* good (not for the shipping company, but for us ordinary human beings), will sweep overboard the great heap of sacks filled with stinking naphthalene piled on the deck. To get rid of my exasperation I am going to stop reading after dinner and do my wash in the laundry. This is undeniably meaningful, and therefore a consoling thing to do in the midst of a crazy world.

September 8

Forenoon. We kept on our return course until seven o'clock this morning, so we have lost another day. Even so, we are running at half-speed, because the weather reports are conflicting. Last night the wind blew furiously. The swell, however, was moderate; the massive rainfalls doubtless calmed the seas to some extent.

I occupied myself with some rather unpleasant reading— a book on the history of the German Church Struggle. Hardly a word in this account about the power of preaching and the ongoing of the kingdom of God in that time of trial. Church history becomes a chronicle of scandal and disintegrates into backstairs gossip. In a macabre way we are told only of those who did foolish things and of those—including the author— who were right in the end. The micrometric screw of scholarship goes on turning in the void.

I preferred "Helen" to this. I exposed myself to her breath and let her blow away the dreary spook. Why is it that I so often have such a hard time with theologians even though every fiber of my being is bound up with theology?

September 9

Forenoon. Almost the whole time, we have kept at half-speed because Shanghai was still reporting the wind velocity at force 12. Besides, a telegram arrived from the agency stating that the harbor was completely filled up and that we should anchor outside and resign ourselves to waiting as long as six days. A fine prospect! On top of this, it is raining incessantly, and in torrents. Then, too, there were two alarms because the electricity failed and the turbines stopped running. However, both times the breakdown was quickly remedied.

During the night we entered the swell of the typhoon. It was an extraordinary phenomenon. As far as one could see through the darkness there was hardly a whitecap. The breakers too were infrequent, though several of them sprang upon us like wild beasts. And yet the swells were such as I have never experienced. It was very difficult to stay in bed without being sent flying. Everything rolled about topsy-turvy. My typewriter, though it stood on rubber props on linoleum, kept hurtling about the room and crashing against the wardrobe and the bed.

Now it is calmer, and we are heading straight for the Yangtze.

September 11

Forenoon. In blazing sunshine we sailed yesterday through the muddy tides of the Yangtze. It is so broad that one cannot see land, at least not in the estuary. Ocean-going vessels can travel up the river for over a thousand miles, and you can then go more than two thousand miles farther by river-boat. Its gigantic scale is beyond comprehension. We had the feeling we were still sailing on the ocean. The captain could not find the lightship that was indicated on the chart. (The Chinese are always altering such positions without giving notice.) However, we at least found the pilot vessel. It was just good luck that it was back at its appointed post—during the typhoon even the pilot ships withdrew.

Again the now-familiar scenes began to be enacted: the pilot and commissar came on board. But—wonder of wonders! —the commissar saluted and smiled. The word went around from one man to another: "The commissar cracked a smile— he *is* a human being." Perhaps he is.

Then, as land gradually emerged on the horizon and as wharves, tanks, and industrial plants stood out more clearly, at dusk we went up a smaller tributary of the river leading directly to Shanghai.

Now the passage up the river began to be tremendously interesting. We sailed past hundreds of junks putting out for fishing, with more and more lights appearing on them. Ships, barges, and rowboats glided past. Whenever vessels overtook us they set off earsplitting whistles and hoots. The Chinese seems not only to be insensitive to noise but to delight in it.

The nearer we approached, the more numerous became the points of light on shore. We saw brilliant fountains of light produced by welding operations; the ghostly fingers of searchlights groped about the cloud-cover. We passed long rows of warships. Most of them were mine sweepers and landing craft. (Are they intended for Quemoy, or Formosa?)

The passage of this large ship through what seemed to me impenetrable darkness on the crowded stream was fascinating. The nearer we came to the center of Shanghai, this enormous city of six million people, which extends over many miles, the more numerous became the chains and clusters of light. Yet the whole effect was strangely dead and dark. The captain told us that in the past the entry into the harbor had been quite different. The illumination of the city had set fire to the sky itself and made it look like a lighted dome in the distance.

Up on the dark bridge, where the pilot had taken over the navigation, we wondered why the city gave the impression of gloomy darkness despite the vast number of individual lights. It must be because here there is only utility lighting, without advertising lights, insufficient to give that bright, colored brilliance familiar to us in the "capitalistic" cities at home and in America.

It was almost midnight before we made fast between two buoys in the river. We were hardly lying to when lighters came alongside and began the work of unloading. Our concern that we should have to wait outside for six days was therefore unfounded.

The night was filled with the noise of unloading operations and the tooting of ships passing by, so our sleep was restless even though we were very tired. We were obliged to stay up very late; the officials came on board at midnight to set in motion the all-too-familiar inspection ceremonies in all their minute detail.

This morning I am sitting on the boat deck in the midst of

an animated stream. We are surrounded on all sides by junks
where rice is being cooked and washed. The children are
secured with rope or wear little life preservers. The women
are working along with the men in the maneuvering of the
boats. All work together, lending a hand in a very comradely
way. Not for a moment does one have the impression that
any of them is thinking: Here is where somebody else can
jump in and lend a hand. Everyone falls to and does what
needs to be done. They also keep jumping from one boat to
another. It is as if the boundaries between the families were
fluid.

The people here appear still to live in relative freedom
from constraint, since the families are still together and it is
impossible to have a police spy on every boat. There are
some remnants of a family life that is simple, but still intact.
It is pleasant to see here a mother rocking her whimpering
child and there a grandmother feeding her grandchild—
pathetic remnants of essential humanity threatened, like
Philemon and Baucis, by the clutch of the emperor of the
world.* The desert lives and the desert grows.

Though we are lying about a hundred to a hundred and fifty
yards from either shore, even here the loudspeakers can be
heard roaring above all the racket of the harbor. Still the
noise does not hit one's eardrums so directly as it did in
Tientsin.

Afternoon. Towards noon the state Intourist agent returned
to make arrangements with us for motor tours about the city.
He was a friendly young man. When he collected the passports in order to confer with the authorities, he was optimistic,
and we planned our tours as if the permits were already in
our pockets.

After three hours he came back. His attitude was completely changed. Still maintaining polite form, he returned the

* The reference is to the Philemon and Baucis in Goethe's *Faust,*
Part Two. (Trans.)

214

passports to us. The authorities had refused permission to land.

"Including the passengers on the other ships?" we asked. "No, all of the others are permitted to leave their ships. And your crew is allowed to go on land."

When we asked why, he answered abruptly, "When the authorities refuse something, they have their reasons, and they do not need to state them. Neither you nor I have the right to ask what they are."

Then he asked Charles, our Jehovah's Witness, about his vocation. Charles gave him a touching answer, trying to make a witness to his faith, though he did so in a completely relaxed, sympathetic, conversational tone and by no means in a forced, sectarian way.

His mention of the Bible prompted the Chinese to make a sarcastic face, and launched him upon the standard polemical arguments of his ideology, which gradually mounted into a regular propaganda speech.

When I finally told him that the captain wished to speak to him and that he should please go above, he said insolently, "If the captain wants to talk to me, let him come down here to me. I'll wait for another minute."

By chance the captain happened to come in at this point and with an air of ironical superiority really told him off.

I was annoyed by my own miserable English, which prevented me from taking a more active part in this unpleasant colloquy. I cannot deny it, these scenes brought about a feeling of depression. I felt, almost physically, that I could not bear the oppressive climate of lack of freedom. But how querulous and weak that sounds! After all, here on the ship we are living on an island in the "Red Sea."

Evening. Late this afternoon we were witnesses of another wretched scene. Our Jehovah's Witness missionary, who is on his way back to Hong Kong from a meeting of his religious society in New York (over 250,000 people are said to have gathered there), intentionally chose to return by way of Japan, on our ship, in order to visit two of his fellow believers in Shanghai. These two are the only missionaries of the Jehovah's Witness sect left in China. They live in isolation and under the severest hardship—among the last remaining Europeans.

Most of their Chinese brethren are in prisons. They themselves do not know whether they will be expelled or detained by force. In any case, they feel that they are under constant surveillance. They have also learned that the prisoners are being interrogated with the usual pressure methods to secure incriminating evidence against the two missionaries. The Jehovah's Witnesses stick together like burdocks and have many channels of information. Therefore I think it is altogether probable that this information is correct. Besides, Charles is a man of very dependable character who certainly does not talk in an irresponsible way.

In any case, these two Shanghai missionaries are yearning for encouragement, for a chance to talk, for brotherly communication, and not least for an account of the meeting in New York.

The two of them came alongside the ship in a boat to visit Charles. We were all gathered on deck. We were touched by the inexpressible joy of anticipation on Charles' face, and the thought that the same joy was being felt by the visitors. They waved and cheered and shouted the first words of welcome. But already the commissar was on the gangway and drove them away.

Scarcely a greeting and already parted—so many weeks of anticipation, so close together, and yet worlds apart. In this one experience is compacted all that breaks the heart here.

After midnight. Our sailors have just returned from their shore leave. They were called for and brought back in large American (or perhaps Russian?) cars. In their civilian clothes and with their hats cocked at jaunty angles they look quite strange to me.

I invited several of them whom I know well, and whose dependable straightforwardness I have always enjoyed, to have a round of drinks and tell me about their experiences.

They are enthusiastic over the sumptuous furnishings and the spaciousness of the seamen's club, the hospitable reception, the fine food and drink, and the unimaginable cheapness of the things for sale. Formerly this house was the meeting place of high society. It boasts the longest bar in the world, which is kept as a museum piece to remind people of the colonial days long past. Today the house is reserved exclusively for the use of seamen as a shopping and recreation center. Some of these good sailors seem to have felt somewhat uncomfortable in all the splendor while others obviously felt flattered. "It's all propaganda," said one of my companions. But the question is whether he understood the bitter irony of this propaganda. Perhaps all it is intended to say is: "We Chinese have no use for this swank. You go ahead and wallow in it—you ignorant white devils who do not even realize that you are being assigned to an extraterritorial playground. Amuse yourselves only in the places which your fathers have discredited; amuse yourselves and realize that you are being excluded!"

I am glad now that nothing came of our shore leave. If the agent were to come back tomorrow and hand out permits, I would refuse one, perhaps from shame, perhaps from pride.

In the afternoon our men had made a trip through the city. They were shocked by the tremendous crowds of people marching in a demonstration parade, roaring in unison against the Americans and Chiang Kai-shek, and carrying signs demanding the return of Quemoy and Formosa.

In a great plaza, filled mostly with children—the demonstration parade also consisted mostly of children—a theatrical performance was going on. Three huge puppets, one dressed as an American and obviously representing Dulles, another as Mao Tse-tung, and a third as Chiang Kai-shek, engaged in a loud dispute, until finally the supreme Chinese leader knocked the other two down and set fire to them.

Thus the policy of the regime is channeled into the "image-level" of the minds even of little children, and the trauma of colonialism is cultivated because it is needed for psychological strategy.

When our sailors mixed with the people they felt uncomfortable, for they were often followed by venomous looks, and they also heard sounds which were not calculated to arouse their trust. What bothered them most was that they were unable even to cast a harmless flirting glance at the girls. It was but small comfort to them that the girls, who would have liked to wink at them (or so they thought!), were so ascetic and wooden-faced only because of fear of lynch-law.

Everywhere they saw work proceeding at a furious tempo: in the sewing rooms, craftsmen's shops, and stores. "They work like blazes," said one, "but they are not happy at it. They look crabby and sullen." The others nodded in agreement.

I have noticed this same look of strained sullenness among the Chinese who are working on the ship: the guards, the commissars, the foremen, and the coolies. They work like a motor that is constantly being forced to make more revolutions per minute than it was constructed to make. The comparison with an inanimate motor forces itself upon me because they are always on guard against betraying any natural human expression at all (except those connected with the natural processes of digestion!). Every attempt to offer one of them a cigarette meets with indifference—unless he happens to be in a very out-of-the-way part of the ship where it is guaranteed that he will not be seen, nor betrayed by the odor of a European cigarette.

After the men left, I made another tour about the ship; for a long time I leaned over the railing, watching the junks below. The people there had gone "to bed," which means that they were lying on deck beneath the open sky, covered with colorful, often beautiful, quilts. A number of mothers had their babies in their arms—a picture of peace. Here and there an oil lamp was burning. An infant cried, and I saw the mother

—with a long pigtail—get up, pick up the little one, rock it in her arms, and sing a quiet lullaby.

What a reassuring thing is this little gesture after "a long day's journey into night"! There will always be mothers who rock their little ones and sing them lullabies—always—even if we are inundated by a world in which there is nothing left but masks, specters, lemures, and robots.

With this consoling impression of the indestructible order of the world, I went to bed.

September 12

After a short sleep, I rose early and watched the wakening life on the junks. What a sight to see the little children doing their business!—the very small ones right on the deck, where it was immediately wiped up, the older ones in a pot. The adults perform their natural functions sitting on the deck rail, without even interrupting their conversations, not even conversations between the sexes.

There would also seem to be certain class distinctions on the junks in this respect: on some of them there are regular buckets which are collected by a special boat service. When this unspeakable boat comes around, the smells are like those we remember in Tübingen when the liquid manure pumps began to operate.

Right next to all this, sieves containing rice were being let down into the river, obviously with the honest intent to wash the grain. Right alongside, again, washing is done in the same water. Though to our eyes all this looks highly unappetizing, it must nevertheless be admitted that these people are quite clean. I remember that Carl Friedrich von Weizsäcker, the scientist, once said that it is really a miracle (and no philosopher would take your word for it!) that you can make a wineglass dazzling clean with dirty water and soiled towels. In any case, these people on the junks are constantly scrubbing not only the planks and roofs but also their teeth.

With several of the children I established a little system of signals consisting of smiles and winks, and when nobody was looking (for according to the captain's warnings there could be some unpleasantness) threw over some chocolates and bon-bons. With all the primitiveness of the child's nature, these little children are happy. Wistfully I remember the times during the air attacks when my own children played with delight on the rubble heaps around our house, while we adults were thinking of the next night.

Afternoon. To everybody's distress, bad weather blew up in the late forenoon. Stormy winds and torrents of rain passed over us. The work of unloading has stopped altogether. When it started with a great rush, we had good hopes that everything would soon be finished. But they were deceiving hopes. Either the longshoremen are here and the lighters are missing or vice versa.

The cargo officer is complaining about the complete lack of organization. The Chinese contact man for our agency, a nice fellow, is constantly excusing this by saying, "China has too few people." Too few, with six hundred million! "Yes," he says, "they're employed on the development projects. There's nobody left for the harbor."

This troubles me very much. I do not know whether it is correct or not, but I have the impression that the Chinese are thinking: "Let them wait. The whites are so eager for business that they will come back again anyhow. We can safely humiliate them a bit. They do not hate money, and besides, money makes people patient."

The others too are restive over the fact that everything is moving so slowly, that either bad weather intervenes, the lighters fail to show up, or the workers are missing. Even some scare words are passing from mouth to mouth: "Things are going to break loose in earnest soon in Quemoy. The kettle is about to boil over. You can see it by the demonstrations. We are being held up only in order that later all the good ships can be seized."

In this weather and these desolate conditions, how could

there be anything but gloomy thoughts! The river and the ships are now wrapped in a damp gray veil that flutters in the wind. We seem to be in the middle of a big bowl of thick mush. Work has stopped completely. The people on the junks have burrowed themselves below decks. All this pulsing life is hidden away beneath wet sails and damp tarred planks. The Chinese agent has left the ship, and only the commissar, as always, remains faithful to us. The one thing you can depend on is the faithfulness of the inspectors.

Now nobody knows what is going to happen. The captain paces up and down the boat deck like a dethroned potentate. The curses that break from his tormented lips are quite understandable from any human point of view. As a minister, however, I felt obliged to make a mild protest. And since merely negative remonstrances have never yet helped anyone, I decided to use the homeopathic method, that is, to combat *similia similibus* (like with like). So I said to him, "Captain, whenever it hits you like that, just say emphatically, 'Shanghai.' It begins with 'sh . . .' too and will do just as well."

He looked at me gratefully and said emphatically, "Sh—anghai."

I don't want to brag, but I believe nevertheless that by making this suggestion I achieved a great pastoral success. For not long afterward I heard the word all over, and people smiled at me as the inventor of it.

September 13

Last evening, after lying disconsolately in the fog all day doing nothing, I undressed and put on some decent clothes. I needed the strengthening symbol of form. And it did me good. The good "Doc," this extroverted Swabian, could not understand this and thought I wanted to make an impression on someone. He is really a typical Swabian. Like all his countrymen, with their honest solidity, he says, "It's the substance that counts," and he is firmly convinced that form is not a part of substance but rather discredits it.

I am now reading all the books on East Asia that are in the library, and in the quietness of the smoking saloon I am making out very well.

Unfortunately, however, the cigar supply has been exhausted. The radioman and I have managed to do this all by ourselves. We lovers of this symbol of masculine culture are indeed a dying breed, but in both of us the pleasant passion still leaps from the dying embers. And we have polished off more of the good weed than the managers in Hamburg provided for both passengers and crew together.

September 14

Yesterday the ship was almost emptied, despite the slow pace of the work. Now the real loading is to begin. How are the more than three thousand tons of soy beans we are to take on ever to be gotten on board at this tempo?

At all events nothing at all is being done at the moment. It is now evening, and the ship is lying in ghostly stillness. It is illuminated with many lights, but, except for the commissar, not a soul is visible. Everybody is in his cabin, and the workers failed to show up. The only human sound comes from the inhuman loudspeakers that keep booming across to us.

One A.M. A number of us spent the whole evening in the radioman's room, having an exhaustive religious discussion. Along with the whiskey and soda, it did us good, considering the soggy weather around us and the futility of standing still and getting nowhere.

Every day now the two Jehovah's Witness missionaries come past at some distance from our ship in a public shuttle boat. Cupping their hands about their mouths, they exchange shouted greetings and bits of information with Charles. Actually, they have only a few seconds in which to do this. They intend to come back every day.

The representative of the shipping agency who saw this happen today was not happy about it. "I know the two men who are standing behind them. They are detectives," he said. "Why do they do such a thing? They are only endangering both of you!" This was the only time Charles became somewhat vehement: "That's exactly what makes us different from you. We don't ask whether a thing is dangerous, we do what we think is right."

Later on a professor from the technical school came on board with a group of quite young students to look at the ship's engines. He wanted to take the blueprints with him, ostensibly to show them to the students in his classes. Our conjectures were naturally quite otherwise. The captain therefore remained unyielding and refused to hand them over. The professor had studied in Zurich; he spoke perfect German and was a relaxed, cosmopolitan type of person. We invited him to a meal and had a fine conversation. To our astonishment he said—despite the presence of the commissar, who follows him like a shadow —"I am not a communist." But he, like the others, spoke of the present regime only in positive terms.

How well he knew German came out in a little exchange with the doctor. When, in reply to his question where he came from, "Doc" said Württemberg, he answered like a shot, "Ah, then you are a dirty Swabian [*Sauschwab*]." It was a delight to hear this from the lips of a Chinese.

September 15

Early this morning our agent informed us that from now on two gangs would continue the job of loading. This is still far too few, but at least something is going to happen. How much longer will we be here?

At the same time a telegram arrived stating that, on the heels of the wild lady "Helen," typhoon "Ida" was now announcing her coming. Hence it may be that we shall get a week of wind and rain, and the snail's pace of the loading operations will be replaced by a complete standstill.

Finally, still another piece of Job's news arrived, to the effect that in consequence of our delay we must pass up Hong Kong on our return voyage. How we were all looking forward to seeing it again!

I have been making an effort to counteract the pessimistic mood that prevails. But now I am not in a good frame of mind myself, though my daily Bible reading, especially my study of the Prophets, has gained in intensity. The stillness and the strain impart to these texts a heightened power of illumination, as it were.

For hours at a time I can look at the river: its animation makes it look like an artery in the circulatory system of the world. An unseen heart keeps beating in unremitting rhythm through the bloodstream. Ships from all over the world pass close by us, and whenever they are German ships the reminder of home in this alien world touches us to the quick, and we wave with all our might.

What strikes us above all is the tremendous number of manually propelled boats. We see not only junks but also great barges and even whole strings of rafts that are moved by hand.

All of these have a great bent oar manned by three men. Women and half-grown youngsters also do their part in the rowing. The one who is at the extreme end of the oar can exert the greatest leverage, but also has the greatest distance to travel. He therefore does not take hold of the oar directly, but rather moves it by means of a strap or rope. In doing so he must keep running forward and backward in time with the stroke of the oar, and as he leaps backward he often throws himself so far back that he almost touches the floor.

These athletic gymnastics strike us as being nothing short of homicidal, especially since they are performed with machine-like regularity; yet they were necessary in all the boats we have observed. It is hardly conceivable that these people can endure this for hours at a time, especially when one considers the miserable diet they live on.

Likewise, every day we are astonished anew by the enormousness of the burdens the people move by hand and maneuver with amazing deftness through the stream of traffic. It is true, of course, that in doing this they take advantage of the tides. They go along with the ebb and flow of the tide and augment it with just enough human power to enable them to steer the burden.

I wonder whether the Chinese are not also utilizing the political tide, the ideological incline, and adding just enough of their own impetus to maintain the maneuverability which will enable them to steer their way to survival. What is going on behind their strained, silent faces cannot be seen. One sees only their slender bodies bending like elastic wands. As they row, they sink to the floor and then rise again. It is probably more this elasticity than brute strength that enables them to move the tremendous burdens—also their regular, steady motion, which reminds one of the play of steel pistons.

On the banks, there is hammering and welding going on in improvised wharves, and human points move like ants among the cascades of sparks.

Today Doc's playing of chorales in this world of never-ceasing labor is like a sound from another world. "I stand here and sing in perfect peace secure." * It was like the silence of eternity breaking into a never-ending concert.

I thought of the time I stood on the tower of St. Mary's Church in Danzig. The bells were ringing and booming all around me, so that I felt the whole world must be filled with the overwhelming force of this sound. Far below, however, I saw the street workers, who did not even look up but went on their way unmoved. Only my reason told me that, because of all the noise of their pneumatic hammers and concrete-mixers, they did not even hear what was almost toppling me over with its power, though it seemed to be shattering the world with its clangor. So it was with me today: the sound of the Word of God, that moves and rules and holds the world together at its inmost center, the sound that almost painfully fills me to the brim, is heard by nobody else. The dockyard hammers keep throbbing and the rowers bend in undisturbed

* From the third stanza of *"Jesu, meine Freude."* (Trans.)

225

rhythm, when all the while the very ground of the universe is ringing and tolling in our midst. And yet—a few do listen and catch the sound of it. A few . . .

The visit which was to have been arranged by my guests at Tientsin and of which I have already been notified has unfortunately not yet occurred, and I have so many questions to ask.

September 16

Yesterday afternoon the shipboard-psychosis, which may be compared with "barbed-wire blues," reached its high point. Again nothing happened, and the few laborers who were assigned to us sat on their haunches like dumb idols in the gangways or slept.

Pessimistic predictions buzzed through the air: "We'll never get out of here." Announcements of the coming typhoon did not conduce to lifting our spirits.

From land we hear the droning clamor of the daily mass demonstration. May the government not lose face if it brings the kettle of hatred to a boil but does not then proceed to act, that is, take actual steps toward military aggression? The voices of the loudspeakers seem to be becoming even more lashing, more aggressive and vituperative. If they go any further, tomorrow they will flare into the glossolalia of ecstasy. May that not be the moment when the superheating brings on an explosion?

We have time to listen to all this and let it have its effect upon us. Or rather, does time not have *us?* How defenseless we humans tend to become when we are condemned to passivity and compelled to play the inhuman role of a stone, which cannot move and must wait till someone takes it up and throws it!

Again I think—as I did in times past when I lay for long periods of time in hospitals—of how much easier we "intellectuals" have it in such situations (as long as we have not lost all our foundations, in which case the inflated sails of our intellectuality reduce us to unusually helpless playthings of the elements): we at least are able to sublimate our physical help-

lessness and mobilize our inner activities. We can devote ourselves to intellectual exercises, we can conjure up memories,
we can meditate, and we are sufficiently skilled mentally to see
at least the outlines of the fundamental things of life.

This dare not be merely an act of self-control which causes
us to radiate composure; it must be more. Simple souls like
those with whom I am closely linked on this ship are exceedingly quick to sense when we are genuine and when we are
not, when we are producing mere moralizing lectures without
having first ingested the raw materials.

Toward evening the captain returned from a visit to a physician. He gave us the same story as the others who have been
on land concerning the demonstrations and the routine political
puppet show, which is apparently repeated daily in various
places. All who have witnessed it seem to be dismayed and
depressed by it, for watching it requires a certain inner defensive power. Nobody can remain merely a spectator; everybody
feels himself being "engaged." And even the counteraction of
thought requires strength. It is part of the "moral" strategy
of ideological tyranny to wear a person down by keeping him
in constant conflict with himself, and by subjecting him to
increasingly dramatic mental dialogues to soften him up for the
capitulation which will give him back the peace in which there
are no conflicts and no decisions to make.

Since late last evening the loading of soybeans has been
going forward. A whole host of junks and lighters, each carrying only from one to five tons, is fastened to the ship. Cranes
lift up sacks of soybeans from the boats and set them down in
the hatchways, where they land upon grated frames. Then the
coolies cut open the sacks with knives and dump the contents
into the hold.

All these manipulations require a great deal of time. With
the pneumatic conveyors used in European harbors the whole
operation would be finished in from twenty-four to thirty-six
hours.

The constant rippling sound of soybeans pouring into the hold pursues us even in our sleep. To pass the time we calculate how many soybeans would go to each Chinese, then to each inhabitant of the earth, and then to each inhabitant of Germany and the individual states. Soybeans, soybeans, soybeans . . . And all this is to become soy sauce and appear in innocent bottles on homely tables. We begin to feel like starting a boycott.

The expected guests still have not appeared.

September 17

Yesterday morning there was a knocking at my cabin door. The two gentlemen for whom I had been waiting so eagerly were there. They had had to go through a great paper war and many negotiations before they could get to me on the ship. Since they were businessmen, they had been able—quite legitimately!—to declare that consultations with the ship's management were part of the purpose of their visit. They were staying in Shanghai only temporarily to take care of some business matters. The one was an Englishman, the other a German. Both were "old China hands" who had after some years' absence been back in the country for almost two years.

I immediately returned to the same subjects that I had discussed in Hong Kong and Tientsin, in order to supplement my impressions and define them more precisely. Essentially, they were all confirmed. Both gentlemen were very strongly impressed by the achievements Red China had made in development and construction. They were impressed above all by the fact that even the interim period, before the erection of great technical installations, was successfully utilized to carry forward production, and what is more, with means so primitive that they are almost unimaginable to the Western world.

As an example they mentioned the production of steel by manual power in village furnaces. I told them about the similar operation I had seen in the Suez Canal. There, too, vast earth-moving projects are being accomplished by manual labor instead of dredging machines. The superiority of the West through its machines appears therefore to be exceedingly relative, particularly since year by year even this advantage is being offset by the East.

The thematic axis of our conversation was the comparison of Russian and Chinese Bolshevism.

I brought the conversation back to the ideological difference between them that I had learned from the literature on the subject, namely, the fact that Mao Tse-tung, in contrast with the Kremlin, speaks of possible antagonisms between the leaders and the people. For Mao, this antagonism results from the fact that in China the implements of the rulers and the ruled are not the same; consequently, Communism of a different stamp emerges, above all a different ideological superstructure.

Mr. L., my German partner in the conversation, was familiar with this difference. He had had philosophical training, and in interpreting phenomena he always distinguished very precisely between the specific ways of looking at them. It frequently happened that he brought out sharp distinctions between the historical, psychological, and ideological aspects of the Chinese Communists' understanding of themselves. I was therefore interested in how he would interpret this difference on the basis of his personal observation *and* deeper reflection upon it.

In order to lure him out of his shell, I immediately blurted out my own opinion—using it as a kind of irritant—and said that, though Mao was here employing ideological arguments, he obviously did not believe in them himself, but was pursuing quite different aims. For, after all, he had based his action "Let all the flowers grow" upon this "antagonism between the people and the leadership." He supposedly started this action for the purpose of relieving and relaxing the dammed-up antagonisms by quickly creating an atmosphere of liberality, thus providing a safety valve of free discussion. But his *true* purpose was undoubtedly to lure the hitherto concealed spirits of contradiction from their hiding places, and scotch them.

Mr. L. immediately leaped upon this provocative thesis of mine and, though he did not deny it, warned me against over-simplification of this situation. It would certainly be an un-allowable simplification for me to think that Mao made a *merely* tactical misuse of the ideological argument. With such a doctrinaire theoretician, and one who is, besides, on his way to becoming the papal teacher of infallible Communist doc-trine, with nobody to equal him in the Soviet Union, this would be quite impossible. On the other hand, however, the fact that he takes Marxist theory seriously need not rule out the possibility that he may at the same time have had in view quite *different* aims. After all, this occurs very frequently in life. It is called "killing two flies with one swatter."

When you are willing to subject yourself to a bit of self-criticism, you are glad to accept a challenge to make your dis-tinctions more precise. And yet Mr. L.'s criticism—though it was made very courteously, almost affectionately — was not altogether convincing to me. I therefore asked him whether there were any other indications in Mao's communistic theory that he was taking seriously this theory of the formative power of tools and also seriously *practicing* it.

"Certainly," replied Mr. L. "He actually does this *so* em-phatically that at this point he departs from the principles of Soviet Russian society. Even in the West there has been talk for years that Russian society today has social class distinctions to a degree and of a crassness that is hardly to be found any longer in the 'capitalistic countries.' The material advantages with respect to influence and living standards possessed by the so-called favored classes—the higher officials, the specialists, and the recognized upholders of culture—have been growing steadily in the Soviet Union. One might even say that the tendency in the Soviet Union is the opposite of that in the West: in the West class distinctions are being increasingly leveled, whereas in Russia they are being deepened. Mao has very clearly observed this tendency, which is, of course, radically inconsistent with Marxian goals, and he wants to check any

Mainland China

such erroneous developments in China right from the start. And in this concern of his the theory of the formative power of tools actually plays a decisive role."

"To what extent?"

"To the extent," Mr. L. went on, "that he is seeking to preserve or establish the homogeneity of the whole nation, or better, the whole 'society,' by causing all its people to be molded by the *same* tool or instrument. Naturally, he cannot expect to mold a coolie by means of fountain pen and dictaphone. But the reverse is probably possible: he can subject every Chinese, no matter on which rung of the ladder of society he stands, to the stamp of the plow, the lathe, the shovel, and the pickax, in order to achieve the desired standardized form for all. In line with this the authorities are clearly working towards having every 'higher-up' Chinese step down from his hierarchical level once each year to perform four weeks of physical labor. Even the officers, from second lieutenants to generals, are required to serve as common soldiers for one month each year. Naturally, it is never stated publicly, but it is very easy to suppose that the erroneous developments in Soviet Russia served as a warning example, and that the purpose is to correct this deviation in the name of a *better* maintenance of Marxist theory."

I must admit that this struck me as a very plausible refinement upon my rather roughcast statements—just as this conversation as a whole served less to furnish new information than to provide adjustments. Mr. L. knew how to apply the micrometer to my thinking.

In the same way he also helped me to arrive at a more precise attitude with respect to the thesis that the family is being broken down by means of implements. (I have noted earlier that family tools, such as cooking utensils, are being taken away.) It is true, according to Mr. L., that these tendencies have been, and to some extent still are, very crudely and brutally carried out. To judge such radical measures properly, however, one must consider the approximate "chronological point" that has been reached in the process of Bolshevization. Despite its attempts to accelerate the process, China is still in the adolescent period of communism, perhaps still in the age of puberty, which, after all, tends even biologically to be rather stormy and to produce radical proclivities. Russia too went through this period of hostility to the family during the corresponding phase of its development. It is well known how lightly abortion and divorce were dealt with for a time. But just as a revocation of anti-family action took place in Russia, signs of a similar withdrawal are appearing in China along with the beginnings here and there of very slight freedom in personal life, even in the peoples' communes. It would appear that they have recognized that China's tremendous birth rate represents its biological opportunity as well as its strongest potential. China, he said, has too few rather than too many people. And this too may have contributed to the fact that the policy of encouraging birth control has been relaxed rather than intensified."

When I asked Mr. L. for examples of this and—again as a kind of stimulus—also confronted him with what I had recently heard about a rationed limitation upon the number of children, and thus a state interference in the sphere of personal life, he informed me that already this very thing was being disputed. The phrase "family planning" was being heard less and less, and he considered it possible that in the not too distant future this action would be called off altogether.

"But then there are two things I do not understand," I interposed. "In the first place, I do not understand how Red China can reconcile her backing down with fidelity to Marxist theory. You are the one, Mr. L., who has been emphasizing Mao's strict ideological consistency. And, according to strict Marxist theory, all these social ties and potential cells of resistance must be radically destroyed and replaced by communistic social structures, as indeed Mao has hitherto attempted to do in his campaign against the family. In the second place, I do not understand why the Chinese should be following the Soviet

Russian line of development with respect to the family, whereas they are actually repudiating Russia's line of development with respect to the newly evolving class distinctions."

I was really posing a catch-question to Mr. L., for I am not quite so helpless on this point as my two questions might seem to indicate. I had my own answer up my sleeve and was delighted that he reacted exactly as I had expected. What we worked out as an answer to both of my questions in a very lively exchange, in which we were able to expand on what we had said, may be briefly summed up as follows:

It is true that there is a certain inconsistency with theory at this point, and it is also true that here the Chinese are taking advantage of Russian experience. However, the inconsistency is inevitable, because this is precisely the point where Marxian theory reveals that it is contradictory to the elementary facts of life—and breaks down. The fact is that there are certain fundamental elements in human life that have a kind of indelible character and therefore cannot be eliminated. Among these basic elements are marriage and the relationship of parents and children. This elemental order of life is stronger than any artificial order synthetically produced in an ideological laboratory. Therefore, in any battle between theory and life, life will always win, not only because it is stronger—the category of dynamics is not quite adequate here—but because a theory which is in contradiction to life is simply *false*. A theory may be ever so desirable ideologically—like, for example, the thesis of T. D. Lysenko and I. V. Mitshurin concerning the inheritance of acquired characteristics—but ultimately everything depends upon whether the theory is true or not, whether it is a theory in accord with life or one *contrary* to life.

From here our conversation advanced deep into the region of theology and touched upon the question of *which* elements of being in this sense are in principle indestructible, constituting solid granite on which the beast of ideological tyranny will break its teeth. Are personhood and the freedom of man such indestructible elements? To what extent can man be transformed into an ant, and the state into a termite state? Does *humanitas* have an indestructible character? To what degree can it degenerate? Was Pascal right when he said that man cannot get away from himself no matter how far he falls, that he must always remain the king of creation, though with "faded purple" and a "broken crown" and thus in a negative *modus*?

This is the great thing in every serious encounter with communism: it compels us to ask the most radical questions and really gets down to the "roots." We are compelled quite simply to declare *which* truths we hold over against it (which truths hold *us*!) or admit that we have nothing to say. But that which compels us to ask the ultimate questions is not to be denied a certain dignity. By exposing humanity to the ultimate test it is performing a mission for us Westerners: it is subjecting us to a searching Socratic examination. Who are we? Woe to him who does not know who he is and why he is here.

Towards evening, as I accompanied the two on their way out and waved to their departing boat, this conversation continued to tremble within me for a long time afterward. I went up to the deserted bridge and looked out over the river and the land. We ought to pray that we may not fail to see the hour of our visitation. And we ought to pray for those who have been visited . . . for this whole country spread out before me.

September 18

Since yesterday afternoon the work has been proceeding without interruption, though with only two gangs. Soybeans, soybeans!

More and more boats approach us. It is inconceivable how much will go into the belly of a ship. I am going to suggest that after supper we figure out the number of carloads we already have within us and how many more we will still take on.

The first officer has a remarkable influence upon the men. Never for a moment does he lose his fresh and lively spirit. For him it is a kind of spiritual sport to maintain a cheerful composure in the face of what cannot be changed anyhow. A man with strong inner reserves and radiant humanity. We talk for hours about how he is going to raise his little son Wilm-Volkert and what the little fellow is going to become and how bright he is already. Already he is carrying the ripe old age of nine months upon his shoulders!

I spent the day setting down yesterday's conversation. As I did so, a thought occurred to me which I have often expressed before, namely, that every once in a while I am overtaken by the strange certainty that Bolshevism will be overcome or undermined by the women. It is not the great doers who will conquer it, but rather the preservers. The elemental things are guarded and preserved in the realm of mothers. What we saw on the junks, where the mothers were rocking their children, is more than a sentimental scene. It is perhaps a vision. The temples may be demolished, faith may move into the catacombs, and humanity itself may hibernate in subterranean dungeons or temporarily forsake the land and escape to the junks. All these goods may be preserved like bulbs in the hard earth or in earthen vessels deep beneath the surface; they may appear to have no life at all, to be robbed of all fertility. And yet these are the seeds of life that will survive in dark places of refuge.

September 19

Noon. At six o'clock this morning the main winch broke down. The motor refused to work. Now we have laborers and cargo, but the machines have gone on strike. So we were not spared even this little cross. Besides, the weather is bright and the work could be proceeding at full speed. How long will the sun shine? Typhoon "Ida" is still on the march.

I watched our crew desperately trying to make repairs while the coolies, visibly delighted with the unexpected free time, looked on with interest. When people are so bound together as we now are on this long voyage, everything that happens is experienced far more intensely. The electrician, who heads up the repair gang, has become a real friend. Nobody can laugh

235

with such a deafening roar as he can. His experience as a refugee, his family, his very earnest questions about life — I know them all. Now I saw him working grimly under the eyes of the coolies. No longer am I really a pure spectator and a mere passenger. I have become a part of the ship and its people.

Midnight. A wonderful evening, the echoes of which still linger and prevent us from sleeping. The young agent of the Hamburg-America Line was here with his wife. He has studied music and has a good classical education. His wife lived for a time in Tübingen, and we recalled concerts we had both attended, though at the time we had not met each other. They brought with them Bach, Mozart, and Schubert records. The captain had the best wine brought out, and we luxuriated in bliss the whole evening. What did it matter that the electro-winches kept on droning and interrupting the venerable masters with the worst kind of static? The fact that the motor was operating again and the work was going forward was additional music to our ears. We listened to intricate scores as if we were sitting in a comfortable concert hall at home.

When our guests left, we were jerked back to reality. The Red guard examined every individual disc minutely and compared it with his list. The same had been done when they came, and the officials on land had not been easily persuaded to permit this musical transaction.

September 20

Evening. Our friend Charles, the Jehovah's Witness, has been in an abominable situation all this time. Every day his friends come and wave and shout to him, without his really being able to meet them and speak an undisturbed word with them. The futility of his journey is now made even more grotesque by the fact that we cannot call at Hong Kong. Not only is the way to his goal fruitless, but the goal itself will not be reached. Our next station is supposed to be some obscure port in the Philippines. How is he going to get from there to Hong Kong with all his baggage? He has been bearing it all bravely and doubtless senses that we are all being as nice as possible to him and sharing his concern.

Suddenly yesterday a way out appeared. It seemed that he might be able to transfer to the Lloyd's ship "Schwabenstein," which is now lying in the harbor and will leave before we do, stopping at Hong Kong. We trembled to see whether it would work and whether his demonstrative conduct in the daily scenes of salutation had turned the authorities against him. For it is clear that he must be under grave suspicion.

But behold, today at noon the miracle happened. Charles was called for. And with what ceremony and luxury!

Already at ten o'clock our Red inspector began carefully to examine his numerous pieces of luggage. We all lent Charles a hand and sincerely envied him. His passport was found to be in order, and then we waited to see whether the improbable would really turn out to be true.

Sure enough, at eleven o'clock two boats arrived—actually, two boats. One was a launch intended especially for him, on which he was to be transported in isolation like an infectious bacillus. The other launch contained the police escort. Then everything proceeded very swiftly, and Charles, waving wildly to us, was elegantly conducted away like a chief of state in a convoy. He was a good comrade.

This afternoon there was some glorious excitement. I had left my telescope—we are again allowed to use telescopes in this port—lying on the boat deck, and now it was gone.

I mentioned it to our Chinese contact man, who happened to come by, and tactfully tried to conceal my obvious suspicions, at least not to express them. He immediately read my innermost thoughts, however, and hotly assured me that nothing was ever stolen in China. Anything could be left lying about. If anybody ever attempted to steal anything, he would—and he made the gesture of cutting his throat. I believe him, too. Whereas in all the other ports the captain ordinarily took great pains to impress upon us that we must lock our cabins, here he left it up to us to leave them open or not. The penalties for theft are so Draconic that, actually, nobody steals. During the last few days we have heard almost unbelievable things concerning the honesty of the traders, waiters, and others.

At brief intervals the Chinese agent looked me up to find out whether I had found the telescope yet. Sure enough, suddenly it was found. The captain, careful father that he was, had taken it and for educational reasons had let me flounder for a while.

Midnight. This evening I again furnished a round of beer for a group of my sailor friends in order to give them an opportunity to tell me about their experiences on shore. Some of them were brimful of what they had seen yesterday.

As the meteorologists had predicted, the Yangtze had overflowed its banks and flooded the adjacent parts of the city a yard deep. Actually, nobody should have been ashore on this day, especially since it was no simple matter to find means to get there. But a few of these fellows had managed it nevertheless. They had to take boats part of the way, and the rest of the way they waded through the water. They looked upon the whole thing as a lark, and at first had no idea of what they would experience.

As usual, a mass demonstration had been announced for today—this time for the women of Shanghai. They were summoned—again, as usual—for a demonstration against Chiang Kai-shek for the return of Quemoy.

Though the flood had been predicted, the demonstration had not been called off. In totalitarian dictatorships nobody seems to want to assume the responsibility for calling anything off— he might be denounced for sabotage. So the ghostly procession of thousands of women went plowing through the muddy floods. They held banners, shoes, and parts of their clothing high above their heads, often walking through water up to their chests. For Mao, people not only march, they also wade.

238

The usual ceremony went off according to plan. A precentor read the required versicles from a note-pad in a stentorian voice, and the women responded in "liturgical" chorus. For them the floods seemed not to exist at all, and the whole thing had the appearance—or rather, was intended to produce the appearance—that the spirit of the ideology was triumphing over the elements. A macabre giantism . . .

The sailors saw strange secondhand markets where ancient military bags, dirty light bulbs, and torn shoes were offered for sale. The familiar term "shortage-goods" from the time after the war came to our minds as we heard the story.

In other respects too they were struck by the way Shanghai differs from all other non-Chinese ports: no amusement establishments, no bars, no suggestion whatever of prostitution, no beggars. And repeatedly they lamented the girls' complete lack of susceptibility to even the most Platonic forms of approach.

They were were greatly impressed by the handsome workers' settlements surrounded by green plots of ground. On other streets, however, they saw miserable mud huts.

Several of them told about an identical scene, which apparently repeated itself at various places and various times. They would see a young man standing at a street corner or in a marketplace. He climbed upon a table or a box to elevate himself and held up large posters with letters upon them, showing them one after another and explaining them to the large crowds of people who gathered about him. Since one of our parties of sailors was being guided by the manager of the seamen's home, they were able to ask him about it. He explained that the young man was generally a student who was teaching the people Mao Tse-tung's new alphabet, which consists of only forty characters. He said that books written in the new script were available in numerous public libraries for everybody's use.

Our men were somewhat doubtful whether the people would have any interest in such elementary instruction in addition to their strenuous work, particularly since these public courses cannot really be supervised and are voluntary—in this case without even "voluntary compulsion." They went to the trouble to visit two public libraries, the addresses of which the manager had given them.

The story was actually true; the people were crowding to get the books printed in the new script. They sat at tables and in the corners, and many simply stood with the books in their hands. It could be seen from their strained and concentrated faces that they were not just idly scanning picture magazines.

Little reports like this one always seem especially significant to me. We may say what we will; we may talk about burdens and pressure and terror; we may be deeply impressed by the drab, gray atmosphere and the blight that has fallen upon all the "blooming flowers"; and yet the dynamic of the new spirit being pumped into the people is not meeting with resistance on their part. On the contrary, it is creating movement and making its impetus felt even where the motor impulse is not immediately apparent and the controls cannot be seen. Perhaps this dynamic operates as an infectious ecstasy, or perhaps it generates a capitulation which leads to a laissez-faire attitude toward the new power and therefore to the paradoxical phenomenon of a "passive activity." Between these alternatives neither these eye-witness reports nor the evaluations placed upon them by the silent listener on the ship permits us to decide.

How modest and undemanding we on the ship have gradually become! Today onions, manganese, and sausage skins are being loaded, packed in crates, cases, and casks delivered by innumerable junks. The change in the kind of cargo we were loading, though insignificant, immediately stimulated our spirits and raised the emotional barometer. We are happy to see something besides the endless bags of soybeans which were gradually threatening to dominate our whole world-view. A change even of this modest kind appears to us to be a testimony to life itself, which goes on moving and producing ever new shapes. In the midst of noisy uniformity even a nuance becomes a sensation, and a single bird singing on the window sill of a city flat evokes revivifying oases in the midst of stony wastes. Beyond water, ships, and beans there is still another world after all!

September 21

Cloudy, oppressive weather yesterday. But at least two gangs were at work. Our charming lady animal-trainer had a birthday, and the captain procured, not without some difficulty, a bouquet of pinks. We stared at the fresh flowers—which reminded us so much of home—as if they were a miracle, and the recipient was completely speechless.

The word went around this evening that we shall be off early tomorrow. The captain, however, predicted that we would still sleep two more nights in Shanghai, and then with all the fervor of one who hopes to see at least the first gleam of dawn he said, "Sh—anghai!"

Happily, typhoon "Ida" has changed direction and will pass us by at a safe distance. A front in its wake has brought considerable cooling, so today despite the sunshine we feel a bit chilly and have dressed in European clothes.

September 22

Five P.M. The improbable is going to happen: at seven this evening, when the tide changes, we shall be moving out.

The hatches are already closed. Daylight is coming into the dining saloon again—hitherto it has been cut off from the outside world by a huge iron shutter. All the junks have left. The officials, who this time made a very lenient inspection and, quite humanly, sat down with the captain for a glass of beer afterwards, have just left the ship. From the radio come the sounds of a Tchaikovsky concerto, which adds to the festive mood.

For now that the tension is abating a general feeling of wellbeing is coming to the fore. I see the dignified captain doing a solo dance. The first officer is calculating how soon he will see his little Wilm-Volkert again. The sailors show me the treasures they have purchased. They all have a catch in their throats and have great difficulty controlling their exuberance.

The dammed-up vitality among the young fellows releases itself in furious polishing, cleaning, and working. The cooks sing as they peel potatoes and stir the pots. The engineers enter their hot boiler room with delight and blow the first puffs of smoke from the stack as a parting salute. The heart of the ship is beating again, and it seems to be stretching as it feels itself coming to life again. The purser is putting his bottles away to cool: "This is something to celebrate!" A bacchantic anticipation trembles through the ship.

September 23

Afternoon. We left Shanghai at eight o'clock last night. So there it is—recorded in my diary!

Though we lay in the Yangtze barely two weeks, it seemed like an eternity to us because time appeared to stand still. Of the two caricatures of eternity that exist in our consciousness—endlessly ongoing time and time that stands still—we suffered the time that stops.

This too is a part of my initiation into the Asiatic experience of time, which hitherto I knew only theoretically—from the idea of Nirvana, for example—and then encountered for the first time in the timeless summer of Penang and the lack of tenses in the Malay language. During the voyage it has become more and more clear to me that our hermeneutics (our science of understanding) is much too meager when it demands only a congeniality between the one who wants to understand and that which is to be understood or when it makes certain basic, given circumstances of existence (anxiety, conscience, responsibility to truth, etc.) prerequisite to the act of understanding. Climate and the historical situation as a whole also determine and limit the possibility of understanding. Perhaps we shall have to invent a new sub-discipline, such as "meteorological hermeneutics" or "geo-hermeneutics." In any case, I shall "receive" Chinese authors with quite different antennae since I have come to appreciate this completely different attitude toward time in these latitudes and tried to acquire it by means of various exercises of thought.

As we speed along in the increasing tropical heat, again on the open sea, veering around Formosa toward the Philippines (the route to Formosa itself naturally is not navigable because of the continuing bombardment), our time of tormented waiting and apprehensions has already become something unreal in the far reaches of the memory. Optical and acoustical impressions leave behind them stronger traces in our memories than do such accompanying feelings, which come in from the background. It requires a certain effort of thought to go back and "lay hold" of them.

I believe that gratitude to a higher hand that has graciously guided us through dark times in our life is an ethical act solely because it can only proceed from this effort of thought. Our mechanical memory reproduces only a very faint film of past events. Ultimately these past events become tangents that touch us only at certain points, whereas once they were expected or unexpected, feared or hoped for, and therefore characterized by the circumstances in which they happened to us. But the tone and color shading which the whole background of our existence imparted to these events is not reproduced by our mechanical memory. This background includes all the concomitant circumstances that are not registered by the photographic plate of memory, which is sensitive only to objects. Which of us still knows what an air raid was *really* like? Who can recall to memory the whole world of concomitant circumstances within which we received the cracking and bursting and which encompassed the cracking and bursting, both before and after the event?

It requires an effort of meditation to reanimate the supporting process of events that go on "between the lines." Therefore, the mechanical memory cannot make us thankful for having lived through something, and so we are actually ungrateful "by nature." Thankfulness rests upon the "act" of memory. Even toward God we can be grateful only if we give the utmost concreteness to his help by making the effort of meditative remembrance. Otherwise even devotion is only sound and smoke.

Our departure turned out to be very exciting. I have already described how thrilled we were two hours before, when we finally had the ship to ourselves again and the stack began to smoke.

Shortly afterwards the pilot came on board with the commissar. Then two tugs approached and made fast to the ship. From then on everybody who was free was hanging over the railing to watch the tide. The current grew slower and slower; it was supposed to come to a complete stop at precisely seven o'clock. We would have to take advantage of that moment to turn the large ship about full circle, so there was not much leeway so far as time was concerned.

I went up on the bridge to see the captain. Rather strangely he was there alone with one of the officers.

"Well, well," I asked, "where are the others?" But at once I saw for myself what was up. The pilot in his snow-white uniform was leaning far over the bow and shouting directions to those below. He kept shrugging his shoulders and raising his hands in a gesture of capitulation or helplessness. Sailors were standing around him, some of them manipulating the anchor chain while others appeared to be shouting advice to those below.

"The men are having trouble getting our chain loose from the buoy," said the captain. "If they don't succeed soon, the tide will turn and we'll lie here for another twelve hours."

I observed a small board in the water. It was lying motionless. Sure enough, it was exactly seven o'clock. The ship's loudspeaker roared continually, and the sounds it transmitted from bridge to bow and back were no gentle flute-notes.

Finally the captain ran down and took command of the confused workers. He made the same gestures the pilot had made before him. The pilot stopped yelling and came up on the bridge.

There I stood with him and the commissar. I could not understand a single word of their loud dialogue. The tugs alongside us tooted impatiently. Their crews too were staring in the direction of our bow. The little board still lay in the same spot on the water. But how long did we have before it moved?

Again the ship's loudspeaker howled. The captain called up the engine-room crew in order to cut through the anchor chain with acetylene torches. The bolts on the buoy had become so bent in the last twelve days that it was impossible to get the chain loose, and all the force of sledge hammers and crowbars had been of no avail. "It's too late for that now," said the officer, making a gesture of submission to fate.

This fresh delay in Shanghai was almost too much after our rapturous orgy of farewell. "Well, we'll have a Dujardin on that," I said to myself, went down into the smoking room, suited the action to the word, and resolved to engage in a little exercise in self-discipline and not worry about anything anymore. I went on reading my book, and forced myself not to let a single sentence pass by me.

When I had accomplished this after several tries and allowed myself a glance out of the window after this miniature triumph over my annoyance, I had the feeling that I was seeing something different from what was there before. I leaped up and, sure enough, the ship was turning. So it had worked after all. Our boys had done it.

I rushed out and up on the bridge. There the exuberance of the afternoon had returned. We were gliding down the darkened stream, past endless lines of lighted ships lying at anchor, many of them wistfully blinking their signal lights at us.

The evening passed like a festive ride down a lantern-lighted stream. There was no end of talk and hilarity. Again and again we thought of the moods and fears of the last two weeks; now they all were suddenly transformed into a dark foil that only set off the joyous light of the moment more brilliantly.

Faraway times of youth were swirled up from forgotten depths by the whirlpool of happiness, and the future too was near, for the joy of expectation and the pleasure of having something ahead of us were also evoked to enhance the delight of the moment. Even happiness feels lonely if it is confined only to the moment, for a dark presentiment tells us that it cannot last. So happiness calls out to the past and the future for help, in order to create—again only for a moment!—the appearance of permanence. This night that bore us down the Yangtze Kiang, homeward bound, again stirred up in my mind the mystery of time, which has occupied me so much on this voyage.

Philippine Islands

September 25

After the relative coolness of Shanghai, the tropical heat is like a sudden assault that leaves us all fagged out. We drag ourselves around and loll about as if we were crippled. At night we perspire until the sheets are wet, and can hardly get to sleep. Today I had intended to get on with the spadework for my first sermon at St. Michael's Church, Hamburg. I had looked forward to this very much, because the first exploratory reflections, before they are overshadowed by the hard discipline of giving them form, are very stimulating. But I couldn't scare up a single idea. Even if I had not known that the idea would simply dissolve into vapor anyhow, I should have been too lazy to grasp at it.

We have now reached the Philippines and made fast in the Bay of Tabaco, where we are waiting for the pilot. On our left, towering majestically, is the Philippine Fuji, eight-thousand-foot Mayon. As the sun came up over this world of water and islands, seeming almost magically to conjure up the first day of creation, the phrase "rosy-fingered dawn" came to my mind. This is simply "true," I thought. It is something that can be expressed only in mythical terms.

The pilot came much too late. In any case, that's what we thought, since, despite all our experiences, we are still under the dictatorship of clock-time. (We have no time, because time has *us*.)

Finally there appeared in the distance an antediluvian boat, and gradually we made out the pilot's flag. The boat was chugging along at a tempo that made a snail look like a marathon runner. Sometimes we thought it was standing still altogether.

When after a long time it finally drew near, we saw that its stern was occupied by a whole group of anglers who were looking for fish and not for us. Since the pilot had undoubtedly assured himself of a part of the catch, he was filled with tender consideration for his companions, and he even throttled down the diminutive motor. The big German ship won't swim away, he may have thought, but the fish may. After all, in this primeval world how can one judge what is important and what is unimportant? A fish on the hook is better than an ocean liner on the horizon. The essence of a thing always lies in small details, and anyone who is seeking to achieve a synopsis of a culture had better get some light on the little things of the culture before ascending the heights of its thought and poetry.

When the pilot finally arrived on the bridge, the representatives of two concepts of time, namely, he and the captain, collided in moderate ill-humor. But the little cloud soon passed away. This paradise of light and color contains no preservative for anger. Even before the anchor was weighed, we were caught up again in the delight of the moment.

On the shore we saw young people bathing. The girls went into the water with their clothes on, which was not exactly pleasing to some of the men on board. "Bathing suits are unknown here," explained the pilot. "You wash your clothes by going into the water with them on."

For a moment I wondered that there should be any such thing as dirt in this paradise of light. The ship affords us just the right distance from land to enable us to dwell on the edge of fantasy and keep our illusions.

September 29

Now it is really true: we are on our homeward voyage. From now on we shall for the most part be stopping only at familiar places. Above all I shall be glad to see my friends in Singapore again. Apart from this we shall stop only in Colombo for a few days, perhaps longer. I have received word from the German embassy that preparations have been made to show me as much as possible of Ceylon and that I am to speak at the German-Ceylon Club.

So it's true: our bow is pointed homeward. So strong are

the mental images of the last few days that they hardly leave room in the overcrowded imagination for what is to come.

After the high point of the days in Japan I assumed that the second part of the journey could provide nothing but a descent. This expectation was also fortified by the fact that in the Philippines we were to call at a little hole-and-corner port called Bulan (who has ever heard even the name of it?), where there was no diplomatic representative, no branch of any German East Asia firm whatever, no railroad, no planes. If only we were at least to land at Manila!

And now this little hamlet on the edge of the world, named Bulan, has become the high point of the voyage. When you are in fairyland you must allow yourself to be carried along like a mermaid who has no plan of navigation but simply drifts with the waves. As I look back, that is exactly how I felt— as if I were drifting through a glassy, azure blue element, as if it all might have happened in a dream.

Even the approach through the island realm of the Philippines with its constant changing panoramas, its broad expanses of ocean and narrow straits lined with primeval forest, was a pure delight, constantly changing in the changing light of day and bewitching the eye in a happy enchantment. Dominating everything towered the cloud-capped peak of the steep pyramid of the Mayon volcano, which is similar to Fuji not only in its shape but also in its majestic position: it is the undisputed sovereign of the landscape; it seems to be omnipresent, like a fixed pole in the changing flux of phenomena.

As twilight swiftly deepened into night we anchored several hundred yards from a small village, a little Erewhon (or Utopia) here given the name of Bulan. It turned out later to be an overpopulated village, or better, a village overpopulated with *children*. The only electric light we saw was the red lamp in a harbor beacon.

Since a large sea-going vessel appears here to take on copra only about once a month, our arrival was obviously a great occasion. In any case, the pier was black with people. In the light of a few dim lanterns we could recognize only a scramble of tiny points. We could hardly wait to go ashore.

In the effort to console one another for having to stop at this out-of-the-way place, which is not really a port at all, we had been saying that here we might gain an insight into the heart of the country which would be totally different from anything we could ever get from metropolitan, tourist-minded Manila. In the next few days, this turned out to be true. The friends whom we found quite unexpectedly a few hours later assured us when we left that we had seen more than most tourists see in several weeks.

The next morning we four passengers ("Doc," the couple who were animal trainers, and I) were taken ashore in a curious motorized pirogue which was constantly on the verge of turning turtle in the considerable swell.

Hundreds of people, mostly young boys, girls, and little children, were on the spot within a few minutes, surrounding us in a thick swarm. Surprisingly, there was hardly any begging; they simply stood amazed at our white skin and our stature, and apparently also our shorts, which we did not wish to forego in the murderous heat. The immigration officer who came over from Tabaco with us had definitely assured us that this would be a bit "peculiar," but that it would cause no offense. Only Mrs. B., our *dompteuse* ("lady lion tamer"), was requested to forego shorts and wear a regular dress.

It was delightful to see these childlike, cheerful people crowding around us. They enjoyed themselves immensely, shouting and cheering with pleasure, chattering noisily in ecstasy over the great sensation, and forming themselves into groups and crowds for us to take their pictures. Some smiled radiantly at the lens, others struck up a pose, and others again grabbed hold of one or another of the water buffaloes standing in the water and put on serious or silly equestrian acts.

I was utterly enchanted by the beauty of the graceful, slender boys and girls with light brown skin, gazing at us with glowing eyes beneath blue-black hair. We were not aware then of what the physician would tell us a few hours later, namely, that a high percentage of them would perish of tuberculosis.

We then wandered through the village, surrounded and accompanied by an ever-increasing swarm. We were amazed at the number of schools, some of them bearing the pompous title of "academy." Since eternal summer prevails here, most of the wooden school buildings have perforated walls, as well as large unglassed windows, in order to allow the air to circulate freely. The cloud of dust and people in which we plodded along and the clamor of the crowd were naturally things with which even the most interesting lesson could not compete. Wherever we passed, instruction was immediately interrupted. No categorical imperative here, and no conscience-rending struggle between duty and desire. Here the rule is that the delight of the moment must be seized whenever and wherever it presents itself.

The children of all the classes rushed to the windows and in the next moment ran out into the street to follow us. Not a single teacher was heard making any admonitory protest. On the contrary, the worthy pedagogues seemed to run faster than anybody else to get to the street and not to miss the rare show. They waved and cheered along with the troops of enraptured children.

As we continued our pilgrimage, slowly fighting our way ahead through this youthful ecstasy, we felt almost as if we were being cast in the role of supernatural creatures suddenly appearing in the land of men. So it went on from street to street and school to school, the avalanche of human beings around us constantly growing larger and larger. We were able to cast only an occasional glance at the luxuriant vegetation in this paradise.

A woman who was at her window and noticed our interest in her house beckoned us to come in, while the crowd of youngsters remained outside and continued to surround the place with the babble of their voices. It was obviously a very ordinary house—like hundreds of others we had passed. The walls and floors consisted of bamboo staves, allowing the air to pass through freely. The beds too had this same "airy" structure. The kitchen looked as if it came from a medieval museum. But everything was meticulously neat and clean. We drank a warm lemonade which the hospitable woman offered to us, paid her for it—though she asked nothing of us—and then sailed on in our cloud of dust.

Finally we came to a sun-bleached wooden barracks bearing the promising sign "General Hospital." The waiting room was the street itself. An open veranda containing files and writing materials was obviously the office. The secretary looked up in surprise as we stopped in front of the building, but then calmly went on with her work.

This "General Hospital" naturally aroused our curiosity, and we urged "Doc" to go in with us and introduce himself as a German doctor. In this way the rest of us would also get to see something. Caught between curiosity and Swabian reserve, "Doc" was at a loss to know just how to introduce himself professionally: "It may look like bluffing." He agreed, however, to go in simply as an anonymous traveler.

When we asked the secretary on the veranda whether we might look at the hospital—everybody seems to understand English here—she very obligingly invited us in at once and, after a brief wait, ushered us into the chief physician's office.

We had some difficulty suppressing a certain snobbish superiority when we heard the word "chief physician," in view of the board shack, but we were soon to be ashamed of our pride. For it required only one look at the composed, obviously intelligent man behind his desk to realize that he was a man of high caliber. He greeted us with gentlemanly courtesy in polished Oxford English, with friendly cordiality and without a trace of servility.

After the usual opening flourishes concerning where we had

come from and where we were going, I could not refrain from betraying our little "secret"—that the modest young man next to me was a German doctor. The joy over this was so great that the chief—his name was Dr. Altarejos—immediately ordered up some ice-cold Coca-Cola. After our march through the dust it tasted like nectar. In reply to our astonished question where in the world he had got the ice, since there is no electricity here, he explained that he had a gasoline-powered refrigerator.

Afterwards he took us through the "wards," which were really nothing more than floors and balconies on which the people lay uncovered—often in their clothing. The two doctors were soon involved in professional conversation and consultation. "Doc" was amazed at the number of unfamiliar diseases (or at least diseases familiar only in textbooks) he was able to see here.

The chief physician had studied in America and, as "Doc" whispered to us, was fully qualified professionally in every respect. He used the most modern medicaments, mostly American, and his proficiency was apparent in the way he improvised in those primitive conditions. He himself acted chiefly as the surgeon, while his brother-in-law, whom we met later, handled the internal medicine.

After our tour of the hospital, Dr. Altarejos took us into his garden, and we sat down in a six-seated glider that moved with the slightest touch of the foot and provided a pleasant little breeze.

Meanwhile he had sent word for his wife to come; she was the pharmacist. In her we learned to know a real lady, cultivated in every gesture and warmly cordial. We were utterly delighted to discover such an island of cultivated humanity in this primitive, paradisal world.

It was not long before their little daughter, an adopted child, joined us. She came from school, clutching her sunshade under her arm and a colorful fan in her hand, and carrying her pet dove. When I said that I too had a little girl like her, but that she was blonde and wore long braids, she whispered briefly to her mother and then presented me with her fan, saying, "For your little daughter!"

Finally the chief physician asked the rest of us what we did professionally. When he learned that I was a professor of theology he was delighted. He said that he himself was a practicing Catholic and that he planned to retire soon, since he was "a very old man," in order to spend the rest of his life with philosophical and theological questions, for these areas had been his real intellectual home for a long time. He was quite overjoyed later when I gave him one of my publications in English, and he placed it in his library with visible pleasure.

Naturally we then asked him how old he actually was, if he was already thinking of giving up his profession and entering upon these intellectual and spiritual pursuits. Our question was perhaps understandable, since it was very difficult for us to judge the Filipinos with their smooth faces and thick hair.

When he replied, "Fifty," we were perplexed and chaffed him a bit with our slogan "Life begins at sixty." But he would have none of it. There, he said, people grew old earlier. Life expectation was very much less than among us, and we would see hardly any old people in that country. (He was right; we took note of this later, and during our stay we saw only two really old people.) Besides, in that country to grow old was a dreadful thing; people were exceedingly afraid of it. They would not admit to their age. Dr. Altarejos said that we would not meet a single person with white hair; they all dyed it. In those latitudes a person was old at fifty. The climate too had something debilitating about it. He said that he had long since given up driving an automobile and engaged a chauffeur, because he no longer felt sufficiently elastic, and, with the crowds of children darting about the streets there, quick reactions were required.

His remark that the climate made work very difficult prompted me to ask what the day of a surgeon was like there. He replied that in a profession that required so much con-

254

centration it was impossible to maintain the tempo and the hours customary in European hospitals. He said that he rose at ten and then worked for an hour, though when he was operating he worked from two to three hours. Then, after a light lunch, he lay down to sleep until four. Then there was another brief period of work. Following it he read and played some music. Apparently the people there generally went to the doctor only when they were already about to die; despite the large population in the city, the hospital was by no means overcrowded.

Finally he asked our two animal trainers what their profession was. Then the delight really reached its climax, and when the two actually showed the scars inflicted by their wild animals his jaw fairly dropped in utter amazement. The whole hospital was mobilized so that everybody could see what strange guests were here.

It was a good thing that we had carefully built up a crescendo in staging our introduction, and saved our best scene until the last; otherwise "Doc" and I might well have been overlooked altogether.

In any case, a quite unexpected intimacy sprang up in this brief time, and we were delighted when the chief invited us to go for an automobile ride in the afternoon. He had a large Plymouth, into which we all fitted very comfortably.

Before we went back to the ship for lunch, however, he had us driven to a secluded beach where we could bathe. We sought seclusion because it did not seem particularly inviting to change into bathing clothes in the midst of a howling crowd when even the sight of the whiteness of our heads and legs had provided them with a wonderful show. But it was impossible to avoid being seen in the big car, especially in the outskirts of the town, and soon the children came running from the outermost huts and forest settlements to see the spectacle of those exotic whiteskins bathing.

Though we finally ended up in a remote bay, in no time at all we were surrounded by a whole horde of children, still out of breath from running and almost laughing themselves to death at the spectacle of our changing our clothes.

After our first refreshing dip we heard to our horror that particular bay was frequently infested with sharks and all sorts of horrible things had happened there. The chauffeur, who had not breathed a single word of warning, apparently assumed the sharks had a taste only for the Filipinos and the flesh of the whites was unpalatable to them. Our doctor friend held up his hands in horror when we told him about it later—especially when he learned that our animal trainer had torn his foot on a reef and bled considerably. Blood is an especially attractive bait for sharks.

After luncheon on board the ship, where everybody was exceedingly interested in our news, we hurried back to land and found our friends already prepared to set out. We drove far into this perpetually green country, over hills and through ravines, through little villages teeming with people and through deserted solitudes where there were no people at all—they were neither monotonous nor desolate but full of flowers and vegetation. With loud hootings of the horn the driver scattered children, chickens, dogs, and water buffalo. We drove at a murderous speed around the largest puddles and potholes and breathed a sigh of relief whenever we came to a stretch of macadam which stopped us from jouncing back and forth like rubber balls.

On the primitive wooden bridges along the road, two double boards always formed the track; these our driver hit with deadly certainty, so we were not left hanging on the cross planks or toppled into the stream.

Everywhere there were children, children. We had thought before that the spurting fecundity of Japan and China was unsurpassable. But it was nothing compared to the teeming abundance of children in the Philippines.

Dr. Altarejos pointed out that birth control was strictly prohibited by the prevailing Catholicism. This remark opened up a long, serious conversation revolving chiefly around the question what the result of this unchecked fertility would be, particularly if improvement in hygiene increased the general life expectancy. Where would all these people live, and how would they be fed?

True, the country is still in a primitive state industrially and economically. But will its possible development be able to keep pace with the growth in population? And besides, are not definite limits put upon this development by the climate and the capacities of the people?

Dr. Altarejos saw the danger of this development very clearly, but like his friends in politics knew no way out. Even though tuberculosis takes a terrible toll, the country is barely able to support the modest needs of its inhabitants as it is now. As long as bananas, coconuts, and rice are available, the worst pangs of hunger are kept at bay. But the people go on trusting, with the carefree attitude of children in paradise, that whatever they need will always be available.

We stopped for brief rests at several cool springs and enchanted, solitary mountain lakes, and fortified ourselves with fresh bananas. Here for the first time we discovered what a substitute we must content ourselves with in Europe, and enjoyed the aroma and the fruity richness of this familiar, yet unfamiliar fruit. We felt like discoverers, for nowhere was there even a trace of tourist traffic. We seemed to be traveling through virgin territory, and people stared at us as if we were emissaries from another world.

Finally we stopped at the edge of the jungle. With a mysterious smile, Dr. Altarejos disappeared into an isolated house and after a brief time came back with a friendly older man whom he introduced as the "manager" of a volcanic spring. A visit to this spring had been his secret goal all along. The two gentlemen palavered endlessly in unintelligible Filipino. They appeared to be devising plans and preparing surprises, as one saw by the gestures they made and their smiles of secret understanding.

Naturally, here again a group of curious people gathered

immediately, following the palaver with intense interest. As they listened, they kept looking over at us expectantly, as if they were elated by the consciousness of being fellow conspirators, and were saying to us: You will be amazed at what we have to show you!

Dr. Altarejos, standing there among these people, reminded us repeatedly of Faust mingling with the crowd on his Easter walk. He was greeted everywhere with the greatest respect and with obvious delight; everybody knew him, and he had about him the aura that clings to the man of knowledge and medical skill. Though his features are Filipino, he seemed to stand out from the crowd by reason of his poise and dignity and the "flair" the intellectual man possesses.

We were able to drive a bit farther into the jungle on a more or less beaten path and then were obliged to leave the car and travel a narrow path on foot. Here too we came upon occasional out-of-the-way cottages, and we stopped to talk with little children, when they did not run away screaming from the German giants.

The primitive forest grew thicker and thicker around us. For long stretches we walked through green twilight and despite the humidity enjoyed the sunless "coolness."

Quite suddenly we came to a clearing, and there before us, neatly enclosed, lay a large rectangular pool. It was fed by a hot volcanic spring that came out of the mountain, called Volusan, at this point. At the side of the pool stood an empty but tidy hut.

Mrs. Altarejos spread the table with large banana leaves and unpacked her provisions. There was hot coffee with a peculiar taste and an abundance of native and imported delicacies which we bolted as quickly as possible in order to get into the water as soon as we could.

We put on our bathing trunks while Mrs. Altarejos went into the water with her clothes on, as we had already observed in Tabaco. The water was very warm, and near the spring it was actually hot. We soon recognized that our mourning over not being able to go swimming in cold water in this hot weather was quite unfounded. An indescribable euphoria soon had us chatting at length and engaging in diving matches and general scuffling.

While we were romping about we saw two white-clad gentlemen approaching the swimming pool on the same path by which we had come. Dr. Altarejos said to us, "That's the governor of the province. We are political opponents, but he's a very good fellow."

The governor, who had brought his adjutant with him, let out a yell of surprise when he saw the Altarejos couple and waved us down when we moved to get out of the water to greet him. The next moment the two of them were themselves in the water. Social formalities can be dismissed in a far more pleasant way here.

So this was a Philippine governor: unaffected, lively, young, with a somewhat proletarian face. In any case, he was pleasant and genial and certainly not the kind of man to put a damper on our childish capers. On our way to the pool we had passed a large American car with a special blue light on it, and we had thought at the time: That must be some big shot. Today's story opened out into another episode.

When we introduced ourselves, we observed the order that had proved successful before: our best and tastiest morsels, the animal trainers came last, and again the scars were exhibited. The bathing suit, of course, was also attractively revealing. One could fairly see the governor's eyes light up like flashlights, and in this light the trainers were stimulated to give an account of their most thrilling circus acts.

Immediately the governor attempted (though in the Philippines this was obviously not to be taken too seriously) to interest the fascinating couple in establishing a zoo in his capital city. He became so wrapped up in his imaginary visions, and the pair—themselves carried away—added so much fuel to his enthusiasm, that already they felt that they were almost engaged for the position; they began to draw up legendary plans for their new house and finally even began to talk in economic terms. At this point, however, the governor quite visibly grew more sober, and finally one of us said, "I think it would be better to have another dip." And this we did. When we came to the surface the subject was washed away, never to return. Such is the way of dream and reality in the Philippines.

The governor insisted that he wanted to take us with him this evening to attend a celebration. The temptation was great, but since we had not informed the people on the ship that we would be away, there would be concern and annoyance. We therefore declined. However, we gladly accepted his invitation to take us for a drive in the country on the following day. "Man, are we lucky!" said "Doc" when the governor had departed.

We had grown hungry, sitting in the hot water, and Mrs. Altarejos threw boiled eggs at us which we either caught or ducked for.

Meanwhile, dusk had fallen. A thin but brilliant sickle moon appeared above the palms, and millions of cicadas began to sing all around us in the jungle.

Then we had another visitor. The "manager" whom we had seen before showed up, bringing with him two young fellows. One could not help admiring their brown, well-built bodies. They wore long swords, and between them they carried a mysterious burden in a chest.

Before we knew what was happening they had drawn their swords and skillfully chopped several coconuts, which they then smilingly handed to us in the water. With a few strokes they had fashioned a workmanlike mouthpiece through which we were able to drink the milk comfortably. They gathered twigs and branches and built two large fires to drive away the mosquitoes, which were becoming bothersome. Their slender bodies, with the swords swinging from their sides, moved like beautiful specters in the reflection of the flames.

The crackling blaze and the young men in front of it, the sickle moon, the jungle night around us, and the chirping of the cicadas—all this spun a web of enchantment that carried us away from all the past and future, from time itself, and made elves and trolls seem more real than jet planes, fast trains, and house and garden at home.

When we finally stepped out of the water into the cool night air to set out for home, we shivered and for a moment our teeth chattered. So in the end this day even provided us with the goose pimples we had so long yearned for.

On the way back this tropical night looked out upon us once more with its magic eyes: dim little lights shone through the window openings of the lonely cottages. We hardly dared to talk for fear that the magic would disappear and reality would again take possession of us.

When we returned to the brightly lighted ship late in the evening after a long auto ride, we looked at each other in amazement: where had we really been, how far away from our accustomed world?

Dr. Altarejos had told us, "It is by no means certain that the governor will really come to fetch you tomorrow morning." In this country people say a lot of things that are forgotten the next morning. "Even a good heart does not always have a good memory."

When, as it turned out, he failed to show up at ten o'clock, the appointed time, we waited another hour and then went back to the General Hospital where, as we had already planned in case the governor did not appear, we expected to spend the day. What were we going to do? Actually, there was no question about it at all. Naturally, we wanted to go back to our Volusan spring. And that is what we did.

As we were walking the last stretch of road to the pool, we stopped for a moment to look at a dog and her puppies, and she came running after us. The misery of the poor creature touched our hearts. The animal, like so many other

261

dogs we had seen, was emaciated to the bones, and the puppies appeared to be desperately and vainly trying to suck even a drop of milk from the parched skeleton. We were surprised that the dog had enough strength to get up and follow us.

As we stood by the hut unpacking our provisions she looked at us with such an unspeakably beseeching expression that we were touched to the quick. "Feed me," she seemed to be saying, "it's for my children, and you saw, didn't you, that I am desperate." Speaking in the stead of human beings, this dumb creature told us something about the other side of this paradise, for we had seen only its bright, external side. It is true—one never looks into the same stream twice. The lovely, lulling magic of last night will never appear again in the same way. The "Statue" has suddenly entered the scene.*

After we had given our poor fellow creature a good feeding —the animal went for the morsels in a frenzy—suddenly who should arrive but the governor. He had followed our tracks in a wild chase, determined to keep his word. We hastily invited our friends to supper on the ship, marched off to the automobile, and drove off with the blue light and special horn at breakneck speed, scattering the pigs and dogs to the side of the road.

On the way I asked the governor whether he had a family and how many children he had. When he answered quite matter-of-factly, "Nineteen," I must have looked flabbergasted. Apparently he had misinterpreted my incredulous astonishment, for he immediately added apologetically, "Of course, I'm only thirty-eight years old." So that's why there are so many children in the Philippines! When in reply to his counter-question I had to admit that I had "only" four children, he looked at me pityingly, as if I were a leafless, dried-up tree. He tried, however, to console me: "They may still come!"

As we drove through a village, he remarked that a young man had run his knife through his rival's ribs here day before yesterday. We had already heard such events were not

* The reference is to Mozart's *Don Giovanni*. (Trans.)

uncommon in this country, so we asked him whether what we heard was true. "Oh, yes." he replied, "people here often kill each other. But they don't really mean to be bad. It's just their temperament."

Finally we arrived at the capital, Sorsogon, where the governor resides. It too is a small city by our standards and is distinguished from the other places only by a number of larger stone buildings. We visited his "palace"; all over the rooms officials were sitting, obviously having little to do and not even allowing the presence of the governor to interrupt their pleasant conversations.

For his sake as well as "Doc's," we also had to visit the hospital, of which he was very proud. It was built of stone and was a great deal larger than the one in Bulan, but the plan was basically the same; nothing but open halls where the patients lay on the floor, and here again, no glass in the windows. In the children's section the mothers and grand-mothers squatted beside their little ones. Most of them were lying on the mats with the sick children—a highly unhygienic custom, but the doctors do not forbid it, and in any case it was a touching sight.

Before we drove back we went out to the broad Sorsogon Bay, enjoyed the view, and exposed ourselves to the refreshing breeze. The governor insisted that I have my picture taken with him, with our arms about each other: two proud fathers of a total of twenty-three children!

After a wild drive back we finally arrived at the pier in Bulan, where we were to meet the Altarejos family and then catch the six o'clock boat back to our ship. Here we found ourselves involved in a somewhat embarrassing situation. The boat did not show up, and nobody knew where it was. "Broken down perhaps," said someone from the crowd that had gathered, and that appeared to be as good a guess as any.

We stood there wedged in among the crowd of people, which had grown even larger than before because of the presence of the governor. Nothing happened. Night had fallen quickly and there in the distance blinked the lights of our ship. We had some unpleasant feelings as we thought of the captain becoming (quite rightly) irritated and the stewards and cooks groaning because the dinner was getting overdone and their work schedule was being upset. But these considerations appeared not to bother our friends in the least; nor did they become impatient. What are a few minutes in the presence of this eternal summer?

Meanwhile the mayor, the other dignitaries of the town, and even the police arrived on the scene. Though all the available power and dignity was here grouped about the governor, nobody knew how to get hold of a boat. Perhaps they delayed on purpose in order to savor a little longer the enjoyment of his excellency's visit and the presence of medical authority, exotically garnished with the presence of these Teutons. But we were on tenterhooks.

On the way the governor had told us that another election was coming up and that he was worried about whether he would be elected. All of a sudden the idea occurred to him to turn the gathering of people on the pier into a campaign meeting. He whispered something to this effect to me, and I was greatly interested to see how such a thing would go over with these fiery-eyed young fellows who had not yet been case-hardened and conditioned by professional propagandists and radio demagogues.

"Who wants a cigarette?" shouted the governor, throwing himself down upon the ground among the people in his white suit and holding up his well-filled pack of cigarettes. Obviously he was putting on this rather crazy scene merely to assume the appearance of being original and having the common touch.

He had hardly uttered the words when the whole pack was snatched from his hand, and an unimaginable scuffle ensued. The young fellow who had grabbed the package ran off, leaping among docked boats and lighters and back to the pier again, while the whole mob chased after him. By this time the governor had sprung up again to enjoy the spectacle.

Our "Doc" then thought he would try his luck too, and he held up a boiled egg which we had left over from our lunch. The next moment it had already exploded in the air under the wild onslaught of six or eight hands. Though everything happened so suddenly, the thought flashed through my mind that we could distribute as many eggs as there were people, but that if we did it in this way none of them would receive a single egg. The pier, however, would doubtless be covered with slippery egg custard. A little lesson in the philosophy of democracy—and also a thought-provoking scene for all who think a democratic constitution is a universal panacea.

The governor then proceeded to ask for more eggs, candy, and other left-over provisions. He threw them high in the air, provoking fresh scuffles, some of them amusing and some of them rather threatening. Sometimes he himself grabbed a morsel, held it up in the air with a loud animal cry, and ran off with it in order to get the crowd to follow him and take it away from him. His fine white suit was soon completely rumpled and dirty, but he was beaming with delight and probably thought that he had now exhibited himself in both dimensions: in his role as a representative man of the government *and* as a man of the people whom the people recognized as one of themselves.

We finally asked him whether he could not use his influence to secure a boat, for by this time it was already eight o'clock. It was easy to tickle his sense of power. He whispered to the mayor and the police, several young fellows were sent off, and in a short time a boat arrived. The Altarejos family stepped in first. But before the rest of us could follow, a dozen or more young fellows had already leaped on the deck. They had nothing at all to do with our company, but because of them the boat was full and off it went without us. Even the governor had to stay behind. It was a crazy situation. All European notions of planning and sensible conduct were turned topsy-turvy. The only thing that could help now was a grim sense of humor.

After what seemed an endless time the boat returned. With some difficulty we entered it, but lo and behold, the mayor, the police, the customs officers, and a whole lot of others stepped in too. The thought hit me: Surely they're not coming with us on the ship! What would happen to our eight table settings? But the thought vanished because the swell was considerable and we threatened to capsize. After going only a few yards we were all completely soaked. Our good "Doc," who often suffers from presentiments of disaster, was standing next to me; he shouted into my ear, "If we tip over, just take a good deep breath! No panic! We'll be fished out!" I shouted back, "Don't you worry! Remember, they showed you how a life-jacket works!"

When we arrived at the ship's side the boat kept rocking up and down and we had to jump to the gangway at just the right moment, but it was not long before all were on board. Sure enough, the mayor, some alderman-like personages, policemen, customs men, and all kinds of people had come along and were following me in a long fantastic procession into the dining room. The stewards were close to a nervous breakdown. The white-clad cook, who had smartened himself up to receive our guests, looked around with his eyes popping like jack-o'-lanterns and fled for cover to the kitchen.

I held a brief council of war with Dr. Altarejos, who said, "The governor quite certainly invited these people. He wants to make himself popular. The best thing to do would be to take them into the canteen and give them something to drink." And that was what we did. They stepped into the smoking saloon in wonderment—to them it must have seemed fabulous —and hesitantly sat down in the chairs. The governor could not be persuaded to come with us to the table, saying that he wanted to "stay with his boys." This was a fresh embarrassment, but it resolved itself very quickly. For no sooner had the governor dropped into a chair, his legs dangling over its arms, than he fell fast asleep. Thus relieved of all ceremonial concerns, we ordered up whiskey and soda for the rest, which pleased them very much. Meanwhile, we dined at our snow-white tables. During the serving, however, the steward was unable to conceal a slight trembling in his hands.

During the course of the evening we observed several attempts at pulling off minor heists, apparently the method whereby these people exacted "customs duties" from us. Corruption seems to be as necessary as oil to the machinery of the local bureaucracy. It seems more a natural process than an infraction of the law. In any case, I could not summon up the strength to be indignant; it merely amused me. I believe, of course, that nothing lies beyond good and evil. Was it the climate, was it fatigue, was it surfeit with all I had seen this day that made me quite indifferent to it all and permitted me merely to smile indulgently over the fact that here even a certain amount of corruption—into which these people are seduced by the tempting things in our "show windows"—is not without charm? Navigating through those strange waters, I could not get a grip on my normal ethical categories, and so I merely looked on smilingly. How far away is Europe!

In any case, no shadow fell upon our departure from these lovable natural phenomena, who, in the light of the categorical imperative, seem like prehistoric formations. Saying farewell to the Altarejos family was especially hard. We had come very close to one another. From a distance we can now estimate the loneliness in which we leave these people. Whom do they have to share their thoughts with? Who is interested in the things that move their hearts and minds? Now I understand his decision to go into seclusion and find a relationship to the essential things in composed aloofness.

When I awakened the next morning after a deep, drugged sleep, the first thing that came to my mind was not any of the wonderful things we had seen on our drive through the country but, of all things, the governor's demagogical escapade on the pier the previous evening. The little lesson on the philosophy of democracy that flashed through my mind then must have been occupying my subconscious, and I cannot get the symbolism of that little scene out of my mind.

It was actually true: if we had had two hundred eggs for an equal number of people and handed them out, not one of the people would have received a single egg. Many things in the macrocosm of our world are exactly like this situation: one need only think of the nations, instead of these individuals grabbing at eggs. One need not think of such fragile things as the eggs, one could equally well think of the cigarettes which were distributed. One man snatched the whole pack, ran off with it, and "lived" in the abundance of his riches, while the rest chased after him to get hold of the booty. What a parable of the surfeited nations and the underdeveloped countries! For a moment the Filipinos were enacting before us their historical role.

This example of unreasonable folly also brings up the question of democracy. That man is endowed with reason but not guided by reason could not have been more drastically demonstrated. Even those who may perhaps have been personally capable of acting reasonably and willing to do so had to conform with the crowd, for when a solitary individual insists upon remaining rational in the midst of mass instincts he becomes even less effective than if he joined in the free-for-all and thus at least tried his luck at getting a small share.

I cannot get away from some serious reflections. Is democracy right to treat the great mass of people as rational beings, when they are not rational beings at all? Or *is* the great mass rational in the more mature and more highly civilized countries? (The way the English wait in orderly queues for buses, without pushing and crowding, gives some encouragement to this hope.)

Obviously, an analysis of this little incident teaches that democracy cannot be built upon the premise that people are guided by reason, but must rather appeal to the *potential* reason and thus awaken and develop it. Moreover, the very fact that democracy is founded upon the principles of division of authority and mutual control indicates that it is not without a sense of realism, that it does reckon with the fact that men are guided by their urges and instincts and, above all, by their urge to power. Despite what has been said to the contrary, democracy is based upon a pessimistic view of man which is precisely balanced by its hopes and its ideal goals for man.

Towards noon the cargo of copra had been taken on. The ship was still aswarm with the young workers who were waiting for the departure. I photographed a number of types and enjoyed the pleasure they got out of it. It was a wonderful display of vanity; they never grew weary of playing "roles." Displays of emotion and grand gestures were not lacking either.

They were grateful for every cigarette and eager to show us in every possible way that they liked us. But this was because we liked them too. The kindly immigration officer had tears in his eyes when we said goodby, and shook us by both hands. Everywhere farewells were being said, as when old familiar friends must part for ever.

Then they climbed down into the great, big-bellied lighter, a weaving crowd of young fellows, and among them the officials and several merchants. The waving and shouting never ceased until they disappeared in the distance. As our ship slowly glided away, it was clear to us (and one of us actually said it) that in our ordered, planned world we shall always have a bit of homesickness for this island of children.

For many hours the wooded shore and island after island accompanied us. And now we are again on the high seas.

Type used in this book
Body, 10 on 12 Times Roman
Display, Tempo
Paper: Standard White Antique "R"

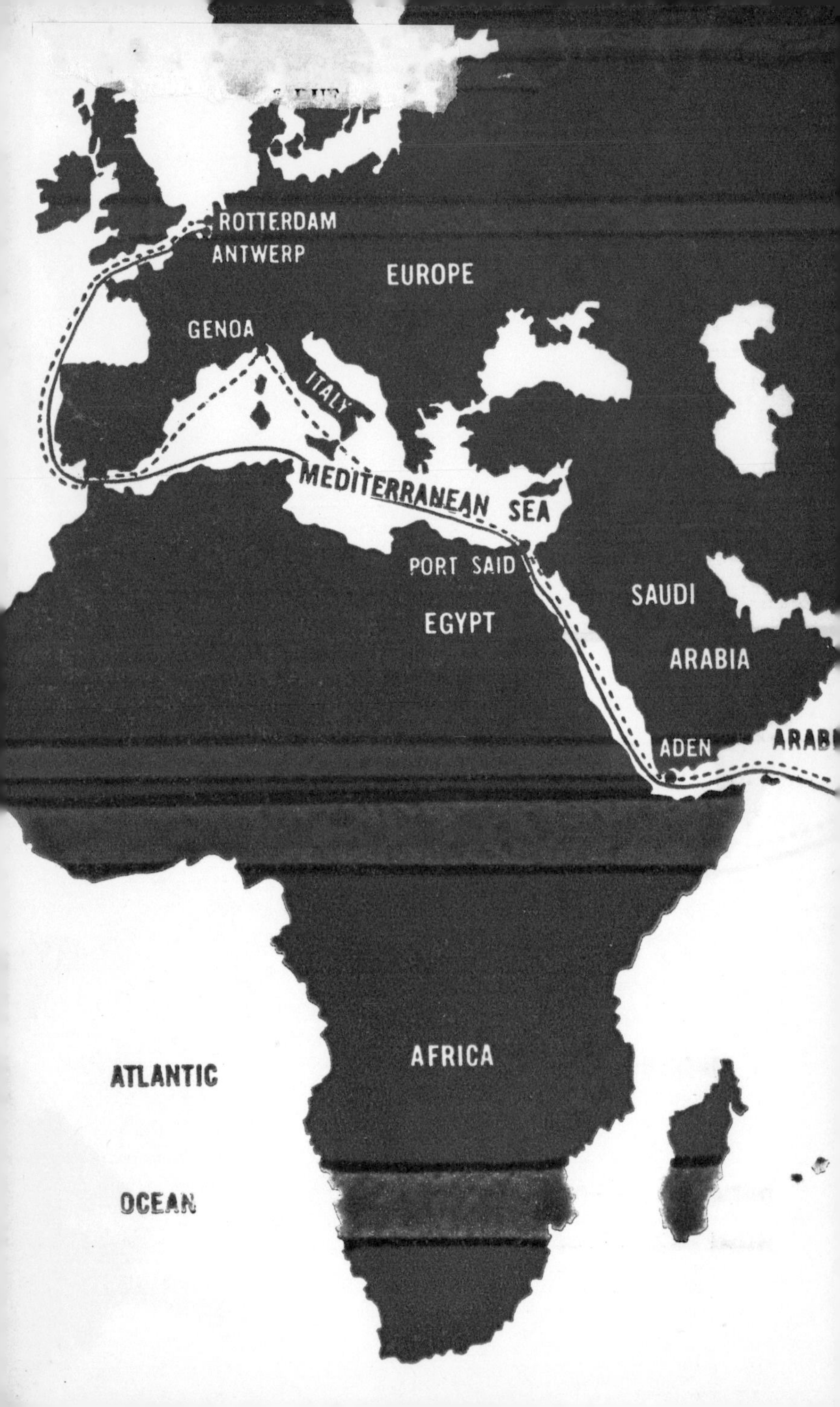
ROTTERDAM
ANTWERP
EUROPE
GENOA
ITALY
MEDITERRANEAN SEA
PORT SAID
EGYPT
SAUDI
ARABIA
ADEN
AFRICA
ATLANTIC
OCEAN